D1526503

*Communism
and the Remorse
of an Innocent
Victimizer*

NUMBER SIXTEEN
Eastern European Studies
Stjepan Meštrović, General Editor

Communism and the Remorse of an Innocent Victimizer

Zlatko Anguelov

WITHDRAWN

TEXAS A&M UNIVERSITY PRESS   COLLEGE STATION

Library of Congress Cataloging-in-Publication Data

Anguelov, Zlatko, 1946–
    Communism and the remorse of an innocent victimizer /
Zlatko Anguelov.—1st ed.
        p. cm.—(Eastern European studies ; 16)
    Includes index.
        ISBN 1–58544–195–3 (cloth : alk. paper)
        1. Anguelov, Zlatko, 1946–   2. Bulgaria—Politics and
government—1944–1990—Philosophy.   3. Communism
and society.   4. Communism and culture—Bulgaria.
5. Bulgaria—Social life and customs—20th century.
I. Title.   II. Eastern European studies (College
Station, Tex.) ; no. 16.
DR93.A54A3   2002
949.903'1'092—dc21   2001006541

for my children

Rada, Vela, Aglika, Zlatko, Kamen, and Bistra

Contents

Illustrations

Preface

My unfading gratitude goes to everyone in the large family I grew up and lived with most of my life. It is also heartfelt for all my friends across the former communist world who go on with their lives there. All of you—with your virtues and faults—inspired me to live, to tell good from evil, and to be humble before the force of destiny.

My memoir is built around the life history of my family, a family of three generations of communists. Although I was able to escape party membership, my personal story shows that I could not live detached from, let alone opposing, my country's mainstream. While by current standards I ought to be regarded as a dissident, a close inspection of my own and my peers' behavior reveals that we complied with the system, no matter what. Therefore, I think that this book has a novel and uncomfortable message. By Western standards, all communist societies were repulsive. However, focusing on the few dissidents hides the fact that for many of us communism was a normal regime. It was a regime to which we had, with varying degree of unwillingness, to adapt. The story narrated in this memoir shows a morally ambivalent world in which survival literally depended upon having dirty hands.

This book is also an account of daily life under communist rule. Throughout this book, I use *communism* as a generic term that best portrays the regimes established in Eastern Europe after the Second World War as "socialist (or people's) democracies." Internally, the adjective *socialist* was largely used to qualify everything in the social and historical spheres, but I feel that *communist* and *communism* avoid confusion with the meaning the term *socialist* has in the West and really single out the unique and infamous features of these societies. Moreover, my use of *communists* stems from the vernacular use of the word in my country to name people who were devout members of the Communist Party and devout proponents of communism as the new and just social order they were allegedly called upon to build. The notion was advanced by party ideologues as defining a morally superior category of people. It had a rather pejorative connotation in the everyday vernacular.

My narrative exposes a world that was less one of heroes and villains than one of less-than-brave, morally implicated opportunists. This social psychology, I claim, has left a legacy making consolidation of democracy far from certain, perhaps even unlikely, at least in the near future. Thus, although mine is a memoir of a world that has passed away, it is also a warning to beware of facile hopes for change in a world whose core is still unknown to the West.

What is a greater challenge, however, is for survivors to cope with life after communism. Those who were fools of fortune under communism are now carriers of another universal message, a message with vast philosophical implications: how dictatorial regimes change our individual fortunes. In a world hypnotized by celebrities—both on TV screens and in books—our fortunes go unnoticed. However, our fortunes are what history is all about. The account of one who was a fool of fortune, therefore, should make a difference.

I wrote this book in the summer of 1995 during my second year of doctoral studies in political sociology at McGill University in Montreal. It would have been an impossible project had I not enjoyed the generosity of my mentor, John A. Hall, who was the first reader of a still embryonic manuscript, and who let me dispose of a whole semester free of course work. My other mentor, Alberto Cambrosio, supported me with tacit respect, which later turned into a warm friendship. I also was lucky to befriend Marc Thompson, a wonderful man and a specialist in English romanticism, who gave of his precious time and editorial talent to look at my text in his capacity of being a native speaker of American English.

Masha Alexander, then working as a literary agent with Lynn Franklin, in New York, was the first professional to enthusiastically stand up for this project, even at that immature phase, and has provided continuous encouragement and networking ever since. I also thank Lynn, as well as the few subsequently contacted agents and editors who did not accept the manuscript, for making me aware of the stumbling blocks in American publishing.

In 1999, following four years of fermentation, I resumed my work on the manuscript, unexpectedly encouraged by my fellow journalist from London, Johnathan Sunley, a former editor of the *East European Reporter*, the magazine with which I collaborated between 1989 and 1992. I am particularly indebted to Johnathan, who offered invaluable insights into Eastern European communist and postcommunist politics.

My dear friend John McWhorter, a linguistics professor at the University of California at Berkeley, championed my manuscript with grace and persistence and cheered me up with his thoughtful e-mails in difficult moments. I am indebted to my daughter Aglika for sending the manuscript to her good friend David Lawrence, writer, editor, musicologist, and wine connoisseur, who lives outside of San Francisco. David wrote one page of comments that opened my eyes to flaws and values of my writing, which I had not noticed before. Then came the ubiquitous Alan Nagel, a professor of comparative literature at the University of Iowa, who—without being asked—simply took a pen and scribbled all over the manuscript his invaluable comments, criticism, suggestions, and edits.

This work would not have come to its present shape without John, David, and Alan. Bathed in their friendship, I will, alas, never be able to pay off my intellectual debt to them. Any remaining snags are, of course, due to my inability or stubbornness to follow all of their advice.

I wish also to thank Stjepan Meštrović, professor of sociology at Texas A&M University, to whom I sent my unsolicited work and who first saw its merits beyond the commercial considerations, and the many helpful staff members at Texas A&M University Press.

Above all, I owe this book—and the shape my life is in today—to my wife and closest friend, Roumyana. My love and care for her can never be adequately expressed in words, even in private.

Communism and the Remorse of an Innocent Victimizer

And our obsession with understanding them on the stage,
To know what they are when they pretend.
—Czeslaw Milosz, "Body"

Prologue

Collapse and Reanimation

It was a nasty day in Sofia in November, 1989. Shortly before noon, I took a famous natural healer to meet Bulgaria's chief toxicologist in his murky office facing a gray backyard. The healer was desperately seeking approval for a new drug he believed would become a panacea for all AIDS victims. He had asked me for help since he knew I was a freelance AIDS campaigner connected with the country's medical pundits. The chief toxicologist was a specialist in mushroom intoxicants. More importantly, however, he was a member of the Central Committee of the Bulgarian Communist Party (BCP).

This official had warned me that he was scheduled to attend a plenum of the Central Committee at noon but that he could allocate ten minutes for my protégé. In truth, it took him no more than five minutes to tell the old man that he would use all his influence in the Ministry of Health to obtain a certificate for the healer's concoction.

I parted with the old man at the tram stop feeling no sympathy for him. Shivering with cold, people around us dissolved faceless into the fog. The tram rails, too, were disappearing into the fog, making it seem even thicker. Ahead of me, it looked like a lifelong existence under the communist regime.

I no longer had any illusions that I would be able to rid myself of a Politburo that watched, bugged, threatened, and decided about my life and my daydreams. I was quite at peace with the thought that no change whatsoever would occur in my lifetime.

That same morning, for example, I had paid scant attention to an unenthusiastic report in the paper that nervous crowds had started demolishing the Berlin Wall at several places and had thus shattered the myth of the Wall's eternity. The short report did not make the headlines, nor did a photo of the event accompany it.

I went home to scribble down a few thoughts from my recent interview with a psychiatric administrator on the issue of psychic healers mushrooming all over the country. By four o'clock, while I was still engaged in that activity, the telephone rang.

"Did you hear the news?" a fellow physician from the Heart Institute asked without any introduction.

"What news?"

"Todor Zhivkov is down!"

"What?"

"Todor is down. They kicked him out today. It will be on the news tonight."

I looked at my wristwatch. It was November 10.

"How do you know?" I asked, still incredulous.

"My boss has a relative in the Secretariat of the Central Committee, I tell you, and he told me they had a plenum today. Todor resigned, that's for sure."

I hung up the phone and went to the other room to see our babysitter, a woman of eighty-one, who was with our one-and-a-half-year-old daughter.

"Todor Zhivkov is down!" I exclaimed.

"Truly?" she asked. She stood up to kiss me. "Happy me to be still alive to see this. Have I told you that I knew him personally?"

"How?" I asked, suddenly puzzled by the fact that we had never talked about him before.

"Well, he worked as a typesetter in the same printing house as I did. This was a long time ago, still in the Tsar's times. He was there for a while when I was very young. This was at the very beginning of my career as a printer. He's probably two years younger than me. I'll tell you, he was a very lazy guy. All the time he pretended to be going to some meetings, so he hardly spent two days back to back in the shop. He wanted to be a leader. Oh, my dear, I can't tell you how glad I am that I've lived to see him down!"

Still not believing my ears, I later tuned in to the six o'clock BBC broadcast in Bulgarian. "Today," the announcer said matter-of-factly, "the long-standing Bulgarian communist leader Todor Zhivkov was forced out of office."

The TV news show also included a report from the plenum. With a trembling voice, the newly elected secretary general of the Politburo was reading his eulogy on how much Todor Zhivkov had contributed to the Communist Party and the country. He declared that because of his advanced age, Zhivkov had handed in his resignation to his comrades with the full awareness that a rejuvenation of the communist cadres was the best direction to take when the country was experiencing economic troubles.

For the most part, the camera stayed with the speaker, but there were instances when it zoomed in on the face of the resigning secretary general sitting in the Presidium. Behind the thick glasses, an animal fear filled his eyes. To paraphrase Tolstoy, all rising dictators are alike, and every falling dictator falls in his own way. The same is true of countries: every falling-apart country suffers according to its own ways. But the link between the dictator and the country he disciplines renders the malaise of both dictator and people alike. The longer the tyrant stands at the helm, the stronger the likeness. Ours had been at the top for exactly thirty-five years.

Sitting there motionless in the Presidium, our phenomenal dictator appeared stunned and frightened. There was no hint of vengefulness or brutality from the audience. They seemed even more frightened than Todor himself. I sensed their angst to see the session end before something tripped the circuit breaker and we were all brought back to face the dark reality.

His ousting looked so trivial. After ruling for thirty-five years, Zhikov sat there listening to the hoarse, banal male voice that muttered gratitude and humility. This was his send-off. I stared at his cowardly face, stunned by the flush of sympathy I suddenly felt for him. An era was coming to an end, and I was watching the dull rites of passage at home on my TV set. Was this the way history occurred? Empty dishes at the dinner table, emptied hearts, speechless minds, the bitter taste of outsiderness . . . and the man who embodied this whole nation staring anxiously at his former subjects. What have I done to deserve their sudden loss of servitude, he seemed to be asking himself.

The first *post*-Zhivkov rally (for it certainly could not have been an *anti*-Zhivkov one) was held eight days later, on November 18. A friend who took part in the behind-the-scenes preparation of that rally told me that Peter Mladenov, the newly appointed BCP general secretary, had authorized it. A small group of self-proclaimed "oppositionists" had been promptly formed, and they negotiated the authorization. Almost all of these people were still party members, but they were rushing to detach themselves from this compromising link. The details of the rally schedule were negotiated with the party's number-two man, Andrey Lukanov, an upcoming prime minister and one of the most gruesome personalities in the incumbent party hierarchy. Those negotiations took place in the apartment of the famous Bulgarian writer Nikolai Haitov, just one floor above the party boss's suite.

The handful of oppositionists at the rally read their ebullient speeches proclaiming communism dead and praising themselves as the harbingers of democracy. We, the populace, were all there, amidst national flags, flowers, and placards written with children's markers at the very last minute. We yelled for the first time in our lives at a rally, angrily shouting "down!" after every mention of a prominent communist name, and "hooray!" at the slightest suggestion of democratic appeal. The foreign TV crews were filming us. We were unexpectedly reentering the world. Maybe we even were reentering history, out of which the communists had dragged us with inviolable revolutionary presumption. At the moment, however, we were hardly able to think of anything. Someone or something had opened the "postcommunist" era in this Balkan country.

Within days of the opening, it became clear that, contrary to all expectations, the fall of communism did not make this country's people any happier. In fact, the people and the fallen dictator alike grew less and less happy as the new freedom began to seem more and more like a new chaos. The attempt to convict the dictator for the pains he had caused during his rule failed shortly. It would only have become a sentence on the people themselves. And what sort of people would imprison themselves? To cause moral pain is not a crime under any country's penal code. No one prosecutes for historic losses. Moreover, there was no evidence of any insupportable pain. The people and their dictator were reunited in unhappiness. As far as I am concerned, we all were still communists—some more, others less, but we all still belonged to the communist reality and dreams.

And so, you see, we cannot claim to have suffered to death under the regime, since it was *our* regime. Like Nazism, communism would have been an impossible creature had the people not embraced it, had it not been an integral part of the families, communities, and meandering biographies of each one of us.

The timing of Zhivkov's fall, however, caught me all too unaware of this. I believed that we had been the perfectly innocent victims of the most oppressive regime in history. In 1989, the domino-like fall of Eastern Europe's dictators was my epiphany! Now, after a number of years, I feel it my duty to disclose what this epiphany is all about.

I kneel humbly before all those who lie in shallow graves or bear scars of torture on their bodies and souls. However, I swear that *they were not the representative majority among us.* In most cases, they were imprisoned at random or by coincidence. Also, the isolated cases of conscious self-sacrifice were not highly praised and wholeheartedly backed by those we might responsibly call "the people."

The stories of pain, blood, torment, and exile are true, but they are the lesser truth. They were not the essence and the meaning of the communist regimes. They skew the scenario of communism in Eastern Europe, distorting it into an image of heroic resistance crushed by merciless oppression. Today, the heroic image merges with the presumptuous idea of a rapidly fading communism to erect a monument of the maimed human spirit. The place of this monument is purportedly in the museum of oblivion, where apocalyptic figures of bravery and knighthood appeal to the imagination and human compassion. It is these figures that occupy the foreground of historic canvases so that the real submission of the people and their amazing adaptability to the regimes remain in the shadow. *The story of abiding and compliance has not yet been written.*

Today, both those who claim to have ruled in the name of the people and those who know perfectly well that they were willing accomplices require that the communist page be turned over as soon as possible. Neither despots nor slaves have any desire to focus on the details, in the name, they shout, of moving on with democracy. No shame, guilt, or remorse is apparent in the postcommunist era. But no precipitous democracy either! Even those few who have indeed fought against the dictators need not keep the communist page open because they are now so enthralled by self-contemplation. The disorientation and fragility of the so-called democratic forces in virtually all postcommunist societies offer undeniable proof of that.

You did not need to be a rugged pessimist to forecast the return (albeit, in most cases, temporary) of former communists to power. It sufficed to open your eyes to the bare truth that their species was not made extinct by the fall of the regimes. Quite the opposite, they have always been out there, resurfacing on every convenient occasion, usually disguised under new party banners, names, or public offices. At the same time, imported democrats are desperately being sought in order for any democratic motion to be feebly pursued. Sadly, a vicarious democracy seems preposterous.

Yet this is how Eastern Europeans are making adjustments to their postcommunist realities, in the face of the contemplated world order. Unfortunately, few people are willing to acknowledge their own involvement in the communism that preceded it. Most of them (slaves as well as tyrants) endure broken destinies. However, all of them claim to be fooled by communism and Western capitalism alike.

As far as I am concerned, this book is my commitment to tell the story of my own communist past. The day of Zhivkov's fall marked a watershed. The forty-three years of communist rule *before* that day matched the forty-three years of my life from birth to middle age, a past which cannot be erased. The years *after* that day are the unknowns that mankind named "postcommunism." For wishful thinkers, postcommunism signifies "non-communism" or "communism-free." I strongly disagree—and I wrote this book to explain why.

This book could not, however, be a cold comment on the communist society; it became necessarily the emotional story of my family and myself. Our destiny was as much woven into communism as communist history was enacted by the very individuals and families committed—willingly or not—to communism.

I am now sitting in my downtown Montreal apartment staring with visceral resentment at the abyss that separates me from my past. I am writing my book, overwhelmed with emotions while not losing my reason. Emotions aroused by memory fuel my energy to write; the cool reason inherent to my new environment guides my pen in analysis.

I chose for myself and for my children to come to America. I wanted us to rejoin in history. I was an outsider to history, as all my former compatriots were, and still are in many key aspects of life. Thus, the meaning I assign to the concept of "insider" refers to being inside history, far less than it does to being part of a particular society. I do not care about my national label, although I am haunted by my native identity. However, because people seem to care so much about being nationally identified, I respect this in all my attitudes and analyses. I only want to make it clear from the very beginning that my personal stance in this world is outside any nation.

I grew up surrounded by books, obtained several university degrees in my life, and performed successfully in academia. I thus cannot define myself other than as an intellectual. I feel rather awkward to be outside a nation. Usually, intellectuals support and attempt to justify nationalistic causes.

The peculiar Eastern European group of people I belonged to—the *intelligentsia*—was very much a people's intelligentsia. It claimed a monopoly on wisdom even prior to any rational knowledge. Standards of "high" morality and stubborn contempt for those who were less moral or less wise coalesced through the ages in different forms of compassion the intelligentsia showed for "the needs of the people." "The people," in turn, regarded the intelligentsia as a group of prophets and moral authorities.

Regarding the communist regimes, the intelligentsia was trapped in a very ambiguous, though crucial, role. Although this role will make part of the argument in this book, it is not an attempt to claim any special status for the intelligentsia. If there was any, though, it was the unsavory lack of true wisdom contrasting with the pretensions of the intelligentsia itself.

In a nutshell, while the purported calling of the intelligentsia was to uphold freedom, the actual intelligentsia was required by the communists to justify the communist regime "scientifically." In complying, we inflicted upon ourselves an unbearable moral curse: we justified totalitarian communism with our surrender rather than with our intellectual work. On a personal level, and in spite of my present wisdom, I cannot dissociate myself from the past deeds and pliancy of the Eastern European intelligentsia.

Consequently, living in the postcommunist era after having survived communism is a painful experience. The nightmares of the communist past need to be reconciled with the challenges of a free present. It is quite hard to be free. Yes, it is hard to be free despite what I have been thinking during the long years of communist imprisonment. But it is worth trying.

When one looks at communism as a personal story, one is shocked by the sudden realization that this political regime irreversibly overturned all human destinies and all human projects it had brushed against. I feel cursed forever by its legacy. After all, I could have perhaps been able to overrule my moral liability, had it been humanly possible to dissent from communism.

Today, both dissidents and conformists see their lives crushed as in a classic tragedy. The catharsis, though, is yet to come, if ever.

PART I

Behind the Iron Curtain

CHAPTER I

Buying Illusions

*A model is by definition that in which nothing has to
be changed, that which works perfectly; whereas
reality, as we see clearly, does not work and constantly
falls to pieces; so we must force it, more or less roughly,
to assume the form of a model.*

—*Italo Calvino,* Mr. Palomar, *1983*

I was brought up by my grandma Zlata. Hers was a rare gift of humanity.
It is such a pity she lives now only in my memory and perhaps in the
memories of a few aging acquaintances of hers. My grandma is my intimate *madelaine* on a Sunday morning, and every time I evoke her memory,
she unveils the happy pictures of my childhood.

The irony is that she believed in communism. She died just before the
fall of Gorbachev, taking to her grave the obstinate faith that what Moscow says is a biblical truth.

She was born at the end of the nineteenth century, in the family of a
Macedonian doctor and a bourgeoise Austrian. Her mother, Klara, was, in
fact, from another mixed marriage: grandma's grandfather, Maximilian
Silberling, was a Frenchman from Strasbourg, and her grandmother,

Wilhelmina, the descendant of an Austrian petit bourgeois family. Grandma's father, Ivan, was the son of a rich leather merchant from Solun (Greek: Thessaloniki, formerly Salonika) by the name of Paountchev (Paountché means "small peacock" in Macedonian). Thanks to grandma's aunt Lucy, who was a painter, the oil portraits of these honorable personalities now hang in an old house in my native town of Varna or are spread in traveler's trunks all around the world. They have excited my childhood imagination a great deal.

In 1895, the family of French railway engineer Maximilian Silberling arrived from Strasbourg and settled in the same town where the young Dr. Paountchev had opened his practice ten years earlier. The engineer was hired by a German company constructing the railway to connect the capital, Sofia, with the country's eastern agricultural land. What transpired shortly thereafter was nothing short of the kind of stories one finds in a nineteenth century *roman d'amour.* The eighteen-year-old daughter of this French family fell ill, and the doctor was called to see her. This formal encounter led rather quickly to a wedding in 1896. In June, 1897, my grandmother was born.

All I know about this mixed family comes from her. Almost no documents are left to uphold my imagination. In Bucharest, where a branch of the family still lives, I have seen the freemason oath certificate of one Dr. Silberling who lived in Paris at the turn of the nineteenth century. And in the loft of my native house in Varna I once found a handwritten letter from the great French writer Victor Hugo dated 1859. It was addressed from his Guernsey exile to Maximilian Silberling, the engineer who, as a devout follower of Charles Fourrier, had asked the eminent French poet to support the Fourrierist social movement after the death of its founder. Finally, again in Bucharest, an invitation for a wedding party—written in Gothic German on one side and in Cyrillic Bulgarian on the other—was once shown to me. This brownish seven-by-seven-inch invitation acknowledged the honor both the Alsatians Silberling and the Bulgarians Paountchev had in announcing the marriage of their beloved son and daughter.

I no longer possess any of this scattered evidence of my family's weird Balkan-European composition. Keeping relics made little sense for anyone caught in the turmoil of changes that gripped the Balkans throughout the twentieth century. We, the survivors and the escapees, are left to narrate from the memory of our souls.

After the First World War, Dr. Paountchev sent the five children born to his delicate Alsatian wife between 1897 and 1904 to *Hochshulen* in Berlin.

Seventy-one-year-old Grandma Zlata with her first great-granddaughter, sitting on the stairs of our house in Varna, summer 1968. (Author's collection.)

*This photograph was taken in the early 1920s in France, when Maximillian
and Wilhelmina Silberling's three grandchildren were students in Berlin.*
From left: *Maximillian (French: my great-great-grandfather), his granddaughter
Claire, his wife Wilhelmina (Austrian: my great-great-grandmother),
Grandma Zlata, and her brother Georgi. (Author's collection.)*

He chose an artistic education for the two eldest, both girls, while the
three younger boys were told to obtain diplomas in healthy, practical do-
mains like economy and engineering. The well-conceived plan quickly
foundered, however. My grandma was the eldest and she went ahead of
the others to study opera singing. When her sister Claire came the next
year and registered in the conservatory's piano class, there was not enough
money for both of them, so Zlata switched to pharmaceutical studies, which
were much cheaper at the time, leaving Claire free to pursue the career of
a pianist. Almost each year thereafter, a new student from the family arrived in Berlin to join the highly intellectual Bulgarian student community. Some of these students went on to become famous philosophers,
economists, and composers of European renown between the two world
wars. Only a few of them adhered later to the Marxist ideology that spread
throughout Bulgaria after 1920.

Claire married one of those students. His name was Todor Vladigerov,
and he later became a corresponding member of the Bulgarian Academy

of Sciences. His cousin was the composer Pantcho Vladigerov. While Claire remained with Todor in Berlin, one of her brothers became an accountant, and another a mechanical engineer. The youngest brother disobeyed his father, who wanted him to become an economist, and studied music theory. None of them had any link to the Communist Party or to the opponents of the communist ideology in Bulgaria during their lifetime. The two sisters, however, brought the communist spirit into the family by marrying communists.

My grandma hastened to complete her studies and return to her native Bulgaria. It was 1924, and her father's career was nearing its end. After ten years as a successful practitioner in Vratsa, he had consecutively been director of the County Medical Administration, first in Lom, on the Danube, and five years later in Bourgas, the second largest Bulgarian town on the Black Sea. After so many years of private practice and medical administration, Dr. Paountchev and the rest of his family finally began to enjoy high social status in Bourgas.

Grandma Zlata began working with one goal in mind: to become a pharmacist and to repay the money her father had spent on her education.

This 1920s photograph is of siblings married to each other. From left: Todor Vladigerov; his wife, Claire Vladigerova (grandma Zlata's younger sister); Claire's brother, Georgi Paountchev; and Elena Vladigerova-Paountcheva (Todor's sister and Georgi's wife). (Author's collection.)

In her own peculiar way, she was a kind of spontaneous and successful homegrown feminist. She succeeded in building and sustaining her own business in a backward country where females remain second-class citizens to this day. In the beginning, she borrowed money from her uncle—Alphonse Silberling, her mother's brother who owned textile factories in Bucharest—and opened a drugstore in Bourgas.

She soon met an insignificant bank clerk who was fully infected with the most recent leftist ideologies. He chased her obstinately and persistently, so that she could not reject him. On the other hand, she quickly realized that her own independence could be sustained only with a male companion who was inferior in both intellect and character. Although she was courted by top eligible bachelors from Bourgas's upper class families and at some point the Belgian consul to Bourgas asked for her hand in marriage, my grandma chose a man who had no social position at all. Their deal seemed fair, and both of them remained loyal to it until they died. He obtained a subordinate role in a successful private pharmaceutical business, and the humiliating stature of a low-class intruder ridiculed in a highly self-rated bourgeois family. As compensation, she blindly embraced the same leftist Russophilia that had thrown him into the ranks of the BCP.

In Grandma's family, the Macedonian father earned the money and was the emblem of stability with his top position in the medical hierarchy. Only a narrow circle of regulars with this family knew, however, that he stopped sharing the family bed with his wife after she refused to become pregnant for the sixth time. His morals barred him from divorcing, but he effectively split with his wife while managing to maintain the appearances expected of an upright family man under a common roof. Paountchev's house was frequently visited by the mundane world of the provincial sea town. The worthy Frau Paountchev regularly scheduled concerts and five-o'clock teas. She retained a hyphenated Silberling in her passport, but in those places that hardly mattered at all. Tea was served in Meissen porcelain, and there was a Zimmermann *Flügelpiano* in the salon of the house.

The local *Bürger* felt flattered and duly elevated when they listened to *Lieder ohne Wörter* from Mendelssohn or Tchaikovsky, or to Beethoven's violin sonatas while sipping English tea and nonchalantly dropping the names of George Sand and Knut Hamsun in between the gossip on the latest love affair of the *Bürgermeister*. All of the children in the family played the piano, of course, and took lessons in French. Despite the striking resemblance in the décor and decorum, this was not the end of a heart-moving era, as Ingmar Bergman implied for Sweden in his film *Fanny and Alexander.* This was supposed to be the Balkan way of integration with Europe, the beginning of a long-awaited prosperity for the people in this Balkan country.

By the time my childhood began, our small house in Varna retained only the fading glow of this short-lived moment of brightness. I remember three or four shoeboxes and two glossy albums full of photographs and postcards. Wrinkleless faces and brilliantine hairdos of the same people aging irretrievably around me, embroidery and crinoline, and the windows in twilight—all forever imprinted on my mind like the images on those fading brown daguerreotypes. I was the only one curious enough to look at them. Meissen porcelain cups and saucers in nonmatching numbers, some of them traversed by blackening cracks, rested in an antique oak cupboard. There was nobody to serve the tea to. The Zimmermann, almost irreverently out of tune, filled a room only twice its size. Were it not for my regular piano lesson exercises, it would certainly have been sold as obsolete furniture. The loft was jammed with disintegrating books, printed only twenty or thirty years before. But it was not so much their physical condition that evoked nostalgia, as it was the fact that their titles were terribly out of fashion. Downstairs, on the only floor my grandparents occupied in their own two-story house, the shelves of two small bookcases were bent under the weight of the *Bolshaya Sovjetskaya Encyclopedia,* twenty-two volumes of Lenin's *Complete Works,* and three thick volumes of Marx's *Das Kapital.* Only at the periphery of the shelves could you find novels by Thomas Mann, poems by Pushkin and Lermontov, and some Bulgarian fiction.

Almost every time I went up to the loft, I met some of our tenants: three families that had moved to the town from nearby villages. The basement and the second floor had to be rented because no one, not even the owner of the house, was allowed to occupy more living space than prescribed by the communist authorities. Thus, Frau Paountchev-Silberling's salon was reduced to a small wooden table packed with vials, small flasks, saucers, and creme boxes. She stood by like a watchdog, quitting only to go to the bathroom, armed in all instances with tampons soaked in methylated spirit. She could not approach this strange new world with bare hands. Everything was *spurkat* ("dirty" in Romanian).

As for myself, my fresh world was natural and their past world was easily packed away in drawers. It was indeed quite odd that, in this tiniest of places, I somehow grew to love small things. Later in life, when I saw

Les Champs Elysées, the Brandenburger Tor, or the square before San Pietro in Rome, I had a hard time accommodating their giant size with my small house and the small streets and small towns of my small native country. But at that early time, I used to spend wonderful hours rummaging around in the drawers that contained my grandma's treasures. There were yellowed letters in German and Bulgarian, sugary postcards, a golden men's Swiss watch with a long chain, mother-of-pearl brooches, a magnificent stick-pin, and, of course, shiny surgical instruments. In a small suitcase that I used to pull out from the dust beneath the wooden double bed, a number of copies of *Economy and Housekeeping* magazine (from the years before Hitler) had been carelessly stashed away. The paper patterns inside each issue had never been cut.

My grandma did not show any time sickness, though. She was proud of her experience, and particularly of the fulfillment of hers and her husband's communist dreams. She never condemned her parents' lifestyle (she was the kind of person who did not know how to criticize others), but she also never praised it as having been better and nobler than the one in which her daughter and her grandchildren were doomed to live. Or perhaps I simply loved her so much that I could not distinguish any difference in her attitudes. That is why I grew up in full harmony with the surrounding communist world, or at least without being conscious of its dark sides. Although I do not recall it happening, I am certain that even if someone had tried to alert me to the drawbacks of the society we were forced into, my grandma's loving authority would somehow have shielded me from this person's words. She protected me against resentment and disbelief, and I spent those innocent years believing that the world was perfect.

Grandma Zlata told me a great deal about my family's past. When the time came for me to get meaning from her stories, they were imprinted in my mind like movie pictures. I realized her biases and was seemingly prepared to take her down from her pedestal and to desacralize her. Although I should at least have been able to put her accounts in the cultural and political perspective where they truly belonged, the full meaning of her stories did not penetrate my consciousness while she was still alive. My grandma emanated such propriety that something of an irrational nature stopped me from showing contempt for her intact ideals. Heaven forbid that her world, which provided security and protection for me, might disappear as a result of my curse on her genuine trust. I did not dare question her propriety, even while I dared to question the morals of the regime she so wholeheartedly endorsed.

She used to be sarcastic with her brothers, who never expressed any affinity for the communists, and she despised her sister's snobbishness. However, she paid due respect to her sister's husband, great-uncle Todor "Totko" Vladigerov, who belonged to the communist elite. This was the kind of elite that the average, noneducated party bosses needed badly and thwarted openly. She was also condescending toward my grandfather but rated highly his antifascist and procommunist activities. These two men— my great-uncle and my grandfather—embodied two characteristic faces of East European communism.

Great-uncle Totko was a scientist. He began lecturing on economics in the late 1920s in Berlin. What he delivered was a Marxist-oriented course highly appreciated by German leftist intellectuals. Who wasn't leftist at that time in Central Europe, by the way? Because of his links with BCP leaders Georgi Dimitrov and Vassil Kolarov, who had recently escaped from Bulgaria, the young Vladigerov also became known to the Soviet comrades and apparatchiks who took over the Comintern, an international association created by Lenin to promote communism throughout the world.

At the same time, *Nazionalsozialismus* was already sweeping through Germany, one of the powers of European capitalism. In 1933, only months after usurping power, the Nazionalsozialistische Partei instigated a fire in the Reichstag, alleging that the communists were responsible for the incident. It so happened that Georgi Dimitrov and two less significant Bulgarian communists were arrested, accused of having settled in Germany as agents of international communism. Allegations against them were filed in a German court, and the trial took place in Leipzig. In spite of the Nazi efforts, however, the three inmates were acquitted. Under Stalin's initiative, the Soviet Union provided asylum to Dimitrov and several other Bulgarian communists persecuted by Hitler. That was how Todor Vladigerov wound up taking a train to Moscow. By that time he was an economic consultant working for the Comintern.

By his own account, during the 1930s he and great-aunt Claire lived in a huge apartment building in Moscow, where he could not help but notice that his neighbors were gradually disappearing. So was his own rational basis for believing that the centrally planned economy under Communist Party rule embodied social evolution. But unlike visiting Western liberals who could go back to their democratic homelands and write bitterly about their own disillusionment, Todor Vladigerov could only keep his eyes wide open to the truth. He had to keep his mouth shut.

His homeland had never known democracy; neither had Bulgarian governments ever tolerated Marxist organizations. In 1934, a technocratic dictatorial regime came to power in Bulgaria by means of a coup d'état to impose political stability and put down the rising labor unrest. By the end of 1935, Bulgaria's King Boris had unseated the prime minister and installed a royal-military dictatorship. This form of government spread across nearly all of Eastern Europe in those prewar years. But even though it was called a dictatorship, major personal freedoms and basic social mobility were not eradicated, as happened with the succeeding communist dictatorships.

Todor Vladigerov could still travel to Bulgaria if the Soviet spy machine provided him with passports to leave the Soviet Union. It was Vassil Kolarov who unexpectedly summoned him one day to his office and handed him two fresh passports, whispering that if he and his wife did not rush to take the train to Bulgaria, they would be next on the list of those who were methodically disappearing from their privileged flats on *Komsomolskaya Naberezhnaya*.

Thus, the Comintern employee's life was saved by a whim of fate. One hot summer afternoon in the late 1950s, I remember him sipping Turkish coffee at the table in our dining room in Varna and saying, "We took the last train to Bulgaria."

Through the open doors and windows, a light afternoon draft barely cooled the small, modest room adorned with oil paintings and a cupboard showing porcelain cups through its glass windows. As a corresponding member of the Bulgarian Academy of Sciences, great-uncle Totko used to spend his vacations with great-aunt Claire in a protected resort at the seashore near Varna. In what had become a tradition, they would both pay a visit to my grandparents and have a bourgeois Sunday lunch.

"Last train." Those two words had more than one meaning. The literal sense was immediately evident to me. It was in the spring of 1941, when middle Europe was already occupied by the shiny German troops, the invasion of the Soviet Union was imminent, and Bulgaria (a traditional, though not entirely faithful, ally of Hitler) was about to cut all commercial and physical links with the vast Soviet Union. The metaphorical implication only became clear to me much later, however. This was the last time a chance was offered to those people who knew from inside how the Kremlin machine worked to get away alive with that knowledge inside their heads.

Professor Vladigerov was not the type of person, however, who would engage in clandestine activities. He achieved tenure and settled in Svishtov,

The Bulgarian commissioner to the UN, Prof. Todor Vladigerov, chats with Soviet foreign minister Andrey Gromyko at the UN, New York, 1951. (Photo courtesy United Nations Department of Public Information.)

a little town on the Danube. An economics university had been installed in that tiny town in the 1930s with a donation from a rich Bulgarian wheat merchant. When the war ended, communists turned out to be the best-positioned—and best-equipped—candidates for leading the small Balkan country toward people's democracy *à la russe.* Professor Vladigerov was soon summoned to Sofia by his Moscow acquaintances and assigned a role on the diplomatic track. In 1948 he became the Bulgarian ambassador to Paris, and in 1951 he was sent to the United Nations in New York as the head of the Bulgarian mission. A year later, the professor turned diplomat was forced to resign from public service because Valko Tchervenkov, the successor of Dimitrov and Kolarov, had installed his own personal regime in 1950 (known as "the cult of the personality") and no longer needed anyone from the "old guard." Professor Vladigerov returned to his academic post and went on working there until his sudden death in 1968.

He never spoke about his experiences in Moscow or as a diplomat, and an aura of secretiveness surrounded his life. Tante Claire outlived him by sixteen years, and even though she was stricken with Alzheimer's in her late seventies, she never breathed a word about her husband's involvement with the Communist Party in Moscow or in Sofia. In fact, the entire family referred to him as "the academician" rather than "the communist." To be sure, both his diplomatic and academic career under communist rule implied two basic considerations. First, highly educated members of the intelligentsia with pronounced leftist convictions were used to present a civilized façade for the brutal and mostly obscure communist reality. Secondly, individuals like great-uncle Totko were only too aware of the actual atrocities that took place in the backyard of the communist realm. They were considered a potential danger, both to the façade and to the smooth infiltration of the dictatorship into the social fabric of the country. Those who offered him service in the regime knew perfectly well that he could not refuse. Had he been foolish enough to do so, he would have been quickly brought to trial on false allegations of espionage for the enemies of the people or the American imperialists. In turn, he knew that while the official count of postwar death sentences pronounced on the rulers of bourgeois Bulgaria by the so-called People's Court was 2,730, the real number of political opponents executed by the BCP amounted to about thirty thousand. He also knew that those who acted, or were simply suspected of acting, as internal party opponents, were thrown in camps without trial. So, for the simple reason that he knew a lot, he could follow suit.

Professor Vladigerov and certainly the whole Eastern European intelligentsia were convenient prey for the brutal party executioners. He had made his choice when he embraced the leftist liberal ideologies, because he believed that Marxism held the solution to the problems created by an unjust, cruel, conservative capitalism. He could not have imagined at that time that in adopting a revolutionary stance on social theory, he would find himself trapped in the most Machiavellian political philosophy—and practice—ever known. According to this philosophy, the ends of the libertarian ideals formulated by the Enlightenment—*liberté, égalité, fraternité*—justify the use of brutal means in discarding those who disagree with the ends or the means to them.

We now know, of course, that low-class murderers abused the ends to achieve their egoistic, philistine ambitions. What great-uncle Totko knew as early as 1938 was that a power-hungry group had gripped the reins of the Communist Party in Moscow and propagated their hard line through the world communist movement. He was aware of their relentlessness and could not possibly have had any illusions about his personal safety. He no longer had the choice to reassess his first choice. To serve and be civilized was the only option available to him, provided, of course, that he could

conveniently forget what he had witnessed before and what he was wit-
nessing now. He realized that he would not be able to use his inside knowledge in self-defense, let alone in organized opposition to the hard line. The
party felt too flushed with victory and the bosses too confident of their
impunity. Every individual act of dissent could easily be annihilated, the
actor strangled in a dark midnight hour. Justice and impartial arbitration—
the ultimate environment for every liberal movement—were simply not
in stock anymore.

The moral dilemma of Vladigerov's life was that he began it as a free
person choosing liberal values in a democracy-oriented capitalist society,
but ended it as a fool of fortune in an autocratic communist regime, which
pretended to protect those very liberal values. His tragedy was in knowing
the extent of the charade. His frustration came when, after having served
loyally, he was expelled from his diplomatic career because the dictator
and his entourage no longer needed him. The latter were busy solidifying
their power by using less sophisticated and more manipulative servants.
But he was still psychologically and intellectually ill equipped to entirely
dismiss his initial beliefs.

This was a point that he sincerely shared with my grandfather. They
both sat at that solid table in the narrow dining room, the door to the yard
left open for the midday August sun to enliven their peaceful discourse. So
incredibly different, socially distant, and intellectually incompatible, they
nevertheless used their trust in Marxism as a common ground. They agreed
every time on one topic: that those who had so distorted the Idea would
one day themselves be dismissed and made to endure the retaliation that
would follow.

As is typical for the Balkans, grandma Zlata and great-aunt Claire held
their own discussion on clothes, children, food, and the weather. They
were different, however: Grandma cooked and served the dishes, while
Tante smoked a cigarette or two and made remarks about improper serving or the lack of certain etiquette. I was able to observe, though, that
neither of them was alien to the men's conversation and sometimes inter-
fered. Great-uncle was a lovely interlocutor, but also a severe man of principles. His authority was recognized at this table, no question about it. But
besides his well-traveled manners, an experienced observer would have
noticed that he was not a free man, a statute that one might expect for a
person of such a high stature.

Believe it or not, it was my grandfather who looked like a free man! It
was sometime during the 1970s when I first encountered a phrase that

*Grandma Zlata plays chess with Granddad Georgi in their bedroom in
Varna, 1967. (Author's collection.)*

offered a Western approximation of this type of freedom. At one time *Le
Monde* published a long article on the prolific secretary general of the
BCP, Todor Zhivkov. The editor in chief, André Lafontaine, who had
conducted the interview with the Bulgarian dictator, characterized him
in a telling fashion: "Zhivkov has the appearance of a person who has
never been tormented by metaphysical apprehensions." Although appealing in its fine irony, the metaphysical explanation was just a guess which,
if accurate, accounted for a small, though essential, part of my grandfather Georgi's background. He belonged, in fact, to a peculiar category of
people who could appear and flourish only in the rarefied Balkan conditions. There, on the fringe of Europe and in such close proximity to the
decaying Ottoman and Russian Empires, smallness was an incubator for
the petit bourgeois, remoteness a fertilizer for provinciality, literacy the
ersatz for erudition, and intelligentsia the local resemblance of an intellectual class.

Frozen within the mentality of a straightened and provincial petit bourgeois, my grandfather was acclimated to life in a tiny Balkan town, where
the local newspaper played the role of an encyclopedia and the surrounding
overgrown hills were mistaken for the entire world. No doubt, everywhere

Grandma Zlata and Tante Claire under an oil portrait of their father, Ivan Paountchev, in Varna, 1971. (Author's collection.)

on earth provincialism amounts to the same restricted mentality, and this is perhaps the condition in which the vast majority of humankind respectfully lives. What makes the difference, however, is where that provincial spirit resides. Sublime causes and events drive great nations toward national grandeur, whereby the unity between historic vision and nation sweeps up the provincial phlegm into a common enthusiastic stream. No such cause, in contrast, is capable of enticing the little peoples into united action. Even more so, the lethargic pace of life in the Balkans reduces every sublime cause to pulp while little causes, from neighborly disputes to ethnic hatreds, stubbornly grow.

So, my grandfather would have been incapable of becoming a male Balkan Madame Bovary even if someone had made him read Flaubert's novel. Spleen and romantic illusions were not the sentiments, which a Balkan petit bourgeois would have considered worthy of sacrificing his life. There were virtually no impulses to bring individual values above social illusions. My grandfather grew poor and expendable. His individual energy was neither abundant nor sophisticated, and no one had great expectations for his life. He was summoned to the army to defend the Bulgarian territory during two Balkan wars and the role of cannon fodder that he was cast to play did not please him at all. He thus joined the socialist circles spread out throughout the country and suddenly forgot his own unimportance. Socialist ideas ranked highly with the provincial intelligentsia. But then again, that same intelligentsia boosted its rating by adopting a socialist stance. In 1917, the October Revolution in Russia brought the Bolshevik version of Marxist socialism to Bulgaria, and my grandfather stood as a fervent follower of this trend that was to become the dominant ideology of the place.

By a stroke of luck he met my grandma. Her world represented the top social layer of this country, even though it corresponded to an average middle-class European level. But these kinds of correspondences can mislead. How could the Bulgarian middle class be a stepping-stone for social climbers when the upper layers were missing? The social conventions were nothing but an imitation of Western European manners that lacked the distinctive social class codes they were intended to demonstrate in Europe. Moreover, the shift in values went downward instead of upward. It was my grandma who would sacrifice her family background to comply with my grandfather's proletarian pretenses. It was she who would rather die as Emma Bovary for the populist sentiments professed by her husband.

It is a sad irony that my grandfather was not even a pure-stock proletarian. Neither was he a romantic. He had never worked seriously. Typically, he spent most of his time in party clubs and coffee shops playing backgammon and chain talking about the advantages of Soviet socialism. He used to help my grandma in the drugstore and later in the chemist shop, but she never told me why he was not allowed a say in the business decisions. Nor can I remember him telling me anything important or memorable about his life and his experience.

After they opened the Bourgas drugstore in 1925 and had their only child in 1926, grandfather became an active member of the Bulgarian Workers' Party (BWP), the legal wing of the BCP. Prime Minister Tsankov outlawed the BCP after the defeat of the September, 1923, uprising. Although clandestine communists performed the Terrorist Act of 1925 in the capital, the BWP was still granted political status. Grandfather Georgi had been elected town councilor for several consecutive years after 1927. During an antigovernment rally on the streets of Bourgas in 1931, a plainclothes policeman shot him in the left thigh. These activities, which evidently jeopardized the family's safety, created serious tension between him and his father-in-law. At the time, Dr. Paountchev was already retired and enjoying the absence of his wife, who had gone to Bucharest with her brother Alphonse, a bachelor.

But the times were troubled, and in terms of precautions little could be done. My grandma, a born peacemaker, decided to leave Bourgas, where her husband had inflicted more trouble than was necessary. In 1934, she sold the drugstore and the family moved to Varna, Bulgaria's largest Black Sea town, where she purchased one of the town's central chemist shops. She also bought a house in the center of Varna: the house in which I was born and where one of my children still lives.

This house bore witness to a major clandestine act in which my grandparents were involved: For ten days in the fall of 1940 they sheltered a high-ranking party functionary sent by Moscow to strengthen the illegal BCP infrastructure in view of the coming war. This man, a member of the BCP's exiled Central Committee, came in a boat across the Black Sea and had to be transferred to the underground party headquarters in the capital. My grandparents were unable to identify him until a decade after the war was over, despite the fact that the police caught him and he had been sentenced to death and executed back in 1942. The revolutionary was, in fact, Anton Ivanov, an "old guard" member of the Politburo. His name was released to my grandparents by a liaison who later served as Bulgaria's minister of the interior for three years during the 1970s.

Indeed, the Second World War years were obscure and full of anguish. My grandfather spent part of this time in a camp for politically exiled foes of the government and its pro-German policy. From what I know about the Bulgarian Resistance—although the truth is, this knowledge was heavily falsified—I cannot claim that he was committed to it. Moreover, I am inclined to believe that the most salient national feature, which hangs like a curse over this Balkan nation, is that neither the nation nor its citizens have ever been entirely committed to anything. There have always been plenty of loopholes available for last-minute withdrawals.

Basically, the people who were hungry for political power joined the promising movement and used it as a vehicle for their ambitions. Until recently, the names of those people were listed in the annals of the Bulgarian communist movement as devoted "Fighters against monarchism-fascism" in Bulgaria. Many still believe they really were. But their names also embody those factions that struggled for dominance after the BCP came to power. So, these people were not entirely committed to defending the ideals of Marxist dogma. They were self-styled professional politicians, and hardly anyone expected them to adhere zealously to their platform, let alone put on a moral political performance. At least, this was the common perception in Bulgaria. Some of them paid for their ambitions with their lives, but the majority escaped intact and fervently joined in the political struggle, a struggle they knew would be merciless and totally dehumanizing.

There were, of course, a great number of people who did not care about communist ideas. Those people simply wanted to fulfill their little petit bourgeois dreams.

Those who embraced the Marxist dogma from A to Z did not enter politics. I count my grandfather among those people. His loophole was my grandma. Her business protected him from poverty, while her father's decent social status protected him from open political persecution. On the other hand, the bourgeois family he belonged to by marriage made him look suspicious in the eyes of his party comrades, who trusted no one but the "crystal pure" descendants of the low-class proletariat. There must also have been other personal characteristics that kept him from clandestine top-party involvement. At the same time, my grandparents' life was a reciprocal two-way street: my grandma was, in turn, influenced by grandpa's ideas so that she could no longer remain entirely involved with her social class. I suspect that she never really wanted to anyway.

The most bizarre aspect of all these complex relations was that Marxism in Russia, and consequently in Eastern Europe, was accepted and installed on an all-or-nothing basis. No alternatives were foreseen, no choices were allowed, and no emulation from existing democracies was forecast. Instead, all of the countries belonging to the Soviet camp emulated the system espoused by Moscow. In terms of psychology, the "bright" model justified the political system, and nothing but the model counted when a person faced his or her own life strategy. This maximalist utilization of the model explains why it has never worked on a personal level. At the same time, however, it explains why everybody tried to find a personal way to adapt to it. The big question is whether the people adapted to the model or the model adapted to the people.

So far, the majority of authors have intentionally portrayed the communist political system through the carriers of its political power. In this regard, heroism, conspiracy, iron will, and Orwellian inevitability blur the traits of the nameless carriers of communist life under this system. Communism was no longer a dream. It had become a life. Only it was a life overshadowed by a model that had been the banner of social daydreamers and libertarian intellectuals sheltered under Western democracy. It became a prison—both literally and figuratively speaking—for innocent people in the open remains of Eurasian empires.

The life stories of my grandfather and great-uncle offer blunt proof of this. They were each tailored differently, but their deal with Marxism and with the party structured on Marxist principles amounted to the same motive: to profit from it for their personal well-being. There was nothing strange or unusual in this motive; what rendered it immoral in Eastern Europe was the communist imperative of absolute idealism and utter personal abnegation. In practice, everyone applied this requirement strictly when passing judgment on others, but found subtle or not so subtle mitigating circumstances for one's own deviations from the imperative. This principle alone sufficiently explains why acting Marxism is a dogma. Marxist-oriented politicians were depicted by communist scholars and propagandists as superhumanly elevated, faithful to the noblest of all noble causes, surrounded by a halo of pathos, given to servitude in the name of some bright future for the people, and embodying an extraordinary ability to suffer in the name of high ideals.

However, when you live under the same roof with such people, you see how ordinarily human they are. With the help of some maturity and fair reflection you begin to realize the bigotry underlying the whole political system. Unfortunately, it takes more time (and for some a lifetime is not enough) to realize the importance of this bigotry; the majority of those afflicted with it simply could not.

My grandfather and great-uncle Totko were both over sixty when they began to meet perennially on sunny, carefree August afternoons. They both knew the key faults of the system, the installment of which they had expected, fought for, and acclaimed in all their public performances. Neither of them ranked very high in the party hierarchy, and outside this hierarchy hardly anything existed at all to measure the achievements of their lifetime. In their youth, they were both free to choose their political orientation. At that time, Marxism was just an activism, a form of critique and denial of the capitalist system, and thus appealed to people who were highly sensitive to social injustice. In their youth, they could not have known that the implementation of this activism into a political system would acquire such monstrous content. Now they knew. But I cannot remember them ever being self-critical or experiencing any feelings of regret or guilt.

The more knowledgeable and, hence, more responsible individual, was the academician. He had a deep knowledge of the world's political economy. He also could not be unaware that the centrally planned economy installed over Central and Eastern Europe was doomed to fail one day or another. Even more so, he was the personal friend of one of the butchers of the Bulgarian party members in Moscow, Vassil Kolarov, who saved his life but sent hundreds of other Bulgarians to concentration camps. He was friendly with a prominent victim of the Bulgarian communist regime, Traitcho Kostov, who was executed in 1949 in Sofia on the false charge of being an ally of Tito and an agent of British imperialism. Finally, he was a diplomat at the onset of the Cold War and knew the true factors that had thrown his country into the Soviet zone of influence. None of this knowledge ever surfaced in their talks. It was as if an unwritten taboo had been imposed on such topics. The reason for this secrecy was not the presence of their wives, let alone of a ten-year-old child. Just the opposite: both of them enjoyed the confidence and esteem of my grandma and great-aunt Claire. This was quite possibly the only real recognition they did achieve in life.

I remember both how pathetic and touching my grandfather was when searching for party pork in his late sixties. After the so-called September Ninth Revolution (of 1944), he turned out not to be related to any of the cliques that had crystallized within the BCP on the basis of their past clandestine activities. He thus did not count among the powerful comrades. A most enviable social status and real money were granted to those who were recognized as "Active Fighters Against Fascism and Capitalism." A special Central Commission reviewed the individual applications and simultaneously filled up the party archives. Every clandestine action had to be evidenced by at least two witnesses, and the confusion was enormous because the majority of people were known only by their nicknames. The commission remedied the confusion rather efficiently, however. Its members tacitly decided to decline the applications of those who were not from the partisan brigade supervised during the clandestine period by Todor Zhivkov, the BCP secretary general. As a consolation, the Active Fighter's title was subdivided into three categories, with progressively less pork for the lower ones. It goes without saying that the less significant Active Fighters—that is, those who could not cause trouble to the actual leadership either at the central or on a local level—were assigned to the second and third categories. After several refusals, hundreds of typewritten letters, applications and reapplications, memoirs, and rendezvous with former combatants, my grandfather finally persuaded the commission that he was really the person who had sheltered Anton Ivanov upon his arrival in Varna in 1940. Only then did they grant him the second degree of Active Fighter. I cannot recollect exactly what the benefits of this title were. But I remember feeling that our family was regarded as "one of us," a vernacular euphemism suggesting favoritism, loyalty, and secure social position.

Thus, my grandfather appeared to be a free man. His simple goals were achieved: he spent his life well protected from a material point of view and, on top of that, his ideological dreams were fulfilled. Moreover, the party, the institution he valued most, recognized his contribution to communism. Global communism seemed robust enough to overcome the hurdles of the Cold War, and his grandchildren would admittedly have a smooth life in a socialist country. I would venture to say that he had no scruples about the deviations of the party. He naïvely believed, for example, that those who were thrown into camps—even in Bulgaria there were several camps—or executed without evidence of any guilt were apostates fully deserving of their punishment. To me, he looked like a genuinely happy man.

In contrast, his brother-in-law looked tormented and uneasy, as if he was constantly hiding something. Writing memoirs as my grandfather did was as much out of the question for him as participating in a plot against the party leadership. He was bitter and irritable during the last years of his life. There were two reasons for this, grandma used to tell me. First, he was writing his "big work," later published under the title *The Fictitious Capital;* and second, he was never promoted to the rank of a full Academy member. The latter more than likely involved some of his personal rivalry since, as the expression ran, it was "because he did not applaud the party line." Great-uncle Vladigerov died of a heart attack in 1968. My grandfather Georgi, who was ten years older than him, passed away the same year because of renal failure after a poorly treated hypertrophy of the prostate.

I still vividly remember my grandparents in their old age, playing chess every day, engaged in an endless tournament yet bored to death by each other. I still prefer to think that my grandma was fatally injured and insulted by his lifelong partnership. Indeed, they debated almost every existential or material subject but one. They both loved and enjoyed everything that happened in the "vast Soviet land" with an irrational zeal, and approved of everything that reflected the Soviet policy on the world victory of communism. They adored Joseph Stalin, then sympathized with Nikita Khrushchev, and finally supported Leonid Brezhnev's rigidity that undermined every attempt by Western diplomacy to obliterate the Cold War confrontations. At the same time, they did not like the Bulgarian leader Todor Zhivkov, but believed that so long as Moscow approved of him, it had to be so. They never delved any deeper into details that might perturb their harmony with the Soviet "building of communism."

This irreparable trust would not seem as bizarre as I see it today if I did not mention that my grandmother was a lovable, self-denying, altruistic person. In all respects she was normal, down to earth, and pleasant, with a healthy sense of humor. She was sensitive to art and beauty and highly literate. In short, she was unquestionably an adorable and respectable lady. But she died in her nineties without ever having attended a church service, firmly convinced that Gorbachev would prove that humanity's future was nothing less than Soviet-style communism. She never attended a Communist Party meeting either, as she had never become a member. Yet it would be an oversimplification to claim that communist ideology had somehow become a surrogate faith for her.

Nor would I say that my grandfather was some rough, primitive, or antipathetic man. He was rather harmless, self-effacing, and simpleminded. Neither abusive nor hostile to anybody, he sustained honest and fair relations with customers and relatives. As a neglected son-in-law, he kept chilly relations with his host family. There were never any violent conflicts in our house. A measure of peace and tranquility marked their otherwise flat existence throughout the stormy decades of Europe's twentieth century. My grandparents and great-uncle were not aware that communism in Bulgaria grew up on the shoulders of people like them. They dreamed about some fictitious brotherhood based on the bookish ideals of an equal and just society. The dreams of many like them across the Soviet system—the so-called old combatants—stamped the real regimes with an aura of humanism tangible even today.

Nothing of this humanism was real. But the shoulders of my grandma and grandpa were real. Real also were the people who stepped on their shoulders. These people continue to haunt me today because they populated my own reality against my will. The following chapters tell the story of how these real contemporaries of mine appropriated my grandparents' dream. And how I became, against my own good intentions, part of the appropriation.

CHAPTER 2

Bad Luck or Bad Choice?

A sharp sword turns away from the bowed little head.
—Bulgarian proverb

My father, Radoslav, was born in 1916 in a small village sixty kilometers southwest of Varna. I know virtually nothing about his childhood since he never volunteered to talk about it. I rarely asked either. A green river full of fish, a thick old forest, dusty country roads, and flocks of turkeys—these were the scanty reminders of an embellished peasant world that he rarely and reluctantly mentioned. My grandfather Georgi (who did not like my father) used to say, "Oh, Radoslav used to pasture turkeys till he was fourteen." My mother, who thought she should protect him from his past, expressed this in another way when she told me my father was "very brainy. You know, as poor as he was, his father sent only him out of the whole bunch of seven kids to the nearby town to continue his schooling at the age of fourteen." Truth is, he was the youngest among his siblings and the only one who graduated from high school. He also became the only active communist among them and he was thus labeled a "progressive" in his native village.

I keep the image of his father, Angel, as a legendary personality. He was bearded and therefore strange looking in a rural community where being shaven was part of a man's posture and dignity. He earned his living as the village tax collector. That was regarded as a sort of third-tier among village intellectuals, after the teacher and the mayor (in the mixed Bulgarian-Turkish settlements the priest and the *hodzha* were not as significant messengers of civilization as they are usually thought to have been). But he was a heavy drinker and an Oriental-style home despot. One day he wagered that he could lift up a square oak pub table with his teeth and won. The story runs that the table was strewn with glasses and dishes and that he had bitten at one of its corners.

Another story relates how his fourth son, Boris, was stabbed to death by the brother of a girl he attempted to steal on behalf of a friend who wanted badly to marry her. One early morning shortly afterward, my uncle's killer was found with his throat slit underneath the team of horses hitched to his cart. That evening, some people remember, the tax collector was not sitting at his regular place in the pub and his wife did not need to pull off his muddy boots as she used to do when he dragged himself back home intoxicated.

A second uncle of mine fled the village after the communist era began. The family lost track of him for years—until a mine accident was reported in the newspapers wherein only a few people escaped death. When his name appeared on the list of survivors, they discovered that he had been employed as a mechanic in the mountainous southern part of the country.

In the Balkans, people usually settle in the plains or in the foothills of the mountains. The mountains thus become a shelter for those who breed cattle or sheep and for outlaws or recluses of all sorts. "The world" is down in the plane, while "to flee the world" means to go up in the high mountain. Or, to put it another way, to exile people from society does not mean to send them away to a remote place, but to bring them up, the "exiled" world being vertically separated from the "decent" world. This is due primarily to Bulgaria's small size, but it should also be taken metaphorically. The asocial and the outlaws are moved closer to heaven, that is, they are more spiritual than the others who are ordinary, philistine, and incapable of heroic acts. This uncle of mine remained the only childless person in a family where seventeen grandchildren were born to my grandfather. He also openly despised communists and chose an asocial lifestyle as his sole weapon of disgust and rebellion. This man passed away in a godforsaken mountain shack, abandoned even by his insane wife.

His elder brother, an uncle whom I remember for his sarcastic sense of humor, was also in permanent conflict with the village party functionaries after they took power. He paid for this with several incarcerations, the exclusion of his children from high school, and unemployment. All of his children had a miserable life (one of them, a handsome restaurant singer, hung himself in the early 1990s because of depression). This uncle's preferred curse was "those bloody communists, they dropped their shit all over this country!"

In a mysterious recollection, I see myself watching him walk away on a foggy morning: his stooped back, his straddling gait, a long kitchen knife in his right hand, and a fat turkey about to be slaughtered hanging down from his left. She had been living well, this turkey, but now the infallible hand of her butcher is about to disconnect her head from her body. The air does not smell of crime. But it is, nevertheless, Balkan air, which envelops the scene with a sense of remoteness and locates it far from any civilized existence. The man in the fog is lonelier than even his desolate figure suggests. He was there, but since no records could be made of him, he was, in fact, nowhere. He was severed from civilization. He was as much a phantom as the turkey whose life he held in his own hands. The moisture of an air full of past crimes and imminent "civilized" vibrations sticks in my nostrils like a reminder of obedience, oblivion, and unimportance. To rule over domestic animals in a foggy farmyard was the boldest act this man could afford.

None of my uncles were obstreperous men. Like my father, they wrapped up their deeds in silence. Following this tradition, my father chose an alternative that would alienate him from his natural existence. Did blood, animal copulation, and village mud disgust him? Or was he simply lucky enough to discover a counterpoint to the Balkan backwardness? Was he smarter than his brothers in accomplishing a breakthrough in this enchanting uncivilization? The fact is that by some kind of a poetic justice his choice was finally dismissed along with his own insignificant lifetime.

In a way, he was the pride of his father. Being the only one with an aptitude for education, he was sent to study at the Varna School of Economics after he finished high school. With about eighty thousand inhabitants before the war, Varna was Bulgaria's third largest city. After graduation, he entered a military school and pursued a career as an officer in the Tsar's army. This choice was an unmistakable sign of the values he had adopted at the time, and these, of course, were the best values his father could have imagined for a young man seeking prosperity in the Balkans. The fact of the matter is that no trace of socialism could be found in his choice of values. The military offered high social status, good money, and undisputed channels for controlling power.

My father had fond memories and several long-term friends from his military years. Unfortunately, he was struck by tuberculosis, which brought an end to his military career. Back in the village, he learned that some of his mates were engaged in clashes with the authorities. It smelled of clandestine activity everywhere. Hitler's troops were besieging Moscow and Stalingrad, and in rural Bulgaria the sympathies in the Fatherland War, as could be well expected, went naturally to the "brothers." I was never told why my father turned toward the communist movement. Interestingly enough, I never bothered to ask.

It was just a fait accompli for me that my father was a party member, as if he had been born with his membership, like my grandfather's "Active Fighter" status (neither of them could be who they were without these affiliations). There was no self-criticism in our family that could have challenged the communist activities of its members. There was, however, a would-be critical attitude toward personalities in the party leadership, locally as well as nationally. But this criticism, I realized later, did not question communist values.

The family regarded my father as a parvenu, and condescension always colored the appreciation he received for his professional achievements. His peasant origins were tacitly ridiculed, and this behavior in my family prevented me from fully understanding or respecting the primitive context in which he had spent his childhood. This means that he did not matter so very much to me, and neither did his communist inclinations.

My father lacked the bravery to engage in the clandestine activities of his closest friends. Shortly after the war he inscribed himself in the local party cell of the youth communist organization, which was the springboard for the party membership he was awarded a year later. His transformation was characteristic of the majority of people who formed the backbone of the BCP during the 1950s.

My father did not match the definition of a peasant. He did not possess land himself, nor had he worked land at any time in his life. He was no peasant, despite his first fifteen years spent in the protean broth of Mother Nature. The corset of education suited him better. After a military career became impossible, his dream was to become a teacher, nothing more and nothing less. His education gave him advantages over his brothers. But it also made him resent their miserable life, their labor in the fields, even their game hunting. My guess is that, on top of everything else, he was physically unfit for this, and emotionally rather aloof from any adventurous lifestyle. When I knew him, he was cowardly and insecure. He lacked an enterprising spirit, preferring instead to sit at his desk and read or write. He was just plain boring.

It was to these boring, colorless, watered-down people that communism, spreading like a puddle over Eastern Europe, appeared as an opportunity. Its faceless ideology of collectivism and collective action; its appeal to the unimportant, unfed, unhoused, and disempowered; and its rejection of individual values on behalf of vaguely defined community ideals felt like a balm to their hearts. Claiming involvement in the clandestine activities and passing from a state of mute nullity into the camp of power reclamation was a mere technicality. Like every technicality, however, it arose from a unique personal context.

In those troubled years preceding the defeat of Hitler's Germany, my grandma came with her daughter to live in a village, fleeing the risk of bombardment by Royal Air Force planes flying missions over Varna. In 1944, the bombardment of civilian targets became routine since Bulgaria was a German ally and, although she stood apart from military involvement on the eastern front, she had to suffer some punishment by the Allies. The bombing raids were limited and caused little damage, but people took precautions, especially in view of the approaching end of the war.

My grandma, whose husband was in a camp at that time, locked her pharmacy and her house and struck out for some remote place where the pace of life had not yet been disturbed by cannonades, fascist or antifascist hysteria, and uncertainty. This place happened to be my father's native village. And the room she rented for herself and her daughter, in her senior year of high school, happened to be in my father's native house.

I have a friend who believes that, astrologically, the occurrence of every single couple is foreseen by destiny and we are deluded in thinking that we choose and command the circumstances of our lives. Even if such fatalism sounds exaggerated, I bestow great importance on coincidences that seem so well staged. At that time, my father was still recovering from his tuberculosis and had not yet found employment or joined the local communist guerrillas. While he gazed sheepishly at the young girl he was about to court, he was also calculating the effect of an eventual marriage that would catapult him out of the peasantry. With respect to the outcome of the war and the readiness to acclaim a communist rule in postwar Bulgaria, he certainly found a consensus of opinion between himself, the young girl, and her mother. Every time I try to imagine them talking in the cosmic silence of the village night, I cannot help but associate their image with my uncle and his turkey. In the air enveloping their conversations about Hitler,

Stalin, Europe, and the approaching communism, I smell the same severance from civilized existence. This severance is the predicament of the Balkans.

Something happens with the big world and we expect it to happen with us, too. We expect it to happen in its mysterious enchantment but outside its true meaning and by virtue of anybody else's energy, not ours. History's meaning comes to our mind distorted beyond recognition. We intercept it like a message about the changes that are about to occur. We take for granted that history's aim is to serve our primitive egos without requiring our involvement in return. For my father, liberation meant saying goodbye to the village, making his petty nest in town, and joining the ranks of the ruling class. He experienced the chronic desire to rule, characteristic of all Bulgarians who have always been ruled. He did not care that he would only be co-opted by the group of rulers without, once again, truly belonging to them. But he was needed as padding for the veneer of democracy and mass support. He was needed and he was in need. Both interests mapped in a perfect harmony.

So, the day after Russian troops occupied the country, my father entered the youth communist organization to which his fiancée already belonged. He actually joined the forces that were forming the backbone of the communist-manipulated Fatherland Front, the future scarecrow of democratic coalition under the caption of the BCP. Because of his relatively neutral position in the years before, the guerrillas who descended from the bush installed him as mayor of the village. Within months he resigned. He was anxious to get married. Indeed, the wedding was held in the summer of 1945. He found a job as an accountant with the Shipyard Society, Limited, in Varna, but also bought a sawmill in the low mountainous area surrounding his native village. This inconsistent move betrays his ambiguity regarding the policy of total nationalization, which was written in the platform of the BCP, which he joined at the same time. Simply put, communist rhetoric and uncertain political developments could not wipe out his semipeasant/semi-petit-bourgeois mentality. He was not a genuine believer. Instead, he tried to maneuver until the situation became clearer. The sawmill business was frail, however, and he soon hastened to liquidate it. Shortly thereafter, he was offered a teaching position in the high school of economics at Svishtov, the small town on the Danube where great-uncle Todor Vladigerov was a professor of political economy. The very next year, 1949, with father's new family's intercession, great-uncle took him in as an assistant professor at the High Institute of Economy.

So began my father's "intellectual" career, which was to provide him with two things: a full professorship within about fifteen years, and a place in the local party nomenclature, both for good. But it did not provide him with celebrity. His career was devoid of brilliance or outstanding achievements. Today, after so many years, and after he is already deceased, I am still startled by the total absence of dramatic events or significance, however ordinary, in this man's life.

Unfortunately, his choices, or rather failures to choose, caused so many troubles in my life. His generation conceived of the rules according to which my generation, the Balkan baby boomers, was ordained to live. His generation was exactly what communism was all about. It was tailored to suit ungifted, morally castrated people who lacked true individuality. These people, in return, supported communism. They were the stuff of which communism was made. Communism was not the product of strong men imposing their wills upon millions of weak and speechless people, although that is its conventional portrait. Communism was produced by a nameless human nature, bred in darkness.

My father was "proper" in all outward appearances: a quiet, harmless, faithful husband; a respected university professor; a law-abiding citizen; an obedient item of the party nomenclature. No private property. Trustworthy. He was no leader in his field, but a hard worker. He had no original publications, only Marxism-parroting textbooks for students belonging to the same peasant-cum-intellectual class bred in the remote obscurity of the Balkans.

Every morning before breakfast, he would reread the lectures he had written the night before, then shave, drink a linden tisane, put on his galoshes, and walk three muddy blocks down to the stony university building. He would hardly notice the gray Danube float, the shallow Romanian bank to the north, or the kids invading the corner cafeteria for a hasty junk-food breakfast. He would climb the staircase, open the door, walk by the library, the dean's office, the party secretary's headquarters, and the accountants' department, and continue until he reached his own desk in the room for professors. He would take off his coat and hat and pull out the sheets on which his lecture was handwritten, and at that moment the bell would ring.

A crowd of progressive young people waited on his every word in the stove-heated lecture hall. He would begin to read monotonously, *sans doute,* and the students would diligently begin to take notes. Lunchtime came slowly and went quickly, after which he would attend the regular party meetings. By three o'clock he would hit the streets and head for home.

His home consisted of two four-by-four-meter rooms in a two-story house. One of them was transformed into a kitchen, while the other served as bedroom for him, his wife, and his son.

His five-year-old son waited for him in the unheated kitchen, where he had been left alone for the day wrapped in sweaters and blankets. He would salute the boy without enthusiasm or apparent friendship, start a fire in the stove, and sit at the table to write his lecture for the next day. Shortly thereafter, dusk enveloped father and son in silence and alienation, but neither of them knew that they were alienated. The father would turn on the lamp hanging over the table, and after a while the mother arrived from the hospital, signaling it was time for supper.

Supper was as regular as the father's labor: salami once a week, cooked beans twice a week, cooked potatoes with tinned vegetables twice a week, and fried eggs, stew, or raw white bacon on weekends. The son was sent to bed in the cold, dark bedroom right after supper. The same routine unfolded at the same pace the next morning. And nobody was interested in the life of this professor, his wife, and his son. Nobody knew they existed. Nobody cared if he or she knew. Except, perhaps, the party. The party set a code of behavior and if the professor dared change one street in his everyday walk to work, he was visited the next morning by a party worker who let him know that his misbehavior had been duly recorded. Whether he had dared to change the street remains a mystery to me. I would venture to say he hadn't.

Anyway, the voice of the party was on the radio. The word of the party was on the billboards. The slogan of the party was printed in its newspaper, the only one that brought the news to the family. At that time the party slogan was "to accomplish in twenty years what other nations did in a hundred." A five-year plan for the country, the first one in a series, was voted at the party congress, and the country worked for its implementation. The professor's lectures explained to the students the importance and strength of the five-year plan and why it was desirable to fulfill it in shortened terms.

Contrary to what some might imagine, the professor was not in a state of metamorphosis and would never become a caterpillar amidst a sweaty nightmare. He was not even aware that such a metamorphosis had happened somewhere in the Kafkaesque world and was about to happen to thousands of people modestly waiting in the daily lines of communism for milk, bread, and marmalade. Neither was he watched from TV screens, caved in the wall of the university room or in his own kitchen.

As a matter of fact, the landscape in which Franz Kafka uncovered existential hopelessness was Mittel Europa. The imperial bureaucracy in Prague and Vienna, and the obscure settlements between these two capitals maintained the futility of common sense, decent effort, and self-righteous petit bourgeois existence. Bulgaria is in the geographic periphery of middle Europe, but communism removed her farther along this fringe. I have always suspected, for example, that Kafka left a tiny shard of self-awareness in the mind of his characters. Eastward, within the Balkan obscurity, you would not be able to find any awareness of a person's pointlessness whatsoever.

Joseph K. knew that he existed in an absurd world. My father did not know this, and did not attempt to know.

Well, years passed and changes occurred, nonetheless. After ten years of assistant-professorship my father was sent to Berlin, East Berlin of course, to audit lectures at the Humboldt Universität. During his stay, Berlin was still a mixed city, so he must have compared the different worlds burgeoning miraculously in the middle of Cold Europe. He returned without epiphany. He reread the same lectures as the year before and attended the same schedule of party meetings. He continued to reread ad nauseam Marx's *Das Kapital* and some of Engels's books; dialectic materialism remained his top philosophical tool.

The next year he went to visit a Polish colleague in Berlin, and during that very time the Berlin Wall was erected overnight, virtually before his eyes. No epiphany whatsoever! He reread his lectures from the previous year with the stubbornness of a pair of oxen that plow the furrows of the same piece of land the same way every spring.

He was a mute witness, not a muted one. He had no skills to confront absurdity. And he had no desire to achieve anything else but a peaceful, haphazardly salaried professorship. In his mind he had accomplished a gigantic leap from the village to the university. By international standards, however, it was actually the university, which had slipped back to the village. Communist ideologues hailed this as the birth of a new communist intelligentsia.

Being a legitimate representative of this intelligentsia, my father prided himself as an achiever. As a matter of fact, after obtaining tenure in Varna in the year following the erection of the Berlin Wall, he sadly continued to lecture new generations of students in the vein of "socialist" political economy till his retirement in 1981. He certainly ate better food. He visited classical music concerts, a string of foreign countries, and art exhibitions.

He was granted some privileges: a double-room at reduced cost each summer in the International House of Scientists near Varna, an occasional invitation to some party celebrations in the party Town Hall on New Year's Eve or on the Ninth of September, the National Day of Bulgaria. But he never wore a tuxedo or gave a speech with a witty sense of self-irony. He wrote no memoirs acknowledging the full failure of his life. The span of his life was so ordinary as to exempt him utterly from any ups and downs.

Life, on the other hand, is about the ordinary. Communism could be born and kept viable because it had permeated the ordinary existence of people with ordinary daydreams and ordinary capacities, like my father. My father took his career seriously and there was hardly anything that could make him doubt his self-respect. He thought of himself as a dignified person, particularly in his uprightness. His honesty, however, stopped short of addressing the moral pitfalls of the regime installed in the country by the party to which he belonged.

In short, he was a coparticipant by proxy. As a member of this party, he was unquestionably a member of the regime. But this facet of his moral character was beyond reproach. It was taboo. He never stole, he never lied, he never enriched himself at the expense of others, etc. As far as he and his relatives were concerned, he was a perfectly honest individual.

It should come as no surprise that he was full of righteous indignation over corruption within the party. About Stalin as well as about some village fellows he was told had abused the party's trust by embezzling. About Zhivkov as well as about the faculty dean who failed to disclose his participation in a fascist youth organization before the revolution in order to get access to the ruling BCP. It is true that my father was upright and consistent in this respect. He never joined political movements apart from the communist one, and he did not resign from his party membership until his death. He called this uprightness.

At first, in his youth he did not care about politics at all. For him, joining a political movement was a move of no relevance whatsoever. Later, when he had calculated the benefits from adhering to the Communist Party, he should have known the price (both political and moral) that he had to pay for these benefits. When he finally became aware of what was going on, the honest thing to do (had he been genuinely honest) would have been to give back his membership card.

Why did my father not do it? Either because he was a true supporter of the party and was not critical, let alone rebellious, toward the form of rule the party exercised upon the country and upon half of Europe; or because, in spite of his critical stance, he had been choosing the social privileges by paying the moral price for this.

If asked about it, my father would probably answer with a question: "Did I ever have a choice?" It is at this point that people who have not violated the written laws advance fear to blur moral dilemmas. People say they were so frightened by the regime that they could not act against it. As a matter of fact, fear is a false excuse. *What* you are afraid of is what is important.

In my father's case, he feared for his privileged position, not his job, since everyone under communism was assured a job no matter how miserable the pay. He feared for his *achievement* (the leap from being a village person to a university professor). And this achievement was possible only under conditions that the Communist Party had created and continued to enforce consistently: the equality of people (not for people); the sense that an achievement is delivered but not won in a fair competition; the morally troubling requirement to sign a contract of obedience with the communist dictatorship.

On one hand, my father was a quasi-believer, and on the other, he was enticed like any imperfect human being by the comfort of privileges. As far as the enticement is concerned, ordinariness is a major factor. My father felt like an ordinary man, a man not called upon to perform brave acts of dissent. He saw that everyone around him felt the same way, so, he reasoned, why bother to be an exception?

Thus, he had neither the intellectual honesty to totally dismiss the doctrine nor the character to totally dismiss the privileges. True, he was an ordinary person: being both an ordinary character and behaving like the majority. Not haunted by scruples or tormented by historic guilt, my father was suddenly stricken with Parkinson's disease at the age of sixty-two. During the fourteen years preceding his death in 1992, this debilitating disease would not allow him to get even with the ambivalent state of his own personality—even if that had been his wish.

At my father's funeral, I saw one of my cousins with whom I had had a special relationship throughout all those years. He had not seen me during the previous two years since the communist regime began falling apart, and both of us knew why. We did not live under communism anymore. The forty-five-year-old order was crumbling apart and with it, the hierarchy established between my cousin and me was falling apart, too. Alas, on that day I did not know that it was to be our last meeting.

It was late February, 1992. The body's expectations of the forthcoming spring made the chill seem more biting than it really was. The rationed electricity forced people to heat their homes economically, so there was no place to hide from the cold except under the heavy quilts of the night bed.

A little over two years had passed from the day Todor Zhivkov was ousted and democratic hopes had consequently flourished and faded in the hearts of a minority of Bulgarian citizens. As for myself, earlier in the week I had received documents certifying that my immediate family had been granted landed immigrant status in Canada, just six months after we had applied.

Five years earlier, in September, 1987, I had lost my grandma, who passed away quietly at the age of ninety. She was happily spared the gradual decay of the communist system. My father, too, hardly understood the ongoing events, since the disease had taken his mind long before his heart stopped beating. At any rate, he could not express himself verbally, and we had no idea what was going on in his head.

The sense of loss was overwhelming, but it would not have been so pervasive had it not been accompanied by a sense of decay. Garbage filled the once picturesque small streets of my native seaboard town. Half-finished construction projects stood abandoned in the chilly wind. Shops and cafeterias remained closed until late in the day. When they finally opened, their emptiness was ugly, sadly reminiscent of the summer joyousness that had once reigned over the place. Even the cemetery, which in this country is a place of ultimate order, was a shambles (old graves covered with weeds, tombstones tilted grotesquely here and there). And then there were the new graves that were dug shallow and not aligned parallel with the existing alleys. The rushed funeral ceremony was held in a marrow-chilling hall (communists did not enter churches, even for a burial service) and nothing trembled inside me when I kissed the dead man's icy forehead good-bye.

My cousin Angel was late for the funeral, since only one flight a day, arriving about noon, was scheduled from the capital to Varna. We were eating the after-funeral lunch, steamy red peppers stuffed with minced pork and rice, when he entered from the backyard. His face was solemn and mournful: everyone knew that he had come to pay homage to his uncle. Everybody knew that his uncle's aid was largely instrumental for the success of my cousin's career. But I knew that behind his funereal appearance, my cousin was shaken to his foundations by the symbolism of my father's death. The village, the party, the privileged position, the meaning of life: all was either dead or dying.

Angel was the most vital, energetic, and cheerful man I had met by this time. He was nine years old when the September Revolution of 1944 hit the country. There was no way he could have been aware that the Red Army was the real carrier of this so-called revolution, much less that Bulgaria had been sold out to communist Russia several months before at a wet bargaining table where two players (Joseph Stalin and Winston Churchill) carved up Europe into zones of influence.

During his teens, Angel was wild and boisterous, fishing, hunting, and horseback riding all day long. He skipped school to play poker, and never gave a dime for politics. Because of his unseemly performance, he had great difficulty getting the grades he needed to graduate from secondary school. Once he did, however, he made his choice. More precisely, my father helped him make this choice. He summoned him to Svishtov and forced him to enroll in undergraduate studies with a major in finance. It was during this period that I first met and befriended Angel.

I say "befriended" in spite of our age difference: he was nineteen and I was seven at the time. On the other hand, my family regarded me as a *Wunderkind,* whereas Angel was thought to have the mentality of a village boy. In this respect, he was different from my father, who rarely displayed the remnants of his village mentality. My father was usually embarrassed by a strong inferiority complex in the presence of urban people.

At the age of seven I read the newspapers and knew the names of all the members of the Soviet and Bulgarian Politburos, who appeared regularly on the front pages. I recited poetry and was the youngest reader to borrow books from the municipal library. I proudly showed the adults a notebook where I kept track of all the books I had read by that time. I wrote letters to my grandma and recognized all of the important cities on the map of Europe and the Soviet Union. My grandma and I used to take the train from Varna to Svishtov when returning to my parents' town at the end of each summer. I remember how the passengers in our compartment were amazed at my ability to name all the railway stations on this particular route. On top of everything, I could speak and read German, because my grandma always spoke to me in this language (German was her native tongue).

To know all these things before starting school was shocking for the people of this country where education (as an embodiment of the abstract veneration of knowledge) ranked very high. The village boy, who knew a lot more things with an inappreciable practical value, could not dream of such an "achievement." It was taken for granted that the achievement was due to the town, to some urban specialness that enables people to be utterly cultivated. No one thought that this could actually be the result of innate intelligence. My father's professorship and "high" career status were also partly explained by his move to the town, not by his intellect. The very notion of intellect hardly visited someone's mind when tackling this matter: people were usually divided into "stupid" and "smart" or "cultured" and "simple."

The mentality of the village boy was dominated by this idea of the self as simple, uncultured, and *a priori* inferior by comparison with town people. It tacitly implied that a town boy would grow up cultured and somewhat smarter than would a village boy. Well, when on top of that predisposition you have a small boy who is famous for his special kind of "cultured" performances since the age of five, it goes without saying that my cousin met me with respect and subordination. This explains why we were friends from the very beginning despite the age difference. The experience that he had was diminished in his eyes by my "cultured" status. For my part, I liked his spontaneity and especially his willingness to play the role of my teacher and protector in physical exercise and games. He spent hours running after my bicycle to keep me from falling when I began learning to ride. I regret that my parents were so narrow-minded that they did not allow him to teach me to play cards. I still consider this a big mistake, since card games give you a good instinct for gambling, which is often indispensable in adult life.

When I grew up, it became clear to me that Angel and I were equally intelligent and able individuals. But this initial inequality could never be effaced between us, no matter how rational we became or how differently our careers unfolded. When I grew up, I also learned about his mainstream activities during the time when he played Ping-Pong with me.

In the first place, he dramatically improved his grades. The sense of pragmatism and probably some incentives provided by my father led him to reverse his idle, high school direction. My cousin obtained high grades in all his courses and there was a qualitative leap (to use the fashionable term in communist society) in his acquisition of economic knowledge. At the same time, he became very active in the young communist league (the Komsomol): at one point, he was elected secretary of the university Komsomol organization. Stories of girls and love affairs were running around, but to me they were irrelevant at this age, and later there was no one willing to tell them again. What I knew for sure was that he had had one serious love affair, which failed to culminate in a wedding, and this caused tension between him and my father. Needless to say, my father was a puritan as far as sexual relationships were concerned. Angel was up to a great career, and love affairs ought to be of secondary importance in the long run. He was fashioning himself in the image of a leader.

My cousin had already been chosen by the party servants to become a cadre member in the nomenclature. Thus, he was pushed to follow a freshly elaborated—but very successful from the party perspective—pattern. Teenagers from families that were thoroughly scrutinized as "clean," that is, bourgeoisie-free and not linked to the "former elements," were encouraged to engage in Komsomol activities. This was their official activity. The promotion of those who seemed promising was manipulated carefully, and at the same time they were introduced to some unofficial activities within the domain of the secret police. They were nonchalantly invited to collaborate by reporting any suspicious acts or conversations of their colleagues and relatives—anything that could be interpreted as an anticommunist mood, frustration with the regime, or inclination toward Western values and lifestyles. Those who engaged in this kind of collaboration wholeheartedly were introduced into the system of watching, harassing, and fabricating files about people. The cream of this cohort of "our boys" was further trained in the art of spying, in most cases as a part-time activity. Indeed, they did not become professional spies, but their official occupation was used as a cover for the clandestine tasks they were required to perform when need be.

Thus, young people who in the beginning engaged willingly and without full awareness of these "innocent" activities were no longer free individuals. The system was so tight and self-controlling that those who might have had the impulse to quit found themselves chained by the very knowledge they held about the system itself. Since the system was perpetuated in all social structures, there was no other place to go. This undercover infrastructure was the most solid social contract ever designed. The whole society was bound together in a huge pyramidal structure, where the person who occupied the upper position could handle each element below. At these early times, my cousin still had the choice to dive into it or to remain an outsider—rejected, disregarded, unprotected, abandoned, and deprived of rights. Or did he?

Human choices are managed by the ubiquitous sense of well-being. Angel was smart, ambitious, and aggressive. He had unpleasant childhood recollections of poverty, smashing labor, and narrow horizons. Lucrative or intellectual prosperity had never been considered chances for him. In addition, the village (or the country town, for that matter) was too small a locus for exercising power. With the Communist Party as a vehicle, however, he felt like he was on the fast track in a career that would provide a great potential for personal well-being, the kind of well-being and success he understood and hoped to achieve.

Angel graduated as a brilliant student and a Komsomol leader. His credentials were impeccable. He was also a member of the BCP and, as far as any investigation into his family history might have revealed, he had no compromising persons or deeds on his record. By party standards, he was the ideal person to be installed and used within the echelons of power. By his own standards, the party was the ideal catalyst for well-being. At the time, the issue of rank was not on the agenda. What counted was that he was labeled trustworthy and promising. It was common knowledge that, if nothing unpredictable occurred, he would be eligible for a virtually unlimited hierarchical climb. It is essential to point out that he was not a well-traveled man, which helped him focus his intellectual power within the narrow Balkan horizons. As a result, his energy could be concentrated on a local model, where it was both explosive and sustained.

The local model of communism, alas, was imported by the Red Army and the plainclothes emissaries of the Soviet Communist Party. They required obedience, social and individual uniformity, and political stability. They did not care how this was achieved, provided it was achieved without fault. The lure in suppressing disobedience and instability was the host of promises taken from Marx's works and fashioned into tempting perks for those who would join the ruling party. I would not call this corruption. It was more like the small piece of cheese in a mousetrap, although the party trap was certainly more lavishly decorated and abundant in primitive comfort.

On the other hand, life in Bulgaria is poor and primitive, so a high price tag cannot be hung on it. Neither can its price be inflated by hopes for a prosperous future or economic flourishing. We know that this is never going to happen to us. We know that we are simple and backward, and we comply with this. The emotional counterbalance here is that we believe in the *joie de vivre*. It is instantaneous, explosive, and, when the moment comes, experienced as if it is the last emotion we are allowed in life. Being rare, these moments are, therefore, acted out with a kind of desperation. Out of proportion, they satiate the imagination long after any gastronomic or alcoholic ecstasy. The birth of a child, the wedding, and the funeral are the happiest occasions in which we explode in a *joie de vivre*. Otherwise, it is entirely missing from the monotonous, round-the-clock, labor-burdened existence.

Learned sophistication, too, cannot add price to life, since it is regarded as a strange, remote feature of those not descending from our rug. The "privileged," who are sent to educate themselves, are regarded on their return as lost forever to the joys of life. They have been transformed into dry, unemotional, and self-contained individuals. It is almost as if the educational process had soaked up their vitality and stopped them from sharing the pagan passions during the rare moments of joy.

Power is also irrelevant to raising the value of life, since power is used mainly to get more money. It is not exercised as a political philosophy or as an extension of an economic strategy. Money, paradoxically, has nothing to do with the price of life. Even if you did get rich, there was very little to be acquired in the common meanness of this place. Your riches were, by and large, meaningless. To spend your money outside the country was regarded as an act of betrayal. If you did, you were virtually ostracized from the community. The insider must remain average. Those who dared to distinguish themselves were no longer regarded as insiders.

All this boils down to a philosophy of desperation and discontinuity, both of which make idleness preferable to initiative. Life is sad, priceless, painful—but we only get one! And it is worth celebrating in forgetfulness its joyful moments, while enduring its constant suffering as a curse over all of us. This is the mysterious chemistry of life: to be dirty and hated, to be entirely in the physical as opposed to spiritual state (which is pain and obscurity), to be mad with joy in those few moments of release from suffering provided by life's key rituals, and to evaporate after your last breath is gone. Mystic forces govern the world, yes, but it is not within the power of the simple man to establish any liaison with them whatsoever. It is the gap between this and the other world that conveys the meaninglessness of existence. Hence, fatalism is the only acceptable existential philosophy. Man is an incident. Only the sublime spiritual might, which manages the world's affairs, is eternal.

This was the genealogy behind Angel's choice. If one may speak of rationality in this regard, it boiled down to calculating his personal capacity to endure the chronic stress of suspicion, secrecy, hypocrisy, and dishonesty. Angel had a sufficiently adventurous flair to decide in favor of his natural talents, even if he might have had some hesitation.

It would not be entirely correct, however, to assume that he was simply seduced by the perks awarded to those who hid their lives in the bosom of the Communist Party. Angel's choice was also due to a measure of genuine trust in the party's mission to change life, society, and the destiny of the disfranchised. This trust, however, was progressively failing to materialize, although it did not fail to justify Angel's social status: "I am a servant with a mission and hence I am fully entitled to the perks."

Angel's biography unfolded in three parallel lives. After he graduated from university, I lost touch with him. I returned with my parents to Varna, while he took an administrative position in the largest agricultural town in the wheat-producing sector of the country. Life Number One, the life that everyone knew about, was his career as both a party worker and an economics professor. In the beginning, my father hoped that Angel would become his assistant in the Department of Socialist Finances, but he switched to administration. It was only later that Angel told me about this surprising decision. It was not his own. Indeed, he admitted that during the forceful collectivization of the land in the early 1950s he had taken part in the gangs, which used to harass peasants who had refused to give their property "voluntarily" to the cooperative farm. Owing to Angel's rural background, the party assigned him the responsibility of overseeing the management of farm production in the Dobrudzha region (in the northeast part of Bulgaria). So, he started working hard to meet the demands of the party's five-year plan and to establish himself as a reliable apparatchik. Meanwhile, he married the daughter of a former middle landowner from the same county. This was a well-premeditated move with regard to housing since the bride's inherited portion of her father's large estate saved Angel the money and headache of finding a home for his newly settled family.

Angel had no scruples about acquiring a bride with a house. This was his chance, so he thought. It would be an overstatement to say that he was emotionally involved with her. Their marriage was violent, dysfunctional, and nearly always at the edge of divorce, this despite their two sons born rather early in wedlock. In all fairness, however, the marriage was also a calculated affair for his wife. She acquired a privileged social status and, interestingly enough, immunity from persecution as the daughter of a former landowner. Their marriage was the most common example of this sort of deal people were forced to strike in their strategy of compliance.

Being a workaholic, and having established useful connections in town, Angel embarked upon a career and life track that suited his personality almost perfectly. As a cloak for his secret life, he took a nontenured lecturer's position in the Higher Institute of Economics in Varna two or three years after he began his administrative work. He began slowly to slide into the parallel career of an academic. Here, too, he was an achiever. Within a turbulent fifteen-year period, he reached the level of full professor without ever having been on the tenure track.

In the late stages of party rule, when we were both reunited in Sofia, I was allowed some insight into his strictly confidential Life Number Two. The initial services he performed for the Communist Party had been officially rewarded with a higher rank in the secret police. Angel's secret rank facilitated his access to the files of the population. This gave him a means of manipulating practically everyone in the region with information that people hardly suspected he might possess. In the long run, his secret life was aimed at the same goals he pursued officially: to conceal his trustworthiness and to outrank peers and rivals both administratively and socially. He collaborated with the secret sections of the local police office in a long-term project that I called "operation surveillance."

The 1950s and 1960s were the years when the party's grip over the populace took elaborate forms reaching perfection, and simultaneously the grip of Secretary General Todor Zhivkov over the party became no less refined and structurally entrenched. Party members watched the outside population, while the more trustworthy party members watched the less trustworthy party members. Competition within the party amounted to climbing from the first form of surveillance work to the second. If you excelled in the first, you were promoted to the second.

Angel excelled in every kind of work, overt and covert. He was cunning, subtle, and unscrupulous. He adapted himself to the system with elegance and proficiency. The system, in turn, condescendingly accommodated him. His ultimate aspirations could never be entirely satisfied for one simple reason: he was not linked to the small clique surrounding the big party boss. To make matters worse, he was unable to find any peripheral channels for gaining entrance into this circle of faithful comrades of Bai Todor, as he was commonly known. Again, *faithful* must be regarded as a very relative term in this context: people from Todor's entourage were faithful to the degree that they were effectively bound by the undisclosed "information" the feudal lord possessed about their past and present. There was also a generational rivalry in which the old guard (being in reality not so old physically) successfully defended the strongholds of power like, for example, all key positions in the military ministries and in the central and local party structures. Thus, Angel's real asset was the network of connections he had established with his colleagues in the party apparatus on the high floors of the city hall and in the police basements. In the bosom of this community he enjoyed his Life Number Three. This life was the delight, which helped him perform and endure the other two.

This third life consisted of wine, women, and hunting. In all lifestyles, wine and women has always been one of the most preferred, and certainly one of the easiest. Hunting added a touch of nobility to the whole enterprise, which, by definition if not by force of habit, began in clean-shaven sobriety and ended in a drunken stupor (normally between the legs of an equally dead-to-the-world female). Admittedly, there was not a single male in the entire community who would not consider himself an expert in this art of "high" pleasures. The irony was that wine, women, and hunting were officially dismissed from the standard of proper communist behavior, and thus possessed an additional flavor of indulging in the forbidden fruit. Some poorly infiltrated Romanesque stereotypes made those powerful guys feel as a select caste, insofar as pleasures were notorious to distinguish the Roman imperial caste. The truth was that nobody selected them or elected them, but that they all felt macho and strained to behave according to their primitive ideas of machismo.

A large contribution to Angel's secret career was his voluntary participation in crushing the Prague insurrection in 1968. As did every Bulgarian man who had spent his obligatory two years of military service, Angel had a reserve rank in the army. Those who were especially trustworthy, however, were honored with an officer's position in the reserve. Among these officers, there was a distinguished elite category for those who held both army and police rank. These men served as party watchdogs within the army, particularly when some special operations had to be performed. Thus, it was in the capacity of army police officer (the official designation was "political" officers), that Angel was summoned to the Bulgarian troops sent to join in the Russian invasion of Czechoslovakia. The whole campaign was publicly hailed as a demonstration of international communist solidarity embodied by "the fraternal armies."

Angel put on the military uniform in May, 1968, by the force of his obligations as an officer in the reserve. However, he also felt that it was his duty as a communist to defend the achievements of Marxist-Leninist socialism. He sincerely believed this, and even told me so later. From a strictly human point of view, he wanted to go into battle. Therefore, I do not hesitate to say that he participated voluntarily in this shameful campaign. He returned proud of the victory, and no remorse showed in his narratives about the campaign when he came to recollect his youth in the early 1990s. On the contrary, he spoke of spoiled bourgeois and thankless lumpens,

My cousin, Angel, working at his villa in the outskirts of Baltchik, a small town on the Black Sea north of Varna, in July, 1986. Angel was director of the Labor Department of the Bulgarian Trade Unions at the time. (Author's collection.)

and there were pangs of just retaliation in his voice. His human judgment centered on a well-performed military adventure, while his political judgment focused on the act of enforcing international communism, which had successfully protected the integrity of the socialist camp. Had a fissure in the socialist integrity occurred, he contended, the well-arranged status quo would have been ruined, and the fissure would never have been mended.

As to his ambitions, their saturation followed a well-established pattern. After a decade spent in the provinces in his many public and covert roles, Angel was appointed department chief for the national headquarters of the Bulgarian Trade Union. Ironically again, the Trade Union was as much a travesty of trade unions as Angel's party promotion was of the professional career he pretended to have achieved as a self-respecting male from the European periphery.

This overall duplicity characterized Bulgarian public life under communism no less than the overall compliance with the communist regime. Both were tightly interrelated. People genuinely complied with communist rule for two major reasons. First, they realized that communists were not some exotic remote stock but their neighbors, the backgammon players in the local cafeterias and the village dropouts whom nobody took seriously. Very often, communists came from one's own family. Secondly, they did not care about communism itself if they could accommodate their existence to it. As long as no one bothered them, Bulgarians knew innumerable ways of existential accommodation. One such mechanism of accommodation was the duplicity of social life.

Duplicity was also the cornerstone of Angel's character. When he took his post in Sofia, his life skyrocketed. The increased power he wielded was proportional to the giant step up in his appointment. For some, he had catapulted to this above-middle level from nowhere, but for those who knew the secret details of his life, this was a deserved promotion. His three lives were promoted all at the same time. On one hand, the life of the country town he had just left was highly dependent on his acts and decisions. On the other, his involvement in the secret intelligence service assumed international dimensions when he was given tasks related to international espionage. These tasks were covered under his participation in scientific events around the world. Last but not least, he was now granted access to nationwide hunting reservations only accessible to high-ranking party functionaries.

Late in 1989, when the communists ousted the long-lived feudal lord Bai Todor, Angel was at the top of his multiple careers, and his personal affairs looked great from afar. He had long forgotten his choices and apprehensions (if he ever had any at all) from the time he had enrolled in this party reality. But if he were to remember his start, and to be fair, he would say that he still had the alternative to reject party dependence. Only one exceptional circumstance must be taken into account: this was not a choice among several competing alternatives, but a choice between a positive and a negative response to one and the same alternative. His dilemma was simply to enroll or not to enroll. To sign a deal or not to sign a deal with the Communist Party stretching its muscles over the backward country.

He signed the deal. He preferred guaranteed personal well-being to uninsured (and not highly valued, for that matter) moral purity. The one thing he knew for certain was that the morally pure were doomed to a degenerating existence. So, he said yes and was ready to pay whatever price was due. Materialism has always been a predictable winner in this part of the world.

Despite Angel's unabashed materialism, God was merciful to him. He sent him a sudden death in a road accident in the summer of 1992. On a sultry July afternoon, we saw him off on his last journey. The noiseless village followed the coffin with invisible anger. Sunflowers on both sides of the muddy river bowed their faces in compliance to the swelter and the human lassitude. While the mournful procession took final leave of the deceased man, it also bade farewell to the communist era. Not only the face of death shocked the humble folk. They were stupefied by the fact that the petty happiness they thought was forever under "their" rule was slipping away. The deceased was just one crucial factor in this happiness.

Walking slowly amidst old women with their faces wrapped in black kerchiefs, I remembered my cousin as a young graduate student and how he used to run for hours after my bicycle ready to catch me if I fell. I felt transported into my childhood, during which I was most fascinated by locomotives, but totally unaware that my heart stood at the crossroads of incompatible values.

At this age, I now realize, the pressure of values had begun. And with it had come the immense brainwashing, from which I still cannot be certain I have been entirely cured.

CHAPTER 3

Victims and Victimizers

The human condition is not pain only.
—Czeslaw Milosz, "Body"

I was born in 1946 at the onset of the Iron Curtain. Rather, I was unlucky to be born on the eastern side of the self-erecting Iron Curtain. And I have been immersed in so-called socialist values ever since. The fact is that I grew up as a child of "socialist democracy."

Is there anyone who would dare deny that childhood is the happiest time of life? You are hugged and kissed and nourished and you are God blessed, although you are not aware of all of it. When adulthood comes, you want desperately to return there, either to flee some life drama in which you have become the leading actor or to understand the roots of your suffering, boredom, or failure.

In the moments when I go back to my happy childhood, I cannot find there any tangible signs of brainwashing. Even the fact that I was not particularly attached to my mother and father, or that they themselves seemed to care little about our emotional relationship, did not bother me. I loved everyone around the whole sunny world and me as if I were the inexhaustible source of life. Nothing on earth, person or event, could disappoint me.

Retrospectively, I suppose that I received in return the amount of love my young soul needed. Some skeptics would probably object that love is by itself a brainwashing, because adult life (and often childhood as well) is rather depressing and deficient in love. These memories of love and exaltation are evidence that even in the Balkans, where hardship is the rule of being, it was in the nature of things to expect good things to happen in life.

The formative landscape for me was the sea. It enhanced, instead of contradicting, my happy expectations. Yellow sand, idle people, the silence of the midday sun, an ink-blue horizon behind the motley array of beach umbrellas—this is the picture of eternity for me. Early in the afternoon, scoops of pink ice cream were served in German silver cups right on the beach, and a little afterward, the morning hubbub sank into a shady siesta. In this hour of paradise, the thin gurgle of a tap left running at the sand's edge marked the beach's silence as if for posterity.

The innocence of this scenery was rounded and smooth, as were the soft hills rolling along the mid-Bulgarian mountains into the endearing sea. Thin rivers meandered between the hills. Land and water and human expectations alike have always been frugal at the skirts of these hills, imposing moderation as a philosophy. For a child, it was all simply magnificent.

Affluence would never characterize my childhood, but misery was also remote. Frugality and moderation prevailed not only in terms of matter but of spirit as well. A child who does not know what luxury or excess or frustration is feels in perfect harmony with such a world—and trusts it.

My grandma owned part of a vineyard on one of the slanting hills overlooking Varna Bay. A small summer villa was built in its middle. Her neighbors were an aging couple with whom my grandparents used to drink Turkish coffee on a terrace covered with gray tiles. The husband was a retired sailor, one of the first captains in the small Bulgarian fleet of merchant vessels and cargo boats. Their terrace had a low iron fence adorned with anchors, lighthouses, and binoculars. In my recollections, it seems to me they had everything they needed. Wicker chairs (I preferred to climb on the rocking chair, of course), fine china cups and saucers, divinely flavored coffee blended with double-baked and finely ground chickpeas, homemade cookies or petit fours, and a lazy afternoon. The smell of sandy earth, retreating swelter, and vine leaves sprayed with a blue Bordeaux mixture. It was all so very French! But it was also mine, and so very Bulgarian, although no one would recognize it as such. But since I am alive and carry it with me, it undeniably exists, despite cruel attempts to take it.

My eighty-nine-year-old great-granddad, Ivan, and me on my third birthday.
Varna, June 18, 1949. (Author's collection.)

These attempts began when I started school. Nothing similar to the fig trees surrounding the eighteen-meter-deep well between the two neighboring vineyards could exist in this school. The clear, poetic, and understandable realm of my first seven years was gone, magically drowned by the flat world portrayed in our textbooks and by our teachers.

The infallibility of this new representation would be achieved by rooting it in history. According to historic materialism, the ultimate goal of human history is to build a communist society. We had gone through rivers of blood, our teachers said, to defeat the exploitation of slave-owning societies, to overcome the unjust inequalities of the feudal epoch, and to replace it with capitalist economic relations. Furthermore, the unbalanced development of the capitalist countries had made them declare war in order to reshape world geography. In the womb of capitalist society a new class had been bred—the proletariat—whose unique historic role, to the best of my tutors' beliefs, was finally to tear apart this history of exploitative relations. The only way to play this role successfully was, of course, anticapitalist revolution. Only revolution could establish the just, new, socialist society. And who could be the organizer and leading factor in this revolution? Inevitably only the Communist Party. And who could join this party? Inevitably again, the blessed were the *most conscientious* representatives of the proletariat. The ghost of communism was enlightenment for these clairvoyants who only initiated the party cells and structured the "most progressive" political organization in history: the Communist Party.

Moreover, the enlightenment offered a tough and viable ghost; it visited the dreams of all humanistically minded persons and obsessed them with the French idea of liberty, equality, and brotherhood—each of them so smoothly achievable on paper through just and progressive revolution. These bright brains of humanity had never asked the question of who had to be stabbed during this revolution. Could this question matter when such a gigantic task was ordained by history to the class whose humble servants they were? The task was to enrich the miserable billions all around the earth and build an unprecedented paradise of supreme happiness.

I was led to believe that my generation was the luckiest. We would take part in the last stage of this historic evolution. But hold on! The emphasis was on "generation," not on me as a person. Of course, I came across this nuance much later. My teenage image of the world was preconceived according to the Leninist historic agenda: first this, then that, and at the very end my generation is blessed by Marx to overcome the failures of the capitalist way of production and to establish the society of honey and butter.

This society would crown history by achieving complete human well-being. It seems so simple and tractable, does it not?

Since dialectic materialism taught us that revolutionary motion was unstoppable, the treacherous question of what was to follow next crossed our minds only momentarily, if at all. Having no answer available—and unable even to anticipate one—I complied with the lessons and fell in with the careless self-preservation of my age.

As a matter of fact, we were taught not history, but the "History of the Bulgarian Communist Party" and "History of the Communist Party of the Soviet Union." Both were part of the "ideological package" that soared from primary school all the way up through doctoral programs. At the latter level, you would have been denied a doctorate in whatever discipline had you not passed the special exams on BCP history, "Dialectical and Historical Materialism," and "Scientific Communism."

All this, I know, is a boring story. For me, it is even more boring and ordinary. But the fact is, it occupied the whole space of our best years of life to the extent that the conventional expression "life is short" has an idiosyncratic dimension for us. My story may even seem meaningless to somebody who sticks to the image of communism created by George Orwell, Aleksandr Solzhenitsyn, and Western journalism, confident in agents' records and sporadic visits across the Curtain. But I submit that the image of "real socialism" did not consist only or mostly of conventional cruelty, abuse of human rights, and political violence. It was, in fact, a most ordinary lie.

This type of society merits the name of mediocracy. *Mediocracy* (or the rule of the mediocre) is probably the most exact and truthful term that portrays most accurately the form of government in the Soviet Union and Eastern Europe.

To make itself workable, *mediocracy* had to reduce the whole system of local and universal values into a new, unprecedented code that would transform even those who were not subservient by nature into docile citizens. The propagation of this code over the whole population was the goal of communist brainwashing.

Without exception, everyone was showered permanently, repeatedly, and stubbornly with this new socialist social code. There was a vicious ambiguity here. The communist doctrine was on the one hand believed, but its aloofness from reality was so flagrant even to the believers that it was on the other hand decreed. The brainwashing was not pure malice; a modicum of genuine trust was alive behind it.

The brainwashers knew all too well that the best time for acquiring controllable victims (that is, victims who would actually *enjoy* their victimhood) was in high school. At the threshold of my conscious age, my father enrolled me as a student in a high school that was both prestigious and elitist: the so-called Lycée de Langue Française, a language school with enriched teaching in French. It was prestigious because French was among the three Western languages, along with German and English, highly valued in Bulgaria. It was elitist for two reasons. First, only academically gifted and trustworthy teenagers were accepted to it. Second, all of the students selected came from carefully verified communist families. Thus, the school was a true incubator of cadres for the security services. I said "my father enrolled me" to emphasize that first, my attending the French school was his idea, and second, that while I was responsible for achieving high grades in the primary school, he knew he (and inherently, the legacy of my grandfather, the Active Fighter) was responsible for the trustworthiness that was about to be passed on to me.

Such a family intercession was the most natural thing in the world. All around me in this school were kids from communist families; I cannot remember a single exception. In regard to the requirement that all kids should have very high grades, however, exceptions were the rule. For example, there were only thirty of us on the official list of accepted on excellence-cum-party merit for the school year 1960–61. A week after school began, some thirty other fellows arrived. As I later discovered, this week was necessary for parents of the additional contingent (all of them party functionaries or with some merits before the party) to call their local party officials and obtain oral permission for acceptance of their not-so-brilliant sons or daughters or nephews or nieces. Party merit always had priority over school performance. It is important for my story that I did not recognize until much later these covert mechanisms, uncontrollable by any independent social or judicial body.

At the time, I did not pay attention to such "details," since I was still enjoying the miracles of the carefree life. Varna is a wonderful town in the summer. I used to spend every sunny day on the beach. Girls began to have a physical appeal for me, and I still used to go to the vineyard, where the cherries had ripened almost black and someone had to eat them right from the tree, or my grandma wanted me to pick apricots for the jam she used to boil and preserve for the winter.

Also at this time, in spite of their relatively low income, my parents had bought a car (a brand-new antediluvian Soviet "Moskvitch") and early each fall they organized trips around Bulgaria. I felt no anxiety around me, since most people lived the same life my parents did. They all seemed content, and they were all promised that life was going to improve year after year—provided they complied with the party line. Life was a commodity, and the party line was offered as the only true set of instructions for its use. So, you had bread and butter, you had clothes, you had your guaranteed vacation in a resort run by the Trade Union, your child had a good school to attend, your family had a free doctor, and you had guidelines for how to live life. What more did you need? This, pure and simple, was the implied rhetorical question.

Indeed, when I entered the language school, I needed nothing more than to enjoy the present, since my future had already been declared guaranteed. An unrestricted future? Yes, if only one single requirement was met. The requirement of toeing the party line had to be done in several ways depending on family status. You complied or simply did not deviate or the expectation was that you contribute actively and conscientiously. Speaking for myself, I had two vaguely realized reasons why I did not mind succumbing to the party line. In the first place, my family foresaw nothing else as life goals, and secondly, at this time, I had no idea what price I would have to pay for it.

Of course, now I know for sure that not every family lived in such complacency, as it seemed to me in my teens. I am unable to calculate the relative ratio of hypocrisy to naïveté in our circle of acquaintance. In no case was it strictly one or the other. In any event, a teenager like me cherished this life and had no reason to grow up resenting it.

At the time, I was not at all aware that my name (along with the names of almost all my classmates) was already on the candidates' list for the party nomenclature. We laughed proudly at the nickname "Red Wolf Cubs of Bulgaria," coined for us by Radio Free Europe. To be sure, Radio Free Europe, we had been convincingly told, was the channel of dirty imperialist propaganda, wherein only traitors of the fatherland served as dogs to their patrons. We were bound to grow up as devoted radicals, determined to defend communist values from the encroachments of rotten capitalism. It sounds artificial and even ridiculous, I'm sure, but this was the jargon that we all effectively utilized: it turned into a vernacular instrument for mental work and political debate. Certainly, personal nuances ranged from sincere commitment to this discourse to simple parroting of the clichés. Sooner or later, every one of us worked out our personal rhetoric just as boys develop new manly voices at the end of puberty. Our puberty, however, was driven forth into a territory of values that turned out to be distorted or altogether nonexistent.

At the time, we were proud of our values. The recollection of this pride confirms my distinct belief that we did accept communism as it was presented to us in the doctrine. Even more so, pride was added to our sense of destiny, historical significance, and a kind of determination to take on the remainder of the capitalist world, fallen behind the times and unable to share our visionary hopes.

How can I forget that April morning in 1961 when our physics teacher rushed into the classroom yelling, "Our man is in the Cosmos!" "Our man" was Yuri Gagarin, and the euphoric mood was due not so much to the fact that mankind had surmounted gravity for the first time, but because that particular cosmonaut was born in communist Russia. It was an achievement of the communist state, and hence of communist ideology. Had there been no communist values, *Sputnik* would never have flown. By contrast, we also experienced anxiety and bitterness that year (and in the year that followed) in response to the Cuban missile crisis. John Kennedy had tried to rob us of our future, and we saw his intervention as an act of supreme malice.

We, the Red Wolf Cubs, lived in a boarding school in close proximity with the town's Seaboard Park. Just as the whole country was sequestered from the rest of the world, so our elite school was walled off from the rest of the town. While our parents worked hard to "build" communism (actually, to brush shoulders with the strong of the day), our preoccupation amounted to dance parties, courting, body fitness, and acquiring strictly scientific means for mastering the world.

I am not at all misled in judging this from a stance, which would require us to build barricades and to become postmodern Gavroches. What I am implying here is exactly the opposite. We were normal, carefree teens who had all the imaginable amusements of this age, except perhaps world travel. Yet the context of our *joie de vivre* was peculiar, unique in orientation, and declared fit for all of us. This orientation was so smoothly and consistently rolled, layer after layer, into our souls that, when awareness of its absurdity brushed our minds, it seemed already too late to turn to another track. How could we build barricades when we saw no foes?

Perhaps I am wrong to adopt the position of a spokesman for an entire generation, or even for a single school. But as far as I am the subject and the witness of this total manipulation of values, I submit that we were awash in rhetoric, safeguards, assurances, good will, daydreams of prosperity, and soporific alienation from the battles and realities of the greater world. Black and white was allowed, the spectrum of colors banned.

But the colors of the sea were still there, appealing and mysterious. Nature's generosity contrasted with the sparse warmth, love, and emotional education we received from our elders. These were never sure whether we would follow the instructions for life dictated from above or even whether it was a good idea to comply with the instructions. These elders were my parents, the parents of my classmates, and our teachers.

In retrospect, I can hardly feel sympathy for them. I can remember none of them clearly. I do remember vividly my relations with wildlife, as if a deserted meadow contained more meaning and attraction than any human being. The company of humans slowly became a burden. Solitude in the remote bush or on a lonely beach was far more relaxing and challenging. Was I really a Red Wolf that longed for the wilderness and solitary victories over innocent prey? I do not believe so. It was an instinctive search for the diversity lacking in our everyday life at school. It was, in short, the certitude of communicating spiritually with something real and natural in contrast to the vacuous discourse of my textbooks and teachers.

Wild nature offered only an escape. I still receive letters from old school friends whose emotional life remained on that infantile level of a sentimental contact with nature. It was no admiration for something bigger and stronger, but the vague pretension of having a mute but all-responding partner. This vagueness raises your very value without competition with others and reassures you of your sensitivity while demanding no effort. There, in the bosom of Mother Nature, you escaped the frustrating relations with human beings. You could impulsively escape simply because of the sentiment you found in the high mountains or a lonely sea. Slowly there developed a philosophy in which any struggle for upgrading your existence appeared aimless, whereas going out to hug Mother Nature offered shelter.

In these postcommunist times, there appear to be two opposing ways of wrongly portraying the postcommunist reality. In one, devastated sympathetic characters fall into debauchery, alcoholism, and cynicism. According to the other, the communist world held all creative individuals and admirable heroes in check by depriving them of professional power and civil rights. In fiction, yesterday's window-cleaning Prague intellectuals are portrayed as today's TV, press, or university tycoons, all of whom are devoid of any political philosophy or civic virtues.

It is not the very existence of such people, which I deny. However, I question the implications that virtuous intellectuals are representative of

Eastern European societies. The suffering assigned to those intellectuals will not epitomize the whole odiousness of the communist regime. This kind of postcommunist standard also implies that the power of those regimes focused on oppressing the brave and self-sacrificing intelligentsia. This is simply not true.

According to popular interpretations, it appears that simple, illiterate, cruel, almost brainless executors of an invisible power (the communist regime itself) were somehow supplied to occupy all key positions. They were the ultimate evil. On the demand side there were the attractive, sympathy- and compassion-inviting, morally suffering smart guys. They were usually lonely, chased by plainclothes policemen, and in perpetual conflict with women. They were the ultimate good. This fraudulent image embellishes a trivial reality. Such an abyss simply did not exist. It can hardly exist in any semicivilized (i.e., nonstratified) society because the carriers of virtues and vices are not so discretely separated as they appear to be in some East European novels and memoirs.

Moreover, such portrayals imply that educated or natural-born talents are *a priori* the carriers of liberal values, global civilization, and morality. In order to become a carrier or defender of such ethics you have to grow up embedded in a tradition that has nurtured the values for centuries. Such a tradition does not exist in Eastern Europe. Where and how, then, could all these features of Western intellectualism enter into the mind and behavior of the Eastern European intelligentsia?

Our elitist *Lycée de Langue Française* was, in this very regard, a mirror of how mixed and undifferentiated the young communist intelligentsia was in the 1960s. Our only common characteristic was that we descended from families in which at least one of our parents was a member of the BCP. In truth, the majority of our parents or grandparents were "Active Fighters against Fascism and Capitalism" or active workers in the party apparatus.

My father and mother were both members of the BCP, my cousin worked in the apparatus and contributed to the "Organs" (the various security organizations), and my grandfather was a recipient of the title "Active Fighter." By what standards can I pretend that I grew up rejecting the values they stood for during their lives? By what standards am I entitled to claim, for that matter, that I was a staunch champion of liberal democracy or the ideas of the Enlightenment?

In my class we were thirteen boys and seven girls coming from all around the country, from towns as well as villages, from the capital as well as the provinces. There were none among us whose parents were workers or farmers. They were administrators, lawyers, physicians, teachers, and mainly party apparatchiks. So, by any standard, we were trained to belong to an intelligentsia, no matter how it might be defined under these conditions. There was no doubt that all of us would pursue a university education and that most of us would make our careers within the bosom of the party. Officially, these would be careers in diplomacy, management, engineering, or the people's militia. However, since all professionals in Bulgaria were watchdogged by the party Central Committee, our job positions were directly dependent on this supreme body of communist power.

Several of my classmates became officers in intelligence and counterintelligence, and some pursued diplomatic careers, which amounted almost to the same thing. Only a minority of us embarked upon traditional professional careers to become physicians, teachers, or economists. Yet even behind the most innocent professional façade (i.e., an editor in a publishing house—state run, to be sure) you would sooner or later discover a loyal party servant.

During these school years, for example, one of my classmates (who was registered in the French school on the additional list of thirty latecomers) studied literature in a provincial university. He could not even make it to a Sofia or Varna university because of his mediocre grades. After graduation he became a provincial journalist with a small newspaper. Two years later, he was appointed deputy literary editor in a relatively big publishing house in Varna, our native town. Not too long after that, his immediate boss, a renowned provincial poet, was forced to resign, and my classmate was fortuitously appointed in his place.

This came as no surprise to all of us who knew whose son he was, but it shocked those who knew only about his mediocre capabilities. His father was the chief gardener of the Euxinograd Party Residency, a former royal palace just eight kilometers north of Varna, and a colonel in the secret services. This luxurious estate was strictly isolated from the public and served as an almost personal resort for Todor Zhivkov and his entourage.

Logically, after spending five or so years in this post, and after a clash between two opposite factions of the local party authorities on another matter, my former friend was appointed director of the Varna publishing house. Let me stress this clearly: a mediocre person with feeble literary judgment was catapulted from an elitist high school into the director's chair of an institution that carried out a great part of this country's publishing policy, controlling a great part of the literature published by the communist regime.

Many of the people I knew well in school turned to secret duties and we lost contact. After Todor Zhivkov fell, they resurfaced as either chief arms traders or retired counterintelligence agents. They were busy opening firms with their old contacts and laundering the old party assets invested safely here and there around the world.

How could anyone living such a life develop a spirit of dissent and revolt? No matter how critical my mind could have been (and I believe I have a natural aptitude for sound criticism) all my youthful spontaneity was perfidiously channeled into the bedrock of communist values, including my knowledge about the physical world. Those values seemed acceptable because their imposition was not related to any direct threat to our well-being. Moreover, we were stripped of any competitive alternatives. We were led to believe that the only authority we would be able to achieve would be an authority that stemmed from party control. Since the party was ostensibly not an ill-intentioned organization, we could find no justifiable reason for running away from such an authority. We could criticize people, but not the system or the party because we simply did not feel the latter was real. We assuaged our discontent, if any, with the belief that deviant people might contaminate the system of authority in the country, but that authority itself was crystal pure, utterly positive, and inviolable.

The authority we faced most immediately, however, was our teachers. We spent week after week in an environment where our teachers were the only adults with whom we communicated. I do not recall any of them ever having pronounced a word of dissent, discontent, or discord with respect to what was decreed, ruled, or tacitly implied. They instead kept a sharp, disciplined eye on our budding sexuality.

Although our dormitories were separate, we had many places where we could meet with girls: the schoolyard, the refectory, the music room, the nursery wing, and so forth. The walls surrounding the school were not too high or carefully watched, so nearby Seaboard Park was another good place for dating. To live in such proximity with girls nourished the appeal of the whole institution. Apart from this ray of hope, the toilets were disgusting, we were allowed to visit a communal bath only once a week (Young Communist League reunions were more frequent!), and the food was insufficient both in quantity and quality.

The *lycée* I attended had teachers from Western Europe. It was an uncommon and appealing privilege to be in touch with living representatives of the forbidden world. More powerful was the act of confidence on the part of the authorities: we were real communist stock, and they must have

A family photo of my parents with my sister and me. Varna,
September, 1965. (Author's collection.)

felt that other views and lifestyles could not pervert us. Even so, our relations with the Western teachers were strictly regulated and controlled.

As to the forbidden world those teachers represented, our tutors used a
pattern based on perfect logic to justify some of the obvious discrepancies.
This world perpetrated two big evils upon mankind: first, the principle of
class oppression, whereby the mass of workers was always oppressed and
underprivileged; secondly, the devastating war on the fatherland of communism. Both the working class and our Russian brothers were genuine
values of Bulgarian culture. The capitalist world had *created* a lot of scientific knowledge and culture (read civilization); we were obliged to assimi-
late it in order to be competitive against our foes in the name of the dialectic of the class struggle.

The instructors who came from the West to teach us French language
and French history, world geography, physics, or math, were, unfortunately,
not the best representatives of the ideologically refuted Western culture.
Most of them were not even professional teachers. Some came along to
satisfy their military duties as teachers in Eastern Europe, while others
were pushed toward our world by curiosity. We even had a French communist from Algeria who was granted clandestine asylum in our country

Here I am with some of my male classmates in the French school's backyard, just before graduation in Varna, May, 1965. (Author's collection.)

because he faced a death sentence for his activities in the former French colony.

But even if they had been professionals, they still would not have been able to perform well. In accordance with our profane programming, the Bulgarian textbooks were translated badly into French, and they had to follow their frameworks. Moreover, there was a general tendency to reduce the number of French teachers as much as possible. For this purpose, Bulgarians were sent to France for six or nine months to learn the language. Upon their return home, they taught it to us. In the 1960s, it was dangerous to dream about sending some of us to France. The country we knew so well through slides, printouts, music recordings, books, and movies was an ideological enemy, and the party feared that our washed brains would be corrupted by the experience of Western lifestyles and values.

Nevertheless, being in touch with these Western features was like finding a little hole in the Curtain through which we could contemplate the untouchable life of another planet. With few exceptions, our Western teachers were decent people who tried to make us feel the charm of free thought and tolerant attitudes. They were never offensive, and many were tacitly supportive of our daring and awkward love affairs. They used subtle ways to convey to us elements of French culture that could be regarded as ideologically contagious by our authorities. In this respect, both the authorities and the townspeople thought of our school as a dangerous territory where leakages in the ideologically pure (and periodically purified) system could potentially occur.

The fact is, the leakage was always bigger than the party watchdogs could ever have imagined. Their low level of knowledge and intelligence limited their own idea of what was perverting and what was not. The entire situation was a big cat-and-mouse game. We were allowed to read Balzac, but we could also acquire under the table Jean-Paul Sartre or Boris Pasternak's *Doctor Zhivago* in French. We were allowed to listen to Adamo and Charles Aznavour, and especially Yves Montand, but recordings of the banned Beatles were also circulating almost freely among the fans in our school. Again, this was unique in town. Louis Aragon was officially in the program, but our literature teacher read to us class texts from François Mauriac, Julien Green, Albert Camus, and the like. We could at least know the names of André Gide and Roger Garaudy. The former was banned because of his book rejecting the Soviet system and probably because he was a homosexual. The latter was bedeviled after he published his controversial book *D'un réalisme sans rivages,* in which he simply pondered a less dogmatic interpretation of socialist realism.

In this cat-and-mouse game, what was banned was immediately endowed with an indefinable glow and attraction, not ignored but consumed in secrecy. Our attitudes and statements, however, kept unmistakably in line with what was required. On the surface, no one could know the real values Balkan people professed.

The intellectual baggage we carried during these formative years was both polarized and inconsistent. The exposure to French culture was insufficient, in my judgment, to elicit criticism. It was sufficient, however, to make those of us who attended this elitist school distinct from teenagers whose windows of learning were kept tightly closed. A single mention of a Western-sounding name of our teachers (Cuomo, Mellinger, Catoire, Bensheikh, Chevalier) has always a tender touch in my mind, evoking something noble, different, and unattainable.

From my personal perspective, the French exposure blended into my family's association with the German culture. I began to associate it with my knowledge of the German language, and my piano lessons. I knew the music

and biographies of all the great German and French composers, and read
the novels of Thomas Mann and Herman Hesse in their original language.
These filled the shelves of our domestic library, where they competed for
space with the works of Lenin, Marx, Stalin, and Sholokhov!

Ultimately, exposure to Western culture was unsystematic and thus devoid of depth. It was duly rivaled by the communist neoculture, which
came almost exclusively from the Soviet Union. The extent of the absurdity in accepting this culture can be illustrated by the fact that even Tolstoy
and Dostoyevsky were regarded as precursors of Soviet-style communism.
I was not anchored to a given tradition, but instead was floating on the
communist waves like a leaf without direction or force of its own. Tellingly
enough, I was regarded within this distinct teenage community as someone strange and enviable because of the veneer of "high culture" that characterized both my family and my performance at this time.

The quantity and fragile quality of our exposure to Western civilization
unfortunately could not provide enough clues to reject our righteous regard for our regime. It was not strategically conceived to give us a clear
understanding of, for example, what the French revolution really was about:
its characteristic political violence was not duly explained, nor were we
taught why the scientific and ideological revolution in the Western world
(in which France was a key player) is known as the Enlightenment. The
concept of enlightenment remained obscure to us, or was awkwardly defined as the love for education.

Did we object to such a state of affairs? Barely. Did we revolt against the
restrictive programming? I do not remember a single act of rebellion, of
dissident behavior, or of basic teenage wrath. Did we try to learn more or
from different sources? Again, the answer is no.

It frustrates me now to realize how big is the loss from such obedience!
We were indeed obedient. We diligently learned our lessons in invented
history. We did not boycott Young Communist League meetings. We were
even eager to prove to our foreign teachers that, despite their cultural superiority and economic achievements, our pristine drive toward happiness
would soon sweep away their bourgeois status quo. This drive would soon
justify our enthusiasm in the socialist revolution, a revolution that was
very close in its ideals to the French one.

CHAPTER 4

Eye-Opening Experiences inside the Prison

Pas besoin de gril, l'enfer c'est les Autres.
—*Jean-Paul Sartre,* Huis clos

In any men's locker room, one can see fathers helping their sons cope with showering, toweling, dressing, and so forth. There are so many different fathers: tall, short, slim, fat, handsome, ugly, with hanging bellies, hunched, or even crippled. Yet all sons, without a single exception, are proud of their fathers.

I was no different. I cherished my father before I became aware of his faults. By the time that happened, however, it was too late. I was myself already flawed in some way or another, and there was nothing in the paternalistic culture of my country that could help me out. None of us is programmed to search for an individual drive to live dissociated from the manger in which we were bred. This feeling is especially strong in the Balkans, where being ruled matters. Then it becomes the drama of our lives to try to detach ourselves from the rule of the fathers and establish a moral law of our own.

By the time I graduated from the French school, I had no idea that camps for political prisoners existed in Bulgaria or that prisons were divided into criminal and political classes. The vague notion of Siberia as a natural prison crossed my mind, but Siberia was no nearer than Japan or the United States, thus the thought that something similar might exist in my proximity never occurred to me.

Crime and violence were completely missing from the newspapers' pages and from the elders' conversations. The word *sex* was not part of our vocabulary. To speak of prostitution or homosexuality (both items from one and the same category of Western-style debauchery) was tantamount to showing your genitals in public. Political diversity was something we could not have been aware of, since order and security were thought to stem from the unitarian political system constitutionally decreed in our country. Incidentally, none of us had ever read the constitution or been taught to think about the social order in terms of a constitution. We took political stability for granted. The very concept of politics was associated only with international relations, and, even more narrowly, with the fight between the two camps: socialist and imperialist. Any notions of Western democracy that managed to leak into our discourse were regarded as a perversion of order, decency, and humanity. We, the equalizers, were the humane; they, the champions of individuality, were vicious.

I shy away from anonymity, so let me elaborate on the use of "we" and "they." Actually, "they" were indeed anonymous, ghosts of a world doomed to be abolished and replaced by our righteous realm. "They" were concealed as negative concepts, as an embodiment of evil. We knew nobody from "their" world personally, including our teachers. We knew only the names of politicians portrayed as embodiments of the Western malice.

But "we" were not ghosts. Although the hypocrisy in our world was not unlike the bigotry that is part of every society, our hypocrisy was mixed with genuine beliefs. In this respect, hypocrisy cannot serve to explain our status quo, as some social psychologists have suggested.

My school world was banal but enjoyable. I am trying in vain to remember at least one of my classmates whose parents were not members of the BCP. We all knew each other's "social situation" well. Accordingly, our school political activity reflected our parents' political status. To a large extent, though, we barely cared about the Young Communist League at that stage. On the other hand, we had tacit knowledge about what was politically permissible, and there were no incidents of politically incorrect statements. The biggest disobedience we indulged ourselves in was dating.

Smoking was the next major issue in the conventional war between teenagers and teachers. It was a ritual to pass the time, because none of the smokers was so ruthlessly punished to force him or her to quit. Alcohol was not an issue, since the generally imposed sobriety seemed to extend over school as well. As for drugs, none of us at that time even knew that such a thing existed.

Anyway, the battlefield where our conflicts with the teachers blew up was our so-called premature courtship. Even a long-lasting, "faithful" affair like the one I had with my first girlfriend was suspiciously watched by the school's Teacher's Council, since the party prescription was to pigeonhole our minds with study and Young Communist League activity. The major part of the literature we were strongly advised to read consisted of Soviet novels and poetry, written in the notorious "method of socialist realism." The key feature, and a crucial requirement of this so-called method fathered by Maxim Gorki, was the portrayal of a leading character whose communist virtues inevitably helped him or her prevail in the fight against the forces of evil and backwardness. These forces were embodied by characters who favored (or even philosophically supported) the decaying capitalist construction. In their turn, communists confessed and projected optimism and trust in the victory of communism.

One of the main virtues of the collective image of the communist was his or her denial of earthly pleasures. This meant, among other things, sexual continence in the name of the just struggle. Sexuality was transformed by communist definition into a platonic love for a companion who shared the vision of communism and could not belong in another class but the proletariat. Loving someone outside the working class would result in a conflict that would lead to a happy, heroic climax and conversion into the ranks of the saintly.

I cannot account for the mental state of the writers who produced socialist realism. As far as the readers are concerned, I can testify that the books were actually read and discussed in class and at other public (or not so public) gatherings. Their publication determined all the significance that literature was prescribed to play in communist neoculture. We were supposed to develop personal qualities like those of the communist characters in the books. However, because the class enemy was not so visible around us, sex became the enemy against which we had to mobilize our moral strengths. We were so taken in that we could not ignore the message or evade its all-pervasive thrust.

Underneath this ridiculous absurdity was a traditional male-oriented moral system. In Bulgaria, the patriarchal family structure had century-long roots, and this structure was reinforced after the country took up the road of capitalist development in the last quarter of the twentieth century. The tragic results of the Balkan wars and the following two world wars heavily undermined the patriarchal tradition. But the corresponding mentality entrenched for centuries could not promptly follow suit. Men were generally allowed promiscuity before marrying age, whereas women were denied that indulgence. Young ladies were expected to remain virgins; wedlock was the only morally acceptable beginning of a female's sexual activities. Extramarital relationships, although tolerated for men, were bitterly vilified for women.

Our school love stories ended up tragically with a break or with a swift marriage. In both cases, the intervention of external factors mingled with the natural fragility of our teen relationships. In rare cases when couples were, for example, caught lying in bed together, the girl was expelled from school regardless of her academic or political status. Other couples, depending usually on the pressure exerted by parents, were called before Teachers' Council meetings and interrogated publicly so that few could sustain their good relationship, let alone love one another, afterward. Those whose love affairs did not reach such scandalous dimensions suffered resentment, house expulsion, chronic quarrels, and so on, and could barely wait for school to end so they could marry. Marriage seemed a moral way to legitimize relationships so poorly regarded by those we considered truly authoritative.

Party regulations invited the intercession of the authorities in our decisions to get married. A number of my classmates did marry soon after school in response to "moral" pressures. To be duly married was to observe decency. Decency enhanced respect and augmented the chances of a spotless career. The majority of our parents lived in marriages based on the *young communist* standards of love and spousal fidelity. Husbands and wives called their partners "comrade," and it was most unlikely that they would betray each other through extramarital sex, let alone a deeper love affair. If that happened, it could rarely be kept hidden, so the whole working collective of the exposed and accused lovers stood up to restore the family's integrity. Yes, the integrity of families, regardless of how dysfunctional they were, was the principal value that outranked even love relations. The common excuse was the welfare of the children, itself revered as a fetish. A traditional feature of the Bulgarian family is that it is highly extended and children receive support until they "take their bread in their hands." It is not rare, however, for the support to be extended beyond the time of marriage and taking one's first job. Communist times helped increase this practice for many reasons.

Our parents naturally expected us to follow along in their footsteps, no matter what. Moreover, marriage was a strict requirement for those who pursued a diplomatic career or service with any of the security organizations. Ordinary citizens desiring to travel abroad were denied exit visas if they were not married. Moreover, party promotions were predicated on having a *healthy* family status in addition to other political, social, and individual standards that had to be met. This meant it was beneficial to avoid divorce.

Thus, at school's end, marriage was a matter of serious concern. There were two others: university education and our forthcoming party membership. To begin with, university education was very prestigious. There was no social layer where it would be questioned or despised. In my family, it was the only track envisioned. So, while I had no problem at all deciding what to do when I finished high school, the real issue was what type of university I would attend. My expectations were vaguely directed toward literature or the cinema, but it would be closer to the truth to say that I did not stand firmly by any concrete option. My father, on the other hand, ruled out anything even remotely related to my humanistic inclinations. His obsession was to exempt me from the obligatory military service, which would be possible only if I pursued engineering or medicine. I staunchly refused to apply to medical school because it was in my hometown. It would stop me from moving to the capital, where university life looked so tempting. Since my mother was a doctor and experienced the negative sides of the profession in the way it was regulated by the communist government, I suspect that my parents decided against insisting on medicine. Instead, they pressed me to apply for the University of Engineering. After interminable debates I resigned for want of arguments, my main weakness being my financial dependence. Bursaries in Bulgaria were given only to Active Fighters (or to their direct descendants) and to persons from families with a very low family income. To have a part-time job was unusual. Above all, however, parents who could not support their child in university were thought to have failed in their duty.

I was accepted in engineering geology, since I excelled in every kind of exam even if it was mathematics or physics. I took the train to Sofia, and my girlfriend remained in Varna. Most of my friends went to the barracks for their military service, but there was a group of schoolmates who entered university studies as I did. Among those who began their military service immediately after high school were future diplomats and secret agents: They were required to graduate in French, Spanish, or another philology and to undergo basic training in the military. A file followed each of us to our university or barracks. Everywhere, the human resources departments (or "Cadre Office" as they were called) took care to thicken it with new information.

The most striking detail with regard to those files was their arbitrariness. The people we usually dealt with every day (the Komsomol activists and assistant professors in the university; the sergeants or junior officers in the army) were the same persons who wrote the reports for the files. The general rule was that the initial information for the family, provided by the neighborhood party activists, determined the character of all further reports, which could arbitrarily hide or reinforce behavior or attitudes inconsistent with a procommunist image. The inverse, namely, that your file be embellished by invented procommunist actions, was practically implausible, since no one would pay attention if you strained to behave as a bigger communist than the average communists were. But it could also happen that your superiors disliked you and decided to taint your file. Or one of them might be related to a personal foe of yours who could have the friend make up some compromising "facts" about your less than trustworthy behavior. In such a case, it would be fairly impossible to check or object to what had gone into your file. This was an arbitrary distortion of your true stance, of which you were unaware: these files were, of course, never shown to you in person.

Sofia opened my eyes to many things, the file story included. However, my file never recorded my true ineptitude at navigating the pitfalls and loopholes of communist reality. I did not doubt for a second that the two strengths I possessed by birth, namely, intellect and communist belonging, would always work in my favor. Nothing led me to suspect that I was a spoiled brat who was poorly prepared to face communism.

From the very beginning, I was disappointed in my studies of geology, and when the first exam session ended at Christmastime, I took my bags back to Varna. My father was furious and threw me out in the street. For the first time in my life (at the age of nineteen) I faced something real: the need to earn my own money. It was easy enough to find a job, but I did not go to the loading dock with all the heavy lifting. I found employment as a pianist in a restaurant band. I remember being full of contempt toward my father's philistinism and childishly proud of my ability to shrug off societal standards with contempt. It was March, a magnificent springtime at the seashore. I was still dating my high-school girlfriend and saw nothing dark on my youthful horizon.

However, while I was floating in my emerald sea of self-satisfaction, my peers looked more pragmatically toward their futures. Some of them engaged seriously in university studies, embellishing their files with records of Komsomol activity. Those who could not rely on professional excellence emphasized their Komsomol commitments. Down the scale from elitist to ordinary schools, teenagers from all social layers tried to enter the best universities they could. The number of applicants soared from year to year. Behind all the rhetoric of equality under communism, the people's common sense told them that professionals would earn more money and that white-collar work is not as sweaty as that of the blue-collar workers. The popular Bulgarian attitude was expressed in the bold phrase, "Go to study, my child, lest you end up a worker/farmer as your father." The young communist dictatorship was still in its infancy at the time, and old norms reigned.

Evidently, few were able to fulfill their dreams of social mobility. Those who went to work in the factories and cooperative farms took great pains

This is me in Varna's Seaboard Park (Morskata gradina), *circa 1965–66. The similitude with Rodin's* Le Penseur *discloses the pretense of the Balkan intellectual to keep in line with European high culture. (Author's collection.)*

to become party members or to please the party authorities, if only so they would be left alone. Of the three concerns that framed a teenagers' horizons, party membership was the most coveted, although the newest and most unpredictable.

During the 1960s, however, party selection was meticulous. The party sieve had very small holes, and only workers and university graduates descended from workers' families (the so-called workers' intelligentsia) received the honor of membership. It was said that the social composition of the party needed to be upgraded by an influx of healthy cadres, and "healthy" implied not belonging to the rotten bourgeois intelligentsia or to the politically ambiguous peasantry. As I have already mentioned, my schoolmates had no problems in this regard. One by one, or in groups, they became party members. And, since most of them were not ordinary party members, they laid the foundation of the party intelligentsia (which was essentially the cream of the workers' intelligentsia). I somehow sensed that my place was not among them, although I could not define where my right place really was. I cannot report exactly why I did not apply for membership, but the fact is, at the time I did not think of it at all. It was most unusual to discuss such topics among ourselves. It was tacitly accepted that everyone cared individually about his or her relationship with the party. We did not discuss prospective professions or jobs since they were guaranteed, and indeed were of secondary importance, to us.

What we did discuss, however, was university and our marriage prospects. Practically all of us were living prematurely as couples and experienced ongoing tensions with our parents. Mom and dad insisted upon radical solutions: separation or marriage. Pragmatic parents used marriage as another way to establish connections with the strong of the day, but our naïveté blinded us to these "philistine" calculations. Therefore, early in my life I fell prey to such a pragmatic strategy. As I said, I was only semiaware of the high status that my family occupied in our town's social hierarchy. As far as some other people were concerned, they were not so flighty as to miss the idea that my social legacy combined old-guard communist fidelity with actual compliance to the flourishing communist regime. Therefore, they had considered me an "eligible bachelor."

Being thrown out of my home and sleeping almost every night at a different place, I came still closer to thinking that maybe it was not a bad idea to marry. Getting a whiff of this perspective, my girlfriend's father decided to encourage me. However, he offered his support on the condition that I enroll in the medical school in town. He even promised to get in touch with the dean in order to ensure my acceptance. At the same time in mid-April, my girlfriend complained that she might be pregnant. This was a clear signal that a wedding party had to be thrown. All of this was a well-conceived plot to trap me, its sole purpose being to preserve her reputation. The plot succeeded, all things considered, because my immediate family was hostile to the idea of marriage in general, and to that girl in particular. I wanted to prove them wrong.

We were married in May, in the reproaching absence of my own parents. She was not pregnant, of course, and by late July I had successfully passed the medical school exams. Thus, I resolved in a very commonplace way two of the three concerns that haunted young communists. For the next six years I penciled in "student in medicine; married" on administrative applications.

I could not have imagined that my initial nonchalance regarding marital issues was indeed setting the stage for my turbulent odyssey. I was twenty when we married. Soon, we had two kids. The two girls were hardly beginning to walk and speak when I engaged in some extramarital affairs. I quickly realized that my schoolmate was too lowbrow for my lifestyle and expectations. It seemed all too natural that I get rid of her. We divorced by mutual consent in the summer of 1972. I succeeded in keeping our daughters with me. I knew that to be a divorced man with two children would not pose any problem regarding another marriage. What really counted was the nomenclature position of my family.

Today, I can hardly justify my haste in getting married again. But at the time, I rushed into my second marriage like a criminal who neglects the likelihood of being caught and sentenced for a crime. I regarded marriage as *the* shelter. I wanted to have an exemplary spouse. As for myself, I was prepared to be an exemplary husband. By exemplary I probably meant to be in a harmonious relationship such as I felt myself to be in with nature. The young lady I was courting was a medical student. We enjoyed good sex, and I assessed her as rather highbrow. Her family, however, did not belong to the communist caste. Quite the contrary, both her mom and dad were bourgeois. I could not have cared less.

This time, both of our parents blessed my marriage. It lasted ten years, and two more children were born. We were such a rarity in Bulgaria (intellectuals with four kids and no apparent dysfunctions) that, a year before I disrupted it, some journalists began reporting about our wonderful marriage in the media.

Why would I disrupt this happy nest? This is the most painful question that I have been asked since. And I have tried so hard to give it a consistent answer that the many answers I could provide almost totally contradict themselves. I am sure that the answer is not male promiscuity. It is, of course, deliberately that I summarize this part of my life in a self-debasing manner. My girlfriends and wives certainly had a say in those decisions, and I tried to respect their integrity. However, I have always regarded my sexual relationships and my marital status as exclusively contingent upon my idea of male spiritual integrity. We, Bulgarian males that is, felt called to make history. Communist ideals were a further call that reinforced our sense of destiny. Their appeal was contradictory. For the period of time one was stupid enough to espouse those ideals, the call was toward commitment to fight for them. Once their cruel bigotry was realized, the opposite call took over one's mind: the call to endure the regime until a miraculous force set us free from it. Since we were temporarily thrown out of history, we ought to wait proudly for our time to come. With a considerable delay, I realized how ridiculously false all this had been.

Today, I feel bitterly ironic toward these former attitudes of mine. At the time when I took them seriously, though, I was at once struggling with and supporting a powerful and relentless adversary. That adversary was the system. It had no face, no shape, no incarnation. It was everywhere and nowhere. Therefore, my struggle was in the abstract.

My struggle was doomed to fail, and I was doomed to a moral condemnation. However, I still did not know that. Some prevailing sense of belonging kept my illusions from destruction. I had a long way to go before I realized the ultimate futility of my stance.

In the meantime, I was possessed by conflicting emotions. On one hand, I felt strongly about my own life and was passionately involved with all the women with whom I had relations. I loved my four children even more strongly. On the other hand, it was impossible not to love an invincible adversary like the communist system. It embodied my country, the people I belonged to, the land and its history, and so many precious things that give life meaning. But because it was such a perverse system, this love was a trap set for naïve individuals like me.

In 1983, I fell into this trap for the last time: I left my second wife. I still believed that one could achieve individual freedom under those circumstances. A man who loved order and stability, I revolted against the order embodied in family life. It appeared as if I wanted to break up the social order established by the communists while it was, as a matter of fact, an individual crisis: a genuine crisis of emotions and relationship. In retrospect, however, I see the added attempt of mine to use this crisis as a means of elevating my own spirits. I was breaking the rules. I was disobeying the norms and spitting in the swamp. No ripples appeared on the rigid surface, though, except that my life changed course rather dramatically.

It was during this time that I met my future third wife. She was divorced and had a son. The deal of love we struck provided a romantic shine over our lives. I will come back to our romance later. My third marriage endured, and we still live together and have a common daughter.

Today, I believe I have built and rebuilt harmonious relationships with all six of my children. Also, the hostilities between my two former wives and me are long over. We have slowly and painfully realized that we were all fooled by the communist system. Our deepest emotions were deviated or torn apart by our dull, compulsory interaction with this system. We survived at the expense of our integrity. We survived because on the rational level we complied with the life that was offered to us. As I will never stop repeating, we complied both because of the brainwashing and because of our genuine belief in communism. However, this compliance cost us dearly on the emotional level.

Today, I bless my intellect (or, who knows, perhaps my nonchalance?) for having at least prevented me from joining the Communist Party. Had I become a servant of the communist regime, this would have been forever, and it would have fully destroyed my emotional integrity.

A real danger existed, though. It would have sufficed that some external event challenged me, whereby I could have responded impulsively against my true nature. My father challenged my sense of independence by showing me the door for disobedience in my studies, and I reacted by getting married. I imagined that this was a revolutionary, nonconformist reaction, whereas, in fact, it was conformism in action, much to my chagrin today. When I was invited to join the party, I probably could have decided that becoming a party member was, after all, a nonconformist deed in response to some other challenge, as for example, being refused entry to the university. Such impulsive intentions are documented in my diaries from that period. What I regarded as nonconformist then was the illusion that if decent and honest people like myself entered the communist movement, the party could be transformed into a "good" institution leading the nation to a brighter future. The extent to which I was remote from my true nature was so depressingly large, indeed. I had reached rock bottom in my fall into the embrace of communism.

Still, it did not occur to me to join in by an individual act of volition. I was responding to the general atmosphere of adherence/nonadherence dilemmas and active recruitment by procrastinating, postponing, and generally claiming that I was too immature and irresponsible to make such a step when confronted by my parents on the issue. Quite frankly, I still suspect that I failed to make the move not out of convictions or principles, but because I hated the idea of being involved with people who were intellectually inferior to me. The fact is that I have never agonized over a genuine wish to apply myself. I was simply not giving in to the pressure to join. And I was sincere in believing that I did not need this membership, an attitude that was an odd combination of exuberant self-confidence and immature political philosophy.

I was definitely immature, but in two contradictory senses. In terms of a man's career in the socialist state of Bulgaria, I was proven wrong, since in the decades that followed I became aware that *the* requirement for well-being—despite whatever cultural terms were used to define well-being—was to belong to the party. Party members were first-class citizens, no matter what. Party outsiders could never be first-class citizens, the few cases of trust, exceptional careers, or paradoxical twists of fate notwithstanding.

On the other hand, my thinking in terms of conscious opposition to party rule proved to be equally infantile. It did not occur to me that any activity implying rejection of the Communist Party as a dictatorial political organization might be the way to deal with my *mal du siècle* feelings.

Being frustrated with my university studies, I focused my energy on building a family. But this occurred at the wrong age for me, and I grew frustrated with my family as well. Meanwhile, I became enthralled with medicine and realized that it was probably the most suitable profession for an eclectic person like me.

At this time, somewhere in the middle of my student years, I was officially invited to apply for party membership. Being already bifurcated in two serious responsibilities (marriage and medical studies) I was actually being asked to add a third one. I did not consider the possibility that party membership might be an alleviating solution instead of another burden.

I did not agonize long before saying no. The only bravery in the negative answer was that I risked ruining my career, and I seemed to be generally aware of the consequences. However, it turned out that I was so self-confident that I underestimated the deep erosion that awaited me. In addition, I held on to the naïve belief that communism itself would "improve" by overcoming the faults of the transition period. I reasoned that I could wait and that it would never be too late to join the party when I finally considered it worthy enough for my moral maximalism.

Yes, the bottom line was indeed morality. My differences with the party were based on moral grounds and did not come out of an antagonistic political perspective or a different philosophical system. The reason for this is that I identified the party with the real people living and acting around me, in a concrete time and space. I regarded the party from an insider's standpoint, in contrast to the entire outside world. Writers, journalists, politicians, and historians from the West have always identified the various communist parties with their notorious secretaries or politburos. Our judgment of the real people who personify a political power is perforce moral; therefore, our judgment about the power itself becomes morally biased. Nonetheless, if we take political power as an embodiment of the political philosophy or social ideals that we embrace, as I did, we may excuse its inability to appear just and efficient because of the low morality of those who act on its behalf in real life.

I grew up in the company of a few friends with whom I shared the belief that a superior morality distinguished us from the rest of our local world. By an incredible twist of logic, we had taken the basics of this high morality from the communist theory about an equal and just society. Our delusion was that we had matched these basics to the postwar reality of a Balkan country. We, however, wrongly attributed the perceived mismatch to small-mindedness, philistinism, greed, and the general imperfections of human nature. We had bought the propagandist suggestion that we were a new generation, called upon by history to build the most just *stroy* (society) in mankind's history. Our nature was allegedly better than the nature of our predecessors. Our self-esteem was so high that we overlooked the real snags of human nature, such as cowardice, bigotry, and subordination to power. However, what we overlooked in the first place, I now realize, was the genuinely wrong idea that communism based on dictatorship can become a superior alternative to civil democracy.

All but one of my former friends joined the Communist Party. All but two of my classmates gave in to the pressure to do so. I have heard so many times the excuse, "I cannot say no because this will expose me as a nonbeliever in communism," that even now I feel sick remembering it. In fact, in the vernacular Balkan language this excuse meant, "I cannot refuse a favor that will make my life easy." Another apologetic stance added to this was, "Everyone else is doing it; why should I be the black sheep?" People actually felt proud that they lacked individuality and could mingle their decisions and deeds with the crowd. A third excuse sounded even more justified: "I make sacrifices to clear a path for my children to be better off." This was, and still is, the most common explanation that our parents and all communists would provide if pressed by criticism about their collaboration with the communist regime.

Marxist communism as an ideology and a prescription for assuaging social pains was taken seriously by almost no one after the teenage flame died down. The Bulgarian people's pragmatic sense suggested two things. On one hand, communism was not fit to "rectify the social mess," but on the other, since communism was what the powerful offered as the social project, the winning strategy ought to be compliance instead of rebellion. Had these people been more educated or vocal, they would have verbalized this existential philosophy.

When initially obsessed with our calf-love of communism, some of us labeled this pragmatic position of our elders as morally inadequate. Although they proved right in their instinctive disdain for communist theory, they were in the wrong regarding the communist practice. To be sure, our true mistake was not that we attributed the mismatch between theory and practice to our elders' moral inadequacy, but that we ignored their correct pragmatic judgment about communism's ability to survive.

The fact is that pragmatism took over swiftly among my peers, and they joined the party ranks with no remorse whatsoever. Although I happened to differ from the majority, I cannot claim that the difference exempts me from my share of the guilt of complying. I was more self-reliant than brave. I was clearly too intellectually immature at the time to distance myself from the communist ideology and the ensuing communist politics. I still had not felt my human rights castrated, my human freedom mocked, or democracy cynically faked all over by the politically immature population of Bulgaria. Rather late in life, I came to realize that this state of affairs was made possible not because cruel and inhumane executors of power harassed the population as they pleased, but because the people themselves met communism with a pragmatic compliance.

Communism got us. But early in life I imagined we had gotten it. During my university years, my moral communism was still alive, so I felt proud in rejecting an invitation to share its privileges. I lived with my elitist illusions, whereas my peers stepped into the real communist elite.

We were parting paths, and I lost track of many of them. My concerns with the premature husband-hood were the main topics of our debates with those who still had not disappeared beyond the horizon. The rest of my energy went into medical studies. In fact, the memory of how hard I was striving to become an excellent physician is the only thing that keeps me from dismissing this period of my life as totally useless.

In the long run, however, I realized that this was, nonetheless, an eye-opening period. It started for real when I began breaking away from my friends. When I saw people abandoning our moral platform, or rather jumping onto another moral bandwagon because of interest, fear, and compliance, I was struck by my twofold blindness. Either they had always been hypocritically sharing my maximalist philosophy, or I had underestimated the appeal (or perhaps, the inescapability) of the communist establishment.

Actually, both explanations were at the bottom of this friendship crisis. In my stupor, however, the value that seemed unchanged was the image of the communist future. As an abstract concept embodying moral elevation and noble well-being, communism existed on a pedestal under a glass cover. Nothing was out there to diminish its shine, and since it was projected into the future, nothing tangible could occur to throw a shadow of doubt over its virtuousness. By contrast, everything that was personified by living human beings was becoming bold, questionable, and missing stable values. It was because communist practice had a real meaning for my peers and me that I had been able to open my eyes to its drawbacks. We could not regard real communism as an extravagance or a violation of humane ethics. Real communism meant to all of us real people, real relationships, and real existence.

No matter how strongly we wanted or could have tried to escape this existence, we participated in it. We had been cast in its roles. Or perhaps we cast ourselves in our roles? Today, I am not entirely sure whether the latter was closer to the truth than the former. Everyone wishes and insists we were dragged in by force. Our participation by coercion is such a tempting excuse. Nevertheless, my reminiscence and a great deal of personal attestations suggest otherwise.

On the other hand, I do not wish to imply that my case of abstention from party membership on moral grounds was exceptional behavior. It was simply not the rule. Later in life, I met a few people who belonged to the class of communist outsiders by birth. They, too, were out of the party, yet they, too, had not lived as "fighters against communism" but, instead, had a more or less nihilistic or escapist philosophy. When I reached their level of repugnance at the communist reality, I realized that I had traveled a longer way, coming from inside the communist ideology and trust in the communist ideals. From the vantage point of their morality (which finally became mine, too), I had things of which to be ashamed.

In that period of my life, though, I did not see any of those people around me. I communicated with renegades who hastened to attach their souls to the flow or with young people who agonized over existential issues, the meaning of life, where and how to achieve happiness, and so forth. My friends called me speculative and high-minded. They became especially angry with me the more they realized that I had not fallen in line with the mass movement toward the "coalescence of the party and the people."

The rudiments of my metamorphosis from a moral communist to a staunch anticommunist can be traced back to my six years of medical school. Again, I did not experience this as an epiphany. It was not related to a dramatic shock that would abruptly pull down a curtain behind which an unknown ugliness stood hidden. I was definitely not a Westerner who, carrying a manipulated image of an exotic reality, steps down from the train somewhere in Siberia and instead of striped and shaven prisoners behind barbed wire sees well-dressed citizens, clean hospitals and posh restaurants. In contrast to him or her, I was not bereft of swaying back and forth from this society's façade to its backyard (a side never shown to the curious Westerner). Thus, these six years I am referring to can be metaphorically described as a trip from the front door to the backyard of communism.

There was not much at the front door, except rhetoric and sheer propaganda, susceptible to which were fragile youngsters or humanistically oriented Western intellectuals. But there was plenty in the backyard. My journey to the backyard was not as painful as one might imagine. I did not uncover the backyard of concentration camps, political prisoners held in psychiatric asylums, and protest rallies smashed by tanks. Not that this part of the backyard was made up by some sick imagination. The truth is that it was a very limited part, and by far not the representative one. My metamorphosis was driven by the observation of people I met every day during my journey. These people either oscillated like myself between the bright theoretical forefront (emphatically embodied in Marx's massive forehead) and the obscure corners of the backyard, or occupied quietly their reserved place back there. What struck me foremost was the comfort with which most people dwelled in this backyard. I am willing to bet that it had never occurred to them that their existence could be compared to a backyard.

From today's perspective, I contend that my metamorphosis occurred precisely because I was not shocked or brought to a paroxysmal suffering. It occurred because I lived among people like me: the brainwashed and the brainwashers, party members and party outsiders, idealists and pragmatists, believers and bigots, compliant and violent, harassed and harassers. Of course, such a metamorphosis, as my experience shows, occurred to only a small number of our brainwashed human species. Communism suited our Balkan people well. Or, to put it even more bluntly, Balkan people were well suited for communism.

I did not feel heroic when I turned down the offer to join the party. Nor did anyone come to shake my hand. Maybe it was an act of civic bravery, as similar deeds have been pompously dubbed by the free press where it existed, or in memoirs. But at the time, I did not much care about its significance. I definitely withdrew from Komsomol activity, claiming that I needed to concentrate on my studies. I did concentrate, in fact, and by my fourth year in medical school, I had become a promising candidate for a career in the Department of Anatomy. I also refused to go to summer brigades under the pretext that I had family duties. It is important to emphasize the verbs *withdrew* and *refused,* because that was all I did. I merely refrained from participating; I never publicly denounced the activities from which I tried to escape. I never actively attacked the principles of their performance. The fact of the matter is, if I had had the impulse and the guts to utter public criticism, my voice would have been the only one heard.

On the other hand, my refusal to join the party and the increasing disdain for Komsomol "initiatives" reflected in my record had no visible impact on my promotions or on my social status as a whole. The tacit family protection worked well. I did not learn until much later that my individualistic "sidebars" were duly recorded in my police file. At the time, however, my "one of us" reputation was not tarnished. This only served to enlarge my delusion that what counted in my life under communism was my performance in science and intellectual work, at least to the extent that I could dispense with special contributions to the Komsomol and the party. On top of that, I felt I had remained true to my moral foundations, which to me seemed ubiquitous. I was law-abiding and could do no harm to anybody, so by all accounts I would not be cheated in any fair competition, no matter how heavily the party assets might weigh.

I was wrong, and again not only in one thing. First, I was wrong to believe that morality stood higher than personal interests disguised as party commitment. Second, I was wrong to take the lack of pressure on the part of my parents and closest would-be friends as a tacit acceptance of my behavior. No debates, no fuss, no scandals; things were accepted as if nothing had happened. Finally, my basic mistake was to delay my decision whether to join the party. I sincerely hoped that this "ideal" social system was simply tarnished by human imperfections. One day, in my lifetime, I hoped, people's morality would be upgraded, and the system would emerge in all its glory.

This state of mind was confirmed by a number of "positive" signs. I continued to have an unblemished authority among peers, Komsomol activists included, and among my professors who saw brilliant prospects for a career in medical teaching and research. I did not suffer any exclusion whatsoever, despite the suspicion that I might have been transferred to the category of untrustworthy citizen. An interesting example is my trip to the Soviet Union, the first trip abroad in my life, which occurred when I was twenty-three.

Each summer, a travel exchange took place between our medical school and the First Moscow Lenin's-Medal-Awardee State Medical University. A group of about a dozen medical students was selected according to two criteria (grades and Komsomol activity) to form a group that would spend three weeks in the Soviet Union. In exchange, a similar group of students from Moscow spent three weeks in Varna. Based on their account, these students were selected in the same way, although more KGB requirements had to be met than in our case before being issued a passport. The official purpose of the exchange was to carry out a short hospital residency in the corresponding university clinics. In practice, our Soviet colleagues fought for the privilege to spend a luxurious vacation (from a Soviet point of view, of course) in a renowned Black Sea resort place, whereas we were eager to visit the famous Soviet capital. Our schedule included an itinerary connecting Kiev, Leningrad, and Moscow by train.

Although I did not meet the Komsomol criterion for inclusion in the group, I never doubted that my overwhelming performance in class and in the clinics would help me qualify. It did, and I obtained my passport and arrived by train in the vast Soviet land to take my next dose of eye opening.

The trip itself was magnificent. Romantic walks to historic sites and Russian Orthodox sacred shrines were followed by Russian-style drinking in someone's apartment. Train love flirtations with the "enigmatic Russian women" alternated with unforgettable visits to museums of fine arts. After getting high on Russian gold in Saint Petersburg's tzar palaces, we were transported into a somber *stolovaya* to be fed with some hogwash made of croup or Russian yogurt. Leaving a porcelain tea party in an old aristocratic apartment, we soon found ourselves on the public transport (bus or subway) squeezed among sweaty builders of communism before being spat out by the crowd at the front door of a miserable student hostel where we were to spend the night. And why not mention the threatening cold of the dean's office where we were once received and instructed in an unabashed official tone on how to observe discipline in the socialist hospital.

Above all, however, I met various Russian people during this journey. Contact with these people who were introduced to me (or, more often, encountered incidentally) provided me with an immediate grasp of the tacit reality, or the "backyard" of socialist Russia, as I had already chosen to call this reality. It is clear to me that today I cannot use fresh-sounding words to depict my grasp because all references to Soviet Russia are no longer images, but concepts. I knew a lot about Russia from the literature, the movies, and the traditional brotherhood that brought Bulgarians near to the Russians. I had my mythology of Russia, a mythology that was at once confirmed and refuted.

I was struck, however, by the brand-new thought that these were the people who had installed communism on earth. And their aptitude for communism was just another face of this people's grandeur, which, alas, I could not bear. This thought further evolved during the multiple visits I paid to the Soviet Union in the 1970s. In 1980, when my second wife returned from her doctoral studies in Leningrad, I decided that I would never set foot on Russian soil again.

Soviet Russia is perhaps the most painful chapter of my life. Russia is even now an unending story of love-hate that aches deep down in my soul. A story so intimate that I hasten to close this digression before it becomes too long and sentimental. Before closing, however, I would like to relate the stories of two splendid personalities I befriended during my first visit to Moscow. They both truly belong to the rare category of extraordinary intellectuals—and in Russia such a distinction has profound meaning.

One was a woman from no special stock, who was bright, erudite, and brimming with energy. Within the space of eighteen days, she gave me lessons on society and hierarchies that I could never have been taught in my provincial country. She also taught me a special lesson about the role of personal values. With great delicacy and tact, she guided me through the contrasts and mysteries of the Soviet reality. Two years later, I met her husband, a brilliant physician with the Central Institute of Orthopedics and Traumatology in Moscow. Both these high-quality personalities were surpassed by Soviet reality. In accordance with Soviet social standards, they were marginalized to the point of suicide. In keeping with the traditional Russian values, they should have occupied a central position, but nobody cared about that. Both never joined the Communist Party, made any concessions to the Soviet regime, or fought against it. They found the required stamina to quit. They have lived happily in Chicago since 1980. After a couple of heated debates and a short period of alienation, our common communist past is no longer a matter of controversy or belated remorse between us.

The other intellectual—a man to whom I will refer only by his initials, P. M.—with whom I established cordial relationships in 1969, was a pure aristocrat. His mother was descended from an old aristocratic family, and his father's lineage went back through several generations of Russian intellectuals. My colleague was brilliant in every respect. He projected physical refinement and beauty accompanied with witty speech and superb manners. His wife, though, was a standard Russian belle of rather limited mental resources. We all admired her like a statuette with whom there is nothing to talk about apart from one significant detail: her father was a high-ranking Soviet military man.

At the time, P. M.'s father was a professor of psychiatry and it was taken for granted that his son would inherit his profession, even his chair itself in one of the central psychiatric institutions in Moscow. The older M. looked depressed all the time, although he kept his posture of a professor whose intellectual authority could not be questioned by anybody from his family entourage. The mainstream attitude toward the Soviet regime in this family was jocular, although it never reached sarcastic tones. Old national values were still highly praised. I felt that something rotten was eroding the family spirit from beneath the lustrous surface, but could not immediately identify it with precision.

An awful explanation came later, when I learned more facts. Old Professor M., by virtue of his central position in the hierarchy of the Soviet psychiatry, was aware (if not himself a reluctant participant) of the misuse of Soviet psychiatry for political ends. On the other hand, there was no power that could force him to sacrifice the career of his son, the upholder of noble family traditions. Thus, his life was already a chain of moral compromises. He could not doubt that even bigger moral concessions with the Soviet authorities awaited his son.

Meanwhile, the young P. M. had not given up Komsomol activism as others around him carelessly did. After graduation, the top Soviet psychiatric institute in Moscow immediately hired him. This institute directed the entire psychiatric establishment under the immediate supervision of the party Central Committee and the KGB. I could not believe my ears when, in the summer of 1990, I was confidentially told that P. M. was not a simple Komsomol activist but a KGB collaborator who had been gathering information about us since the time of our first student exchange trip. I learned this after we had exchanged family visits in Moscow and Varna during the 1970s, where we kept up our snappy repartee as well as our emotional friendship.

During this period, P. M.'s psychiatric career was skyrocketing. I did not yet suspect that this could be due to anything other than his sterling professional skills. I thus had some apprehensions about his alleged connections with the KGB, although my source was the most reliable I could have imagined. My doubts evaporated when I received a letter from him stating that he was working at the World Health Organization (WHO) headquarters in Geneva as a Soviet appointee in the WHO's psychiatric branch. The letter was not mailed but instead was delivered in person by the Bulgarian representative working there. This was a clear sign that P. M. was not willing to expose any of his connections. Such precautions were a professional duty of the KGB staff working all around the world. Besides, it was a public secret that in places like the WHO (and in psychiatry even more so) Soviet representatives were by definition KGB agents. I replied to the letter, but received no answer.

About ten years later, in Sofia during the late Gorbachev era, I met a colleague of P. M.'s who was looking for contacts with Bulgarian healthcare officials. I was the public relations officer for the Bulgarian Medical Academy at the time and often served as a liaison between foreign visitors and the academy board. I thought this might be a good occasion to restore my old connection with P. M., so I asked the Soviet psychiatrist to take P. M. a letter from me. He never answered it. In the summer of 1991, I learned that P. M. participated as the head of the Soviet delegation at the World Psychiatric Association's annual meeting in Athens. He made a plea at a plenary session for the Soviet Psychiatric Association to be readmitted to the worldwide organization, from which it had been expelled in the early 1980s.

In this whole story I was most amused by two reactions. The Soviet psychiatrist, an apparently honest man, abruptly changed his demeanor and rather hastily took leave of me after learning of my former friendship with P. M. He apparently concluded that I belonged to the same category of unidentified (and unidentifiable) turncoats who served the secret police during and after the regime.

Still more ironically, the Bulgarian WHO officer who had brought me P. M.'s letter had the same suspicions about me. As a party and secret police insider, he guessed that I was somehow connected to the Organs, but had to remain unexposed. We did not see each other for about five years after he delivered the letter, although he came back to Bulgaria from time to time. After Todor Zhivkov was ousted, this man was elected president of the Medical Academy in the first postcommunist institutional elections. He in turn picked me to serve as his spokesman, calculating that I, too, was possibly pretending to play with the democrats while at the same time keeping my old connections and perhaps performing some new secret missions. In any event, if I turned out to be a true democrat, it would not hurt him at all to have me as a potential shield against the rising suspicions that he might have played secret games during his stay in Geneva.

Such a mood of common suspicion was not typical during my university years. Then, at least, I was not involved in potentially suspicious relationships. I was still young, with a pristine mind, and naïve. By the end of my clinical residency I was divorced and free of party membership. In other words, I had failed to resolve two rather embarrassing issues: creating my own family and digging my own niche in the partyocracy.

The only security I had was my medical diploma. Receiving it brought a successful close to that early period of my life. Soon, I was appointed to serve as a professor of anatomy in the same medical school from which I had graduated the year before. Again, several awkward circumstances color this episode. One was that when the opening was announced, the other eventual candidates did not apply (or if they did, shortly withdrew their applications) when they learned that I was planning to apply. It was tacitly understood that the position would be given to me. The expectations proved right, since I was the only applicant and performed well on the examination. I felt no remorse; I truly deserved the job. Nevertheless, despite my exam performance, I still had to be approved by the department's and the medical school's party committees. I had no problem with this, either. My family's stature with the party was still working on my behalf despite the fact that my own file (as I learned later) was not as pristine as it should have been.

CHAPTER 5

Selling Freedom

Every particular man is author of all the sovereign
doth; and consequently he that complaineth of injury
from his sovereign, complaineth of that whereof he
himself is author; and therefore ought not accuse any
man but himself; no nor himself of injury, because to
do injury to oneself is impossible.

—*Thomas Hobbes,* De Cive

A notorious slogan decorated *every* office in the state security ministries, committees, and departments throughout the Eastern European socialist camp. It read: "The *tchekist* must have a cool mind, a hot heart, and clean hands." The motto hung as an obligatory side dish next to the portrait of the person who delivered it: Felix Edmundovich Dzerzhinsky. "Iron Felix" fathered the Soviet TcheKa (Tchrezvitchajnaya Komissiya or Emergency Commission), in which the rules were set for the KGB build-up. Communist reality revealed the mind-boggling cynicism in the motto, a cynicism that was perceptible only to my former fellow citizens and me—all potential KGB clients.

Almost everyone in the world thinks they know what the KGB was all about. Typically, those who have heard about communism in Eastern Europe tend to identify the evil of the Soviet system with that organization. But if one really wants to know what the KGB was all about, myth has to be distinguished from reality. And reality was how the true carriers of this system experienced and felt about the KGB.

The Bulgarian branch of the KGB was called State Security, or SS. Pretty chilling name, isn't it? In the Bulgarian vernacular it had become simply the "Organs." I had my first visit from a Bulgarian SS agent when I was in my next-to-last year at the French high school. I maintained a close relationship with several of my French teachers at the time. Despite repeated warnings, I visited their apartments and rode in their cars. I did so not in *defiance of* the regime but because I felt too well protected *within* the regime. I never thought that I was untouchable (as some indeed were), but instead fancied that my mental communist premises safeguarded me enough from the "corruptive" Western influence. For a while, it seemed that nobody was concerned about my relationships with those foreigners. According to the circulating jokes and rumors, their apartments were bugged and even under photo surveillance. Since I had never witnessed anything of the sort, I could not vouch for the truthfulness of such claims (then or now).

What I can account for is that one autumn day in 1963, a man in his thirties rang the bell in my grandmother's house and asked to have a private conversation with me. He gave only his name without revealing what organization or agency he was affiliated with. He took out a folder, opened it, and unscrewed the cap of his fountain pen. His smile was a professional grimace since he did not speak of hilarious things. I was supposed to listen and cooperate. His approach demanded a full commitment on my part.

He said he knew that I felt happy in school and that I was doing well, but wanted me to know that in case I had any problems that needed some intervention I could always count on him. He then gave me a telephone number to call. Who was this man, I wondered, and why on earth should he offer to intervene and help solve my problems? He also knew that I was very much involved with my girlfriend and made a flat remark to that effect. Was I on friendly terms with a French married couple named M.? Yes, I was. Did I visit them at home? Yes, I did. So, what was my opinion of the husband? Well, I mumbled, I can say a lot of good things about him, but what do you need more precisely? He needed to know more precisely whether Mr. M. had somewhat closer relations with anyone in the school, teacher or student, and whether he had voiced any criticism regarding the government of this country. I instinctively wavered in my answer, and he rushed to persuade me that whatever I said would not be used to Mr. M.'s detriment, but only to enhance his stay in our country. He wondered also whether there might be some rift in the relationship between M. and his wife. Who was I to judge? My most vague and general answer seemed to satisfy him so well that he asked me, with emphatic politeness and his perpetual smile, to write down on a sheet of paper all my impressions of M. I was to complete this report in a couple of days, after which he would drop by to pick it up. Ah, incidentally, the report should be in my own handwriting!

This unexpected assignment was my first secret police task. I fulfilled it diligently, though with somewhat mixed feelings. As soon as it was over, I forgot about it. Nothing happened, either to Mr. M. or me. In fact, Mr. M. stayed in the country for another ten years, eventually becoming a French cultural attaché. Three or four years after the SS visit, the couple divorced. Madame M. married a Bulgarian doctor, while Mr. M. brought a second wife from Belgium. After I left school, I had little opportunity to stay in touch with either of them, so our friendship faded. To this day, I am still not sure whether the report I was asked to write went into Mr. M.'s file or my own. A reasonable guess is that if the report had pleased the agent responsible for me, I would have been actively recruited for that type of activity.

I heard nothing from the Bulgarian SS for a little more than a decade. However, it did not mean I was not hearing *about* it. Each and every one of us perceived its invisible ubiquity at almost every turn in our communist existence.

The first sign that I was being carefully watched came in September, 1976. As strange as it seems to me today, I can vividly recall how upset I was over the thought that I had a "bad file" with the secret police. The incident grew out of my plans to attend an anatomical conference in Prague. Before every such trip, private or business, you had to apply for a passport or, if you already had one, for an exit visa at the city police department. The passport office had deliberately restricted hours of operation, so you had to wait in line for quite a while. The waiting room was windowless, dimly lit, and isolated by thick walls from the individual offices in which the clerks worked. When your turn came, you spoke with the clerk at the desk through a square window that framed your head against the wall. You had to come to this window with all of the required documents ready for submission. If the clerk noticed a single mistake in your application (an omitted entry, a photograph wrongly cut, a missing signature), she would return the entire pile to you with a stern warning that your application would be denied if you failed to complete all the appropriate documents in a letter-perfect fashion.

I did, indeed, hand in my documents as required. Therefore, when three weeks later I put my head into the infamous window to ask the police clerk about my visa for Czechoslovakia, I expected anything but a refusal. When she told me I had not been issued the exit visa, it came as a shock to me. I suddenly felt the first fault line in my easygoing communist existence.

I had never before had any problems with the Passport Department. My first passport, for that student trip to Moscow in 1969, was issued without a glitch. In the fall of 1972, when I married for the second time, my wife and I went on a honeymoon trip to Leipzig and Jena in East Germany to visit some remote acquaintances, and again my exit visa was issued without difficulty.

A couple of things had happened in between without my paying attention to their potential significance, however. In the fall of 1974, after my mandatory military service, I let my beard grow. This was viewed as an act of unwarranted liberty in communist Bulgaria. According to the enforced rules, every man's face was to be clean-shaven because a beard was considered a "remnant from the bourgeois past." To let your beard grow was regarded as a claim of differentiation. Bulgaria's decent citizens were scandalized by such behavior, so the authorities had to enforce men's shaving, too. The only way to avoid taking a forced walk to the nearest barbershop was to obtain an ID card with a bearded photo on it. But the photo shops were not authorized to make such photos of ordinary citizens, and if you somehow succeeded in getting one, the police clerk would refuse to file your application.

Out of the blue, my second father-in-law (a nonparty member) volunteered to help me with this issue. He took me to meet a high-ranking secret police officer and, after about five minutes of dull conversation with the officer, my problem was solved. The next week, I was issued a very precious ID with a bearded picture of me on its second page.

By that time, my second refusal to join the Communist Party had no doubt been filed in my police record. I was more resolute the second time, although technically I had simply ignored an invitation. There were no debates, scandals, or official statements involved. Deep down in my heart, though, I had already determined to never become a party member. On one hand, my enthusiasm to pursue a career had been quickly cooled down by the blunt discovery that party members on the faculty were both the most corrupt and least fit for teaching or research. Although I voiced this observation during our obligatory political seminars, nothing visibly changed for me afterward: I continued to teach and to collect my miserable salary.

On the other hand, I was slowly giving up on the hope that the Communist Party's leadership could be improved by injecting moral blood into it. I must have shared these apprehensions of mine with different people, with the nonchalance characteristic of the brood of the communist establishment. I felt above the fray. In a way, I was already poised for an intellectual's apolitical arrogance.

The above apparently innocuous incidents left me feeling quite confident that I had everything square with the Organs. Much to my chagrin, however, my exit visa application for Czechoslovakia failed just two years after I was granted the passport with a bearded photo on it.

My naïveté was confronted by facts. In 1976, I learned, for example, that every factory, institution, ocean liner, agency, and so forth was assigned a plainclothes police agent responsible for evaluating the trustworthiness of the staff. This agent, as an exemplary shepherd, kept files on everyone and set up a network of informers to monitor all the risky moves and utterances within the flock. In the case of the medical school, the agent kept an office in the police building, but used the party committee offices when he needed to meet somebody or issue instructions. This link was not exclusively physical. In fact, the institutional party committee served unofficially (but very effectively) as a fort from which the agent could organize the watch over its subordinate territory.

The agent accountable for the medical school faculty was a young man named Boyan Bohorov. Smiling, polite, even jocular, he also appeared to be well intentioned. He had never summoned me for a "man-to-man" conversation. I had never even been introduced to him. But when we met incidentally in the corridors or on the streets, I always felt that he somehow knew me quite well. By contrast, he was unaware—and possibly did not care—that I knew him as well. The major difference between us was that he had the power to use and abuse his knowledge against me or in my favor, whereas my knowledge of him was strictly personal and helped only to magnify my contempt for him. Philosophically, he hoarded information about my life, irrespective of my personality, soul, or intellect. His only interest was my attitude toward the regime that had hired him to watch, chase, and intimidate. Although I had a fairly clear understanding of his mentality and unsophisticated outlook on life, it served me little. I had to silently bear my visceral repugnance for him and his ilk.

Early one morning, I remember a noisy group of young men in suits and ties bouncing toward the swimming pool where I used to exercise twice a week (it was the only swimming pool in town). I had just gotten out of the blue mineral water and could see this group of plainclothes police officers undressing. "Our" agent was among them. They chatted in loud voices about fitness and a forthcoming trip to Austria. Inappropriate remarks about the legs of a girl they all knew well threaded in and out of the conversation. While they rejoiced in their togetherness, I churned inside and felt my sense of isolation grow with every word they uttered. Smug male nudity overwhelmed the moisture of the dressing room. Pipes screamed and showers ran in the neighboring cabins. The stench of male sweat, so characteristic of the barrack mentality of these men, overwhelmed any sense of privacy. All my life will stink of male sweat, it occurred to me, since my life virtually depended on these nude servants of the regime. I had no other choice but to hope that they would handle my police file fairly. As I learned several years later, however, that was not to be the case.

By 1976, I must already have had another two black eyes in my file: one related to my own behavior, the other owing to family misconduct. The family "dishonor" resulted from my sister's love story. Six years younger than me, she met a French engineer who was working on a construction project near Varna in 1970. When their dating led to a decision to marry, they were hoping they would encounter no problems: Bulgarian law did not prevent marriage to a foreigner. However, the couple had to obtain authorization from the SS rather than from a government institution. No one was surprised when they failed to obtain the required authorization, although my sister's application was not an exception. Other girls had already gotten permission to marry. The primary reason she was turned down was that we were considered a *nomenclature* family, and preserving the "purity" of such families was more important than their personal well-being. At the same time, my father was being considered for the rector's job at Varna's Higher School of Economics. He was summoned many times to appear before the BCP District Committee, where he was bullied and manipulated into trying to dissuade my sister from pursuing marriage to a Westerner. To the best of my knowledge, he did his best to meet this condition, but my sister resisted every attempt to sway her. She even filed a lawsuit asking for authorization to marry a

French citizen. The court granted her request, but the party still withheld its permission.

There was a pattern of hypocrisy involved in all of this. The thought of having a French son-in-law flattered my parents. Thus, they did not work as hard as they might have to discourage my sister. Moreover, they seemed to be disappointed by the so-called party line and the whole perspective of building socialism in the country. Their desire to be well off outside, or rather in spite of, this ideological engagement of theirs clashed with their sense of duty to the BCP. To make matters worse, they were trapped by the party's bylaws and so could not painlessly retreat. Apart from that, my parents were actually quite well-to-do according to the local standards. Indeed, they had to bow to the party mores if they wanted to maintain this status. It seemed, however, that they were not much concerned with the lawlessness of these mores, or with their abrasiveness, for that matter. Only in some very rare cases would anyone have the guts to give up similar perks out of respect for ultimate morality.

My father's failure to prevent his daughter's marriage to a foreigner threatened party security. The latter consisted of disallowing contamination by people or views that did not resonate with the party's expectations. The Stalinist model of the Communist Party was built upon a principle of perfect homogeneity in its elements. Stalin himself physically eliminated heterogeneity whether from within or entering from outside the party. In post-Stalinist times, the various communist parties could no longer be so harsh. They obeyed a model of "moral" liability among nonconforming elements. "Crystal purity" was no longer the critical requirement, but rather a rule of conformity assuring the party monster's immunity against all real or potential contamination.

After almost two years of harassment, the local party authorities conceded to my sister's persistence and granted her permission to marry the Frenchman, though not without serious consequences for my father. He had to remain a nomenclature item, since he was a university professor, but he could no longer be trusted to occupy leadership positions. His "degree of contamination" blocked his eligibility for top posts, although he maintained the right to work, travel, and teach. This was a heavy blow to him, and it only added to his depression and lack of productivity during the six years before the onset of his Parkinson's disease. My sister's happy marriage, including the fact that she left the country legally, seemed to be insufficient compensation for his disgrace within the community he appreciated most: his fellow communist faculty. Moreover, he had come to the realization that his son would never follow in his footsteps, toeing the conventional party line in Bulgarian academia. I cannot tell whether he was concerned with the fact that the westbound departure of my sister meant also a negative entry in my police file. He never discussed such matters with me.

The fact is that I was happy for—even envious of—my sister leaving the communist life. I had merely missed the right time to join the Communist Party. Besides, being a professor of anatomy since the fall of 1974, I had fully neglected any opportunity for involvement with the party initiatives as a nonparty communist sympathizer. My eye opening came brusquely. My mental status was characterized by a frustration that sought exit through two imaginative explanations: either my professional performance would outdo the party's domination over my life, or the "bad people" in the communist hierarchy would be kicked out and we would finally have a communism with a normal human face. Let me say again that my survival ethic was due entirely to my own reluctance to be in the same pot *with the people* who embodied the Communist Party, and not to a conscious rejection of communism as a social program.

This is an extremely important point. The people who could have formed the anticommunist opposition in a country like Bulgaria (and, I believe, the same is valid for the whole Eastern European communist camp) construed their political stance with regard to the concrete carriers of the communist ideology, but not against the ideology itself. Today, I no longer believe that the ideology failed to materialize because corrupted people implemented it. However, in the 1970s, that was exactly my political credo. I never doubted that I belonged in the category of people bound to oppose dictatorial communism. But on an everyday basis, I had always found excuses for my indolence.

How I behaved at this time and how this episode resulted in the second snub in my file remains to be told. It is a story that illustrates the practical fusion between the party and the secret police.

During every school year, a special seminar was set up for the faculty to study selected topics of communist theory and practice. The seminar sessions were mandatory and scheduled after normal business hours, which meant they ate into our leisure time twice a month. A staff member from the Department of Marxism-Leninism, who selected the topic and prepared the syllabus, led the seminar. It is worth mentioning that the professors teaching in the Marxism-Leninism Departments (this name was popular in universities all around the country) were communism-stricken and were usually closely linked either to the party or to the Organs. The simple fact that they taught such a discipline rendered their fidelity to the party unquestionable. For the rest of us, what was unquestionable was their smug straightforwardness and total lack of imagination. In my forced encounters with these individuals I tried hard to perform well enough to avoid suspicion of my belief in communist theory. Nonetheless, I failed to obtain the highest grades in all of these ideological disciplines during my university curriculum. The way they were taught (as newspaper versions of Marxism with an emphasis on Leninism) was repulsive to any normal brain.

During my second-year seminar, I asserted publicly that we did not need these seminars at all because on one hand we were literate people and could read the stuff ourselves, and on the other, we felt competent enough to understand the topics without the elementary discussion to which we were subjected in the seminars. I was simply reacting to the dull presentation of serious social and political problems. But since the very purpose of the exercise was to involve us in dull discourse and distract us from the serious issues, my critique was maliciously interpreted as a reproach to the theory of communism itself. The seminar moderator did his utmost to counter my claims and to move on with his syllabus. One of the topics near the end of that year's program was "The role of the communist in the socialist society." According to the literature listed for the topic, we were expected to discuss the moral virtues that distinguished a party member from the ordinary citizens of our society as it transitioned from socialism toward communism. The material evidence, of course, completely contradicted the topic argument. I could not help attacking the very notion of morality in connection with the party members. "Can we find anyone among the BCP members in this university who is better than the rest of us in any respect?" I asked several times (always supporting my rhetorical questions with plenty of examples). The real examples actually sat in that same seminar panel and kept silent. No one in the room missed the point, although one or two nonparty members took issue with my pronouncements and demanded additional evidence for my claims.

The seminar closed on schedule, the syllabus was fulfilled, and I was conscience-stricken that my contribution had amounted to nothing more than a storm in a teacup. There was a strong element of childishness in my reaction, which might have been accounted for by my idiosyncratic character. Yet such reactions were rather typical of the growing sense of desperation with which my fellow honest intellectuals had been seized. A similar hopelessness pervaded all eventual attempts to raise valid points, to bring

Here I am with a group of professors at the Varna Medical Institute's biweekly seminar for the study of Marxism-Leninism, fall, 1977. (Author's collection.)

serious issues to discussion, or to address substantive criticism over the implementation of Marxism in the communist state. Except in the most flagrant cases, individual criticism was ignored and life marched on as prescribed. The invisible difference after that was that something in the critic's personal life began to run astray.

Thus, when I heard that my exit visa was denied, it struck me that perhaps my file already contained quotations of what I had said publicly during the seminars. These quotations might have come from two sources. The first, the seminar moderator, I had suspected right away. But the second occurred to me only later in life, when I realized that a multitude of informers had lived among us and had reported every hint of criticism toward the regime or its rulers.

Two months later, I experienced another consequence of my meaningless "bravery." At that time, my department had proposed that the medical school's Academic Council promote me based on my performance as a teacher and researcher. At the council meeting, the chair of the Department of Marxism-Leninism stood up and told the audience that I was opposed to the study of Marxism-Leninism and that I must therefore be refused promotion at that time. The council concurred.

Still, there was a touch of irony in all these happenings, or, at least, I tried hard to take them that way. News that I had been refused an exit visa for Czechoslovakia (which was not even a Western country) provoked turmoil within my family. The very next day my father-in-law—notably, not my father—told me that he would see the chief of the Passport Department in person and try to rectify the situation. Shortly thereafter he paid him a visit and two days later the visa was stamped in my passport.

My father-in-law never told me what he said, but since then I have often suspected that he was a covert collaborator with the police. I failed to learn the truth about this man, no matter how hard I tried, but he met all the criteria for the job. He had a bourgeois past and was never openly connected with the communist movement before or after the September, 1944, revolution. He was devoted entirely to his family's well-being. Professionally, he was well regarded as a chief accountant with one of the big factories in town, and he was proud of his modest achievements as an expert in the field. Together, these characteristics made him an ideal candidate for the role of a secret collaborator. At least, he might have been easily recruited, if the education and career of his two children had been threatened. The fact that he was well off without being a party member and that he was privately hostile to the communists, could be consistently explained only on the assumption that at some top level in the police they knew his real role.

My father, on the other hand, was a friend of the Marxism-Leninism professor who had impeded my promotion, yet he would never have thought of seeing him on my behalf. He could only be an overt communist, never a secret collaborator. Although both fathers shared the responsibility for the well-being of their respective families, each complied differently to achieve it. My father-in-law complied with the inevitable, while my father complied with the party discipline. I am positive, however, that neither of them considered any other survival strategy.

Thus, because there was no one to help me with my academic promotion, I had to wait a year and a half for it to happen. In the meantime, I did nothing to add to my tarnished police record and my critical pronouncements in the seminar were gradually forgotten. I am not sure why I silenced my criticism. Was it because I already had four children? Or was it because I came to realize the utter futility of such verbal revolts? Perhaps it was a combination of both. Whatever the reason, I am certain it was not out of compliance. It was, in fact, the beginning of my effort to escape from the trap my elders had unwittingly set for me.

Another six years passed before I completely realized the hopelessness of my efforts to perform as an independent provincial intellectual living in peace with hostile and snooping communist authorities. Although nothing perceptible happened during those years, my diaries reveal that a great deal transpired internally. For the most part, I grew increasingly alienated from my communism-abiding fellow citizens.

After the Czechoslovakia incident, I had no more problems with travel to the Soviet Union, Romania, Hungary, or East Germany. I quickly understood, however, that these trips were not really *abroad.* Uniform mediocrity and abiding communism reigned throughout Eastern Europe. Different nations shared the same gray life of police surveillance and party presence in every family. Suspicion overshadowed virtually all of our encounters, and it was hard to grasp the real political mood of my bitterly jocular "foreign" colleagues. In all instances there was an overwhelming feeling that anyone of us knew some truth about our life, a truth that needed no verbalization. But this obviously common knowledge was fragmented among individuals whose self-preservation instinct kept them on the lookout for one another. You knew that anyone could be a party or police informer and that you looked fishy to everyone. Sometimes you were not even quite sure whether they really *were* right in suspecting you, since speaking and spying were so tightly interwoven that you could hardly be accountable for the final address of the information you disseminated passively or actively. By the end of this chapter it will become abundantly clear how the network of informers could involve anyone, regardless of one's personal morals or volition. Instead of uniting us in our capacity as victims, however, this network turned us against each other and coerced us all into protecting our individual self-interests.

Nevertheless, I had the chance to meet gifted intellectuals (both in my country and in Budapest, East Berlin, and Bucharest) who were eager to break through the walls of suspicion. With these people I could delve deeply into our shared frustrations, and what I saw there, at the bottom, was personal bitterness, the desire to escape (physically and morally), and the ultimate naïveté of believing that an ivory tower could somehow be erected to shelter one's ego. We took the very spirituality as a refuge, as if communism was a triumph of materialism over the human spirit—which it indeed was. By keeping our spirit intact, we believed we could escape the evils targeted by the communist dogma (the social evils established by a materialism-stricken mass). But nowhere can one live as a clam enveloped in a spiritual shell.

To this basic delusion we added yet another, which was no less biased. This was the wrong conviction that in the capitalist world spiritual endeavors triumphed over materialism. With few exceptions, we knew little of the Western world except what we picked up by word of mouth. It is interesting to note, however, that my intellectual friends living in Central Europe were less deluded than I about the betterment of communism itself, although they were more naïve than I was about the humane face of the West. Probably due to my underlying Balkan mentality, I was irrationally reserved about an eventual westward exit. My Hungarian and German counterparts, on the contrary, had definitely turned their backs on communism, seeking an individual solution in immigration.

I submit, however, that among those I knew well, those with whom I had casual professional contacts, or the vocal dissidents here and there, no one stood firmly and uncompromisingly on an *anticommunist* platform. Reformers of the dictatorial communism were abundant, but dissidents fighting *against* communism were hard to find.

Why, one may ask, am I relating the saddening lack of anticommunist endeavors in a chapter dedicated to the Communist Party police? There are two reasons for that, each of which complements the other. First, the communist secret services were structured not to guarantee the state security against foreign subversion or aggression but to spy upon the local citizens. We were the real enemy, not some Western imperialist ideologues or generals. Therefore, it was virtually impossible to remain unwatched, let alone engage in some clandestine activity. Besides, it was clear to everyone that communism simply was not the type of regime that could be subverted by clandestine means. To act openly was equal to suicide and an anticommunist plot (if such a project could be conceived at all) was looked upon as an absurd enterprise. No one dared even think of it. This first rationale is widely known by those interested in East European communism.

The second reason I am suggesting a connection between the lack of an anticommunist sentiment and the party police is far less known, however. If a dictatorial regime does not allow a well-organized plot, the regime is usually eroded by the tacit resistance of its internal foes or by a corrupted style of rule. A break of the elites' unity occurs sooner or later even under the most cruelly imposed authoritarian rule. The communist regime was not imposed; hence, it had no internal foes. The communist regime was chosen, or if not chosen, it was accepted, tolerated, or regarded with indifference. The communist regime spilled over from the Soviet Union as a fake democracy, cynically called people's democracy, and only gradually did it develop into a dictatorship. Wherever an early anticommunist resistance was promptly driven, like in Hungary and Czechoslovakia, it was due to anti-Russian sentiment, rather than any conscious anticommunist strategy. The spontaneous uprisings there were crushed mercilessly, so that all heads were bowed to the feeding trough of the Communist Party for good. In the other countries, it took time for the fake to be uncovered, and the eye opening occurred in pain and ambiguity. The seductive prospect that we, the moral and worthy people, might one day implement a humane political and social theory slowed down the rising frustration and protest.

And here comes my point: Who was around to form *a front* against our national and local dictators? I could easily identify a network of informers, but where were the people willing to build a network of protesters? I could become an informer to survive, but I could not survive as a protester. Even if there were people who had the guts to initiate an anticommunist movement, they would not have found disciples or supporters. A political power does not emerge from an individual effort. It needs a platform, a front, and a political philosophy. None of these foundations were available in Soviet-dominated Eastern Europe. Worst of all, a consistent anticommunist political philosophy was nowhere to be found, on either side of the Iron Curtain.

Let me put it bluntly: a handful of intellectuals thought communism was a predicament that had to be endured. But an end to our suffering ought to come sooner or later. We fancied that somebody in the West knew of our pain and that victory over this type of communism was only a matter of political calculation. Of course, we did not even dare to assume that the vast majority of our fellow citizens liked living under our brand of communism. Ironically, I know of no historiography, sociology, or political theory that claims a political power could survive without the support of the people. Soviet-style communism survived well over seven decades, and it has still not been entirely overcome.

All of this leads me to believe that communism came at a time when it fit the political mood and mentality of nations fed up with backward imperial bureaucracies. Despite this timeliness, it decayed before schedule. Smothered in fierce economic and military competition with the Western free market, communism eroded from the inside out because of squalid party management.

By 1981, at the age of thirty-five, I was halfway to such an assessment of the system in which I lived. I already knew all too well that a lot of people in our camp complied with communism and that we had a ubiquitous people's secret police that invisibly watched every attempt to question such compliance. But there was no way I could have known what the other side of the Curtain looked like, since I refrained from applying for permission to visit such areas. On one hand, I did this because I was unsure I would get the desired permission. Refusal might have utterly destroyed my morale. On the other hand, I may have intuitively suspected that a visit to the West would shatter my hopes that a communist East could become a normal place in which to live. Like a child, I feared the unknown shine of the West. As it happened, I had been unable to foresee the real extent to which this shine would influence my mind and soul. I did not yet realize that the differences went beyond purely existential concerns.

Yet, as George Bernard Shaw put it, I could resist everything but temptation. The international gatherings of medical researchers constituted one such temptation. After many hesitations, my wife and I decided to attend an immunology conference in the Netherlands to be held at the beginning of June, 1981. Such a trip posed two basic problems: passports and hard currency for lodging and food. As for transportation, we were offered my parents' car, a red Soviet Lada, which would also serve as our sleeping accommodation while we were on the road.

We applied for passports in due time. Within four weeks I got a refusal, while my wife was graciously presented her passport. No explanation was ever given for the refusal. We were perplexed and could think of no solution. We did not want to abandon our project of driving to Gromingen through Austria and West Germany. A day or two passed in confusion, but then suddenly my mother-in-law gave me a hint: Why not call the general, she suggested, and ask him for an appointment? Word had it, she added, that he was a humane person. The general she referred to was the chief officer of the district secret police, and he had the authority to overrule the decisions of his subordinates. This was really a chance, I thought, and picked up the phone. By some rare twist of fate, the general was in. On top of that, his secretary made no attempt to turn my call away under some false pretext. My voice was trembling when I briefly explained my case, but he reacted very matter-of-factly and gave me an appointment. Hope and humiliation struggled in my heart up to the day I met with him.

This was my first and final visit to the notorious district police headquarters. My wife and I went to the meeting together. We were allowed to enter following a strict passport check, after which a captain led us to the general's office. No doubt, the boss played cheap popularity by demonstrating accessibility to the public once a week for two hours. He knew full well that the risk of delivering passports to both members of a couple like us was minimal. Only several years later, did I realize that this circus was little more than a subtler way of keeping people like me under control.

There was a formal, but not legal, rationale for the refusal. The police rule maintained that both spouses were prohibited from traveling to the West together: if one spouse traveled, the other would have to remain behind as a hostage. But there was something unusual in our case. I was the one who needed to make the trip to a Western country: I was registered to present a paper at a medical conference. Yet it was I who was refused the passport. They knew, moreover, that I was the only one licensed to drive the car, and that my wife would not travel alone. She could have taken a plane, but it was doubtful she would have paid so much money to go alone to a conference where she had no paper to present—or so they must have reasoned. The trap should have been obvious to me on the spot, but I did not discover it until much later. If we decided to comply with the refusal, the travel would never take place (they really did not give a damn about this), and it would have been one less thing for them to worry about had one of us failed to return. However, if we decided to push to get my passport, then I would become dependent on their "generosity" (their indulgence of granting me an exit visa was in violation of the rules, for which no specific reason would be given). None of these tacit trade-offs were very clear to me at the time.

Indeed, the general did bless my exit—and he made it seem like a service he had rendered to me personally, because I turned out to be so sympathetic and decent. After he greeted us from behind his large desk, he invited us to explain our case. We did this in an awkward way, sensing that this was part of the ritual. Then he asked whether it was true that we had four children. Yes, it was indeed true. "Oh," he exclaimed, "how rare and patriotic!" And so we digressed for five minutes on the subject of kids, care, expenses, and parental bliss. Worries, we assured him, were also part of the bargain. "Well," he concluded suddenly, "since you are such a brave couple to raise so many children, I'll grant you my authorization to travel *this time*. I do believe that you will hurry back to be with your kids." His last words sounded more like a question than a statement.

What else could we do but "hurry back"? Quite frankly, I did not feel at all relieved; instead, I had the sneaking suspicion that this would not be my final meeting with this organization's officials. There was some satisfaction, though: I was so eager to go to this conference and to the forbidden

West that I overlooked the pitfalls of the situation in which I was trapped. I was again naïve to believe that we had simply passed through a loophole in a system designed to be primitively flexible. Moreover, I could not help imagining that my obtaining the humiliating permission was somehow the result of the impeccable behavior, social harmlessness, and lack of professional misconduct I had demonstrated at the time. To be sure, my family was also a factor.

In my blindness I even forgot to think about my worsening file; perhaps our return would be rewarded with some positive points. This thought had occurred to me once or twice. The irony was that the plainclothes officer in charge of the medical school summoned us for the delivery of our red passports. Of course, I paid no heed to the spiteful smile he wore as he instructed us on how to behave in the Wild West if someone were to approach us with provocative intentions. I thought he just felt uncomfortable because his supreme boss had overruled *his* decision to keep us home.

As for the money, it was a strictly private arrangement. We really did not intend to go with a one-way ticket. In any event, we enjoyed our trip euphorically, despite our relative status as poor beggars among self-esteemed colleagues. We returned praying that our Soviet motorcar would not give out in the middle of a long road, as it had already done twice on the way there: we were expected back no later than the date stamped on our time-restricted visa. Upon our return, we enthusiastically told everyone about the trip. It gradually dawned on me that the few Bulgarians who had been granted the gift of a visit to a Western country were usually reluctant to relate the small pleasures they enjoyed abroad, particularly to those who had never had a chance to get out of the country.

During the trip, a few amazing things happened. At first, my eyeballs started hurting because of the colorful urban and rural scenery. I had never seen so many colors before; even the dashed line in the middle of the highway in Austria was yellow.

When we reached the outskirts of Munich, we needed some road instructions, so we stopped at a rest area to ask. We approached a man with a transplanted jaw who strikingly resembled the great car racer Niki Lauda, and asked him how to get to Stuttgart. He pulled a map from his car and, after showing us the route, gave it to us.

Then, in Heidelberg, parking was a problem for us because we did not want to pay for it. We arrived on Friday afternoon and I found a spot among other cars on the sidewalk of the old town square. I pulled the car over, disregarding a sign that banned parking during the weekends. The next morning, as I was entering the square from the opposite side, I froze when I spotted a policeman walking around our shabby Lada, which was the only car left in the square. Overcoming my immediate impulse to turn and go away, I slowly went closer. "Is this car yours, sir?" the guy asked politely. "Yes, mine," I said. "Look here," he answered and pulled the driver's door open. "You forgot to lock your car, *mein lieber Herr.* You could have been robbed like this, you know! There is a camera here, and a purse. I asked over the walkie-talkie for someone to come and watch your car." I thanked the policeman, still not believing that he was not writing me a parking ticket. The notion of private property was foreign to me, as was the idea that it was a policeman's duty to protect it.

Our car broke down shortly after Bonn on our way to Cologne. I hitch-hiked so as to be on time for an appointment with a colleague I did not want to miss, while my wife stayed with the car and waited for Road Assistance. Not only was hitchhiking easy, but it also turned to be fun. A middle-aged teacher who took me to Cologne stopped along the road and offered me a drink. The man who took me back to Bonn invited me to his home and offered me a bottle of wine from his own vineyard to take with me. And when I finally returned to the place where I had left my wife with the car, the work was done and we were able to hit the road again.

All that happened to us was in stark contrast with the propaganda and police warnings we had been given. We returned to our quotidian lives with a business-as-usual mood. A wound had opened on the inner lining of my soul, however—a wound I no longer had any desire to heal. My eyes had finally and definitely been opened to my own cosmopolitan nature. All my standards (existential, professional, political, and philosophical) had to be changed. It was clear to me that I could not alter the system. There simply was no "we" to work together with on such a glorious project. I could, however, alter myself. My trip to the West was more of a catalyst than the cause of my decision to change.

I began to realize that I had been misdirecting my energy. I was in the wrong place. I was doing the wrong thing. I deluded myself in thinking I was useful. Was this by design or was it entirely my fault? I have records indicating that during these rather dramatic years I blamed my failure, as well as the failure of the communist system, on human imperfection. Psychologically, I was not mature enough to reject communism in principle. On the other hand, enough years had passed to successfully dismiss any hope that the party leadership could be replaced with "better" communists or that any change whatsoever in the status quo might occur.

Unfortunately, changing myself meant shaking up my links to the people who depended on my presence. I had spent thirty-six years in the same place, gaining imperceptibly from what little I had hatched and coveted, yet bound to so many people and committed to countless projects. Not yet to my own, though!

The principal object in my destructive desire for change involved my profession, which had brought me far more frustration than comfort. My tenure was secure, and it was considered madness to resign. This was not because I could not earn more elsewhere, but because of the high social status and enviable quietness of the job. Nonetheless, resignation was the logical choice if I was truly determined to change.

Thus, it came to pass that in February, 1983, I moved to Sofia, found a temporary post as a general practitioner (GP) in a suburban clinic, and embarked on a new career as a freelance journalist. This move was not without consequences for my second marriage. Before the move, my wife and I had lived with my parents and grandparents in my grandma's house (in keeping with the Balkan custom of maintaining the entire extended family in one house). In my desire for change, however, I severed connections with my native home and my wife and left my four children behind.

For many, this divorce story, which took almost two years from start to finish, obscured the essential reasons for making the change. According to public opinion, I had defied the most sacred and traditional values by forsaking my children's welfare and giving up a secure and elite university career. The gossip on the matter blew up with sadistic overtones. The condemnation was severe.

Today, I view this simultaneous change of profession, family, and place as an attempt to fight cowardice: I could not rebel against the system, so I ceased being what the system wanted me to be. The majority, however, saw me as a sheer philanderer. Under Balkan communism you could be as adulterous as you were able to afford, on the condition that you did so in secrecy and kept your marriage intact. Divorce was regarded as sexual slackness. The relative significance of my divorce was also inflated out of proportion because no one viewed the profession as an issue. We were granted professional status inasmuch as there should have been a justification for the rationed money we all received owing to the party's clemency. As far as I am concerned, however, the communist system modified our sexuality a great deal. In one sense, one could sexually overreact to the existential restrictions. In another, though, one's sexual performance could be inhibited in keeping with the overall despondency of communist life. In their broader aspect, as an expression of human individuality, sex and love were subdued to a collective norm adequate to the minimal degree of freedom allotted. My own marital relations clashed with this norm, but their broken character was also due to it. I did my best to be an integral personality, that is, to follow a model set up by myself. I ended up falling to pieces.

My change of place was as important as the other changes. The communist rule ordered that every Bulgarian citizen be assigned "town-citizenship"; that is, you could live, work, and own property only in the community to which you "belonged," or (more appropriately) to which you were confined. This was usually your native place. Town-citizenship restrictions worked on a bottom-up principle: you were allowed to move from the capital to a smaller city, or from a bigger town to a smaller one, or from a town to whatever village you chose, but not vice versa. The rationale for this rule was to maintain easy access to your police file. The main effect of this rule's implementation was that communist citizens were stripped of the right to move about and choose freely where they lived. Town-citizenship rules did not, however, apply to party functionaries, the police, or the military. As usual, there were always loopholes available.

I was a citizen of Varna, hence, the move to Sofia did not mean simply taking the night train and arriving fresh at my new place of work the next morning. It meant that I needed special authorization before even thinking of being hired. Fortunately, it just so happened that my cousin Angel worked as department head of the Bulgarian Trade Union's Department of Employment and Manpower. Before handing in my resignation to the rector of the Higher Medical School in Varna, I first met with Angel and asked him to arrange for me to get a job permit for Sofia. I used "personal connections" (one of the most dishonest acts according to local moral standards) to obtain a permit to which I would not otherwise have been entitled. This was also an occasion to restore my old friendship with Angel. Despite our long period of alienation, he used his influence to get me a six-month, renewable permit for a GP job in Sofia (a position that was not at all in demand). Blood relationships had always been Angel's Achilles' heel. But the town-citizenship matter was far from settled after I obtained this permit.

I intended to establish myself in Sofia for good. After a few months, the woman with whom I had decided to live joined me there. By chance (and despite the fact that she, too, was from Varna), she had a passport issued by a Sofia regional police department, and this became our only hope. Even Angel could not promise me full Sofia citizenship. First I needed to finalize my divorce; then I needed to remarry. Only then could I apply for permanent Sofia citizenship based on my new spouse's status. And only after this application was approved, was I entitled to buy an apartment.

It took me two years to obtain a divorce. During that period Angel renewed my job permit four times. My companion and I lived illegally in the outskirts of Sofia. We rented part of a wonderful private cottage in a quiet neighborhood where foreign ambassadors had resided during the Second World War, and where high-ranking party officials now lived with their lovers in the same posh mansions behind closed iron gates. Private properties, communist bosses hanging around, cherry trees in fenced green yards, and our absurd involvement in a chain of bureaucratic happenings— all this was the decor of our début in the capital.

My companion's citizenship was the result of her marriage to a Sofia citizen. The irony was that her first husband was the adopted son of a Sofia-born "Fighter Against Fascism and Capitalism" who, at the age of sixty-five, married his mother. Thus, following the mother's marriage, all her dependents were also entitled to Sofia citizenship. My companion's first husband had never thought to claim this legal right until his young spouse prompted him to do so. It is still not certain whether she was clairvoyant or had simply acted on common sense. Anyway, they both acquired citizenship status in the capital. They divorced three years later, but she retained her Sofia passport. When we were conceiving our project to live in the capital, she tested its validity by successfully renewing it. After that, we regarded my getting a divorce as the only remaining obstacle to my own Sofia citizenship. Our future together depended on a piece of paper.

When I finally obtained the divorce, we immediately married and applied for my Sofia citizenship. To our amazement and luck, this official procedure was not handled by the police department, but by the municipal administration. I walked along several cement corridors before lining up in a somber waiting hall. When my turn came, I approached the familiar narrow window and waited while a gray-haired woman took the pile of documents and inspected them slowly and carefully. After several long minutes, she gazed at me and said, "I'm afraid, comrade, your wife is no longer entitled to her Sofia citizenship. Her divorce occurred before the fifth year of her marriage." In that instant, my entire sense of humor vanished: adieux, brave hopes for a change. My minirebellion was about to be put down by a paper blow.

The woman behind the glass paused for a moment and sighed. "However," she added, "there *is* something that may help you. I see here that she has a four-year-old son. Does he live with her?"

"Yes!" I exclaimed, still agonizing over the outcome of this conversation.

"The decree makes an exception," she continued, "for divorced mothers who keep custody of a child born in wedlock. They are still entitled to their Sofia citizenship for the child's benefit. What you must do now is bring me a document certifying that the divorce was not blamed on her."

I saw myself entangled in a labyrinth of cunning departmental sentences, in which only one hair-splitting exit could be found. "With someone's help," I repeated inwardly with a hammering rhythm. "With someone's help." I rushed to call my third wife. Thank God! She told me that she had a copy of the court's decision showing that her divorce was based on mutual consent. "Life is beautiful," my heart chanted under the golden autumn elms. What superb joy our mother party provided us humble communist citizens! This joy would never have been possible had our whole existence been boringly happy. I loved the oldish woman behind the glass, and for a while I almost forgave the party police since they had so generously and unwittingly provided me with an exit from the labyrinth.

Just to be sure, we bought a special and expensive present for the middle-aged clerk on the day we returned to pick up my citizenship certificate. We believed that she had given us Sofia.

Sadly, this small victory over the administration did not end my relations with the police state. My file followed me wherever I went, including Sofia.

I considered my freelance activities as only an overture to a prospective career as a staff journalist. As part of my job search, I applied for a reporter position with the Bulgarian Telegraph Agency (BTA), the state-run news agency, which controlled the input and output of political information throughout the country. A former guerrilla, a good-humored old man who radiated conversance with the corridors of power (which in Sofia were the corridors of the BCP Central Committee), ran the Cadre Department. He sent me on two thematic tours with foreign journalists as a kind of probation and repeatedly assured me that as soon as an opening occurred, I would be first in line for interviews. I grew somewhat suspicious of his assurances, however, after nearly a year had passed and my application remained in his office. I asked my cousin Angel to make an inquiry regarding its status through his "special channels."

Not long afterward, Angel came to our house with the bad news. "Your file is full of compromising data about what you've done and talked about," he said without hiding his disappointment. He then quoted some pronouncements that I had indeed made in a conversation with the BTA photographer who accompanied me on my first journalistic trip. Their meaning was put into another context, but there was no doubt that this individual had recorded or written down our friendly chat about the development of the Bulgarian chemical industry and had reported it to the police. Worse yet, I was flabbergasted to hear that my file had been transferred from Varna with a résumé of my personal qualities, which characterized me as a completely untrustworthy individual. There were a lot of fabricated facts put in there with the evident purpose of denigrating me.

The story was a typically Balkan one, mingling personal with institutional relations. My former wife had a boyfriend, and this boyfriend was a close friend of the police agent in charge of the medical school in Varna. Vengeance took the form of a file misconstruction through such a simple private mechanism. Ironically, if I were to pursue a political career in Bulgaria today, such a file would support my claim that I was, indeed, considered untrustworthy by the watchdogs of the communist regime. At that time, though, I was neither proud of myself, nor happy with the findings. Simply put, my bad file impeded my ambitions to find a relatively good job. In reality, those who watched me closely persisted with their blackmail.

During the next year I found a job in the country's only medical newspaper, whose deputy editor in chief was a former cop, and whose editor in chief was a communist zealot. Since they both approved my hiring, I could be sure that the police had given their okay.

The mood at the beginning of 1987 was disturbing when my third wife and I decided to go to Tunisia and France on a summer vacation. Once again, after a six-year intermission, I had to fill out long questionnaires, get the signatures of difficult to reach people, put all the family administrative records and papers in impeccable order, and line up for half a day in the waiting hall at Sofia's central police office. All this labor was in vain, however. Six weeks later, on the night of my return from a twenty-day military drill for reserve officers, I found my wife in tears. I will never forget her words: "Oh my dear, I am so scared. We are buried."

It was the end of April, perhaps the best time of the year in the Bulgarian capital. We had decided to have our second child, my sixth. Both of us had good jobs, she with the University of Sofia and I with a reputable newspaper. We did not care for the regime anymore; rather, we accepted

My third wedding. On our right are my wife's parents, Bistra and Ivan, and our female witness, Rina (a good friend of ours). On our left are my cousin, Angel (our male witness), and one of his students. Sofia, August 7, 1984. (Author's collection.)

the idea that our lives would get no better under communism. Deception, desperation, helplessness, call it what you will: the result was a peace of mind, if only we could enjoy our simple style of life.

They could not allow us even the resignation. Again, I was refused an exit visa, while my wife was issued one. The decision of complying with the verdict or struggling to overrule it was left to us. As always, this was a tough moral decision. Complying meant accepting the life sentence passed on me for no crime, and praising myself for my clean conscience (a masochism that repulsed me for its fruitlessness). Struggling for my right to travel, on the other hand, resulted in the equally repulsive intercourse with police agents. Worse yet, it required playing a game with no rules and in which victory was always achieved through some form of servitude. No middle way seemed available. Struggling for myself and my freedom actually resulted in compliance with the system.

Today, I can theorize broadly on this moral issue, but then, I instinctively made the decision to do my best to get the visa. Life is stronger than moral considerations, and human rights become an imperative in certain extreme conditions. Injustice is unbearable, as far as I am concerned.

With my wife Roumyana in front of a café in Sidi Bussaid, near Tunis, during our summer trip to Tunisia and France in June, 1987. (Author's collection.)

On the next working day, I telephoned my cousin and asked him for an appointment, knowing that he refrained from discussing serious topics on the phone. When I deliberated on the issue during the walk we took at his suggestion (walking was the best way to avoid eavesdropping) he seemed for the first time hesitant in his assurances that he could "arrange matters." Nonetheless, he promised to try, even though he failed to specify his exact intentions. A week later he dropped by and told me that I needed to apply for an appointment with the head of the Department of Passports and Visas during his office hours. "He will be told to handle your case favorably," my cousin added to appease my anxiety. "Just mention that you know J."

So I did. I also declared my loyalty to Bulgaria and promised that I would return without fail. I extensively reviewed my professional plans, my commitment to the key national issues, and my family status. The youngish-looking colonel could barely stop me from talking. "But you have had too many wives," he said, implying that this must have been the reason for their decision to bar me from visiting Western countries. "But I have also too many children," I countered, "and they remain here, and I am taking care of them, so I cannot think of abandoning everything just for the sake of my egoism."

Did he really care about my family and me? This question would forever remain unanswered. Did he believe what I said? Nobody knows. He pretended to. There was a secretary in the room, who nodded approvingly at what I said and seemed quite compassionate about my case. But there was also an undercurrent that made me suspect that our conversation was being recorded, that they were both all too accustomed with this kind of theater. The colonel wrote something down in the pile of papers on his desk and told me that he had decided in my favor and wished me a good trip.

That was in mid-May, 1987, three years into the glasnost and perestroika era. By the end of the month, my wife told me that she was pregnant. A month later, at the end of June, we took the plane to Tunis via Rome. But we spent the whole of June dragging ourselves through the lines at several foreign consulates, and we still would not have obtained all the required visas had not luck helped us at a critical moment. Regulations strictly forbade our visiting the foreign missions; a special office in the Foreign Ministry processed visa applications. However, I decided to go personally to survey what was going on. In spite of my intervention, the last Friday before our Sunday departure (our tickets had already been bought and confirmed) we got our passports from the respectable special office with-

out Italian transit visas on them. We ran to the Italian embassy and discovered that the visa desk worked from 4 to 5 P.M. It was 3 P.M., and we
needed three photos each. Photo shops in Bulgaria never made instant
pictures. My wife stood by to keep our place in the line and I took to my
heels to fetch a distant friend with a Polaroid camera to take pictures of us
ex tempore. When I reached the suburban factory where my friend used to
work, I called him up from the checkpoint and pushed him into the cab.
Of course, the camera! We directed the taxi to a private address in the
vicinity of the embassy—which was a stroke of luck!—and he retrieved
his camera. At 4:15 we leaped out of the taxi to the amazement of my
depressed wife. My friend took the pictures as we stood in line. Mine
showed drops of sweat on my forehead. And then came another twist of
fate: we had just finished cutting our photos to the dimensions required
when the consul came out and took the applications of all who were
standing in the line and assured us that by 5:30 we would be getting our
visas. What happiness!

Our trip was an enjoyable one, even though we were penniless as usual,
and, like our Eastern European currency, we felt inconvertible. Tunis seemed
unapproachable. Marseille and La Côte d'Azur looked hostile. Paris was
forbidding, and Lausanne high-minded. Even the two hospitable Swiss
women I had hitchhiked with were unable to dissipate my bitter conclusion that we somehow no longer belonged in the free world, and this was
an irreversible fact of life. My eyes, though, again ached from the scenery's
wealth of color.

Half asleep in a dirty wagon, crossing the interminable Yugoslavia from
Trieste to Sofia, I said to myself that our world was here, in the backyard
full of trash, among murky individuals who shovel in it, using their inge-
nuity for survival. I was simply complying with fate. There was nothing
left to sustain my self-respect but the delusion that I had not yielded to the
communist gang. The upcoming events demonstrated that I was, in fact,
bound to comply with the communist reality, which I subconsciously refused to identify with fate.

Since I had not had the guts to leave communism, I had to live with it.
All the more so, I had not given up the ambition to avoid social exclusion,
thus I was logically forced into deeds amounting to compliance. Today, I
admit the moral fragility of my position. I am more than convinced that
no midway could exist between living with and leaving communism.

Then, one fresh September morning in 1987, I received a call from a
soft-spoken person who invited me to meet in a children's pastry shop in

downtown Sofia. Believe it or not, I did not know who the male caller on the phone was and apparently I did not care. What is crystal clear in my memory is that the person expected no other answer from me than "okay." I also remember his words: "This time it is all for your own good." This vague pronouncement was made without any context or frame of reference.

On the appointed date, I was in the pastry shop just across from the Interior Ministry building when a tall, handsome man came up to me, shook my hand, offered me tea with pastry, and asked me nonchalantly about my trip to Paris. He behaved as if we had been friends all our lives. Obviously satisfied with the information he had compiled on me, he asked nothing that would indicate he had any interest in knowing me better as a person. The talk was nonsense from my point of view, but I still had no clues as to why I was forcibly involved in it. Ironically, it seemed that it was meant as an expression of gratitude for my safe return. From Paris the conversation jumped to my journalistic intentions, my colleagues, what kind of links I had in the Ministry of Health and in the academy, the lot. It was the sort of talk good friends engage in while frittering their time away.

At one point, he asked me if I had any interest in reporting on Red Cross activities. I had none, but I had forced myself to search for links between my AIDS reporting and the new role the Bulgarian Red Cross might play in AIDS monitoring. He then told me that he could be of help if I decided to publish something on the topic, and that he would soon provide me copies of the Red Cross's international publications. "By the way," he went on in a very businesslike manner, "write down my telephone number. You may call me at any time during business hours. Just ask for Emil." I took the lack of a business card as a requirement of his profession. His office was across the street, no doubt, in the square stone building where no entry was granted to the common citizenry. In one of our next meetings, he also gave me his home telephone number, and to my astonishment it appeared in the telephone book next to the name of Emil K. This fact certainly challenged my suspicion that Emil was just a nickname.

After I wrote down the telephone number in my notebook, he engaged in a long monologue. It boiled down to his interest in the overall moods within the medical and journalistic communities (in both of which I had permanent professional access) and how much he had hoped to find some- one who could help him know more about the subject. I replied that I indeed knew a lot of people and had good observations, and that making a résumé of what I knew was no trouble at all for me, provided I did not have to mention any names. I had two motives for this reply. First, I sincerely believed that his request was the result of my travel permit, a privilege I had been granted by Emil's fellow policeman, and it would consist of only a single report. Secondly, the task fit so well with my straightforward approach to social knowledge that I saw in it an opportunity to convey my personal conclusions about what was happening in the country to an allegedly responsible and powerful institution. He was visibly content with my readiness to collaborate, and immediately set up our next meeting, at which I was expected to hand in my report.

The next time we met I had three standard, typewritten pages with me. We met in a small coffee bar on a quiet corner not far from the Interior Ministry. I asked him what explanation I might provide if, say, my deputy editor in chief saw us together. "Oh, that is no bother at all!" he exclaimed. "He knows that I deal with the central medical institutions, so if he asks, tell him that you know me from school and that I met you to discuss an article of some sort." It was, of course, absurd that the deputy would ask, but I pretended to agree. He again began by taking issue with some recent news in the press and leading me in a circular manner to my concrete relations with people. I wavered on how to deliver my report, since we were being squeezed by a lot of regulars who were sitting shoulder to shoulder at the bar and at the few small tables around us. His style of talking was utterly foggy, so I decided to avoid giving answers that were too precise. I simply tried to share his opinions. It would have been far more difficult for me to sustain the same tone of abstract responses if he had asked me specific questions, but that was not one of his tactics. He made a lot of promises concerning my career, and at one point I instinctively decided to slip my three pages over the plastic cover of our table. We talked for another two or three minutes, after which he collected my report and rose to leave. "I'll call you soon," he said and disappeared.

Ten days later we met in the basement of a strange club known only to him. It sounded like a club catering to retired army and police officers who enjoyed hunting. This time he began by saying that he liked my report very much but that I needed to rewrite it because regulations demanded that all reports be handwritten. In addition, he insisted that a report is not convincing enough without the names of those who had provided the information or opinions. He gently asked me to use formulas like, "When I saw S., he was talking to M. about such and such," or "These days L. conferred with me about," or "I was told by N. that," and so forth. "That will make your reports more realistic," he concluded with a large smile. He was actually a rather pleasant thirty-five-year-old guy, and for the first time I felt sympathy for a policeman instead of disgust. "Well," I said, "if that is the rule, I will comply with it." There was one other detail: I had to sign my reports with a pseudonym of my choice. I chose Ivan Peev, the most insignificant combination of Bulgarian names.

After this "clandestine" meeting I had no more illusions: he was engaging me in a regular collaboration. I explained the situation to my wife and asked for her opinion. "Go ahead," she said without agonizing too long. "As far as I know you, you will do harm to nobody. On the other hand, if you refuse, you will be buried for good." That was simple, pragmatic reasoning, something of which I was not capable myself. But it sounded very, very reasonable. She did not tell me what would happen if I consented, however, so I agonized a few days over the issue. When I could find no assuaging arguments, I decided to take the bait, come what may.

The twenty-year-long game of cat and mouse was finally over. They had judged me from the very beginning to be an ungovernable character, and had adopted a technique of mild but persistent harassment. They knew that I would never go so far as to become openly rebellious. Thus, they aimed at my basic vulnerability: my craving to expand my personal horizons and to travel. By gradually increasing my indebtedness, they counted on challenging my genuine loyalty. In 1987, the final blow had been struck with me: they had granted me an irregular permission to make my trip, so now it was my turn to pay them back with my loyalty.

So be it. I edited my first report in accordance with the instructions, rewrote it by hand, and called Emil for a fourth appointment. Until now, no one except my wife knew about my deal with Emil. It lasted for two years, until November, 1989, when the party was forced to be involved in the play of democracy, and the whole party/police construction was shaken to its very foundations.

This deal brought me almost no gain in the material sense, but it taught me some lessons. Before it happened to me, I did not want to accept the blunt truth that life requires practicality and flexibility: characteristics that need not necessarily contradict one's moral principles. The vast majority of people live happily this way, so now I was bound to become one of them. Moreover, I am indifferent to power. More precisely, neither my confidence nor my happiness depend on my having power over others. Also, I usually do not care when someone tries to exert power over me. I regard my indifference as a basic moral principle, since in any struggle for power you inevitably cross others' interests and thus get enmeshed in moral interactions.

From this point of view, my so-called reporting was simply a way I had chosen to be left alone. The truth is, I reported nonsense, as far as I am concerned. I had worked out a scheme. Usually, Emil asked me to write something on special occasions such as the public pronouncements of Todor Zhivkov or the recent move of the Central Committee to upgrade the country's economic indicators. I had never taken the initiative to report something on my own. Every time I was asked to write something, I made up some happenings, added the names of some real people, and expanded on my own critique against the party establishment. I assumed that those named by me could not be harmed either because they had no bold presence in any political activity or because I knew they were too well protected by their family status or by their own collaboration with the party. On some occasions, I put this critique into the mouths of renowned communists whose nastiness was repugnant (my editor in chief Golemanov, for instance). To be sure, no report was ever based on a true story or had even a remote association with the real activities of the people mentioned. I also never knew of any, even the slightest, changes in those people's lives—let alone any job setbacks—that I could associate with my reporting. After the first three or four such reports, none exceeding two handwritten pages each, I started wondering why they still needed them. My rational assessment of the information I provided was that it could serve no purpose.

The awful thing in the whole story is that all these activities were dependent on purely subjective assessments. What gave me the right to judge who was repugnant and who was harmless? How could I prove that my information was evasive and ridiculous? Why was I certain that my critique against the regime was justified? Why did I think that my personal opinions on communism matched the attitudes of the community toward it?

The only meaningful justification might involve common sense and the perception of human nature. All this would have indeed looked absurd, had it not been associated with one of human nature's strongest mechanisms for survival: compliance. Compliance does not mean indifference to the power exerted on you. Quite the contrary, compliance is a way of assuaging the pains caused by that power and at the same time acknowledges that you are unable to oppose or escape it. In a nutshell, you give in to the power in order to share it. That way nobody can claim they are powerless—a condition unacceptable to the communist doctrine that proclaimed that communist power should be embraced (and shared) by all of the people. You were expected to join the powerful by complying with their vision of society, especially when (as was the case with Eastern European communism) their vision of society has not been negotiated with you or the community to which you belong. You must adapt by imagining that the imposed vision is exactly like yours. Those who could not do this ended up with a bent will, in a condition of apathy. And those in power always welcomed apathy.

The secret police network was the tangible transmission of a power available to everyone. It enabled communist power to maintain a large social base. Even more, it was proof that communism was built on a large social base.

A strong argument in support of these assertions appeared during the early years after the Eastern European communist parties loosened their grip on power in 1989. At that time, the prevailing collective emotion had been the obsessive preoccupation with squaring accounts with the secret police legacy. The implication was that *it* was the evil, the essence of the communist reality, and that it could serve as the watershed between a shameful past and a seemly future.

Extremes ranged from fervent disclosure to the silent closure of party police archives. No one has asked for redemption. Public voices have been eager to support either monstrous allegations or the criminal dismissal of archived files. There were no legal grounds (and hardly could be in any jurisdiction) in the penal codes of any of those countries to justify the prosecution of former policemen and active informers.

I submit that this represents another piece of strong evidence for the tacit contract signed between the party/police state and its citizens. Granted, violence and the threat of physical annihilation were certainly part of the mechanism that sustained compliance. But these tactics were applied only in the beginning on a limited scale and were later used only when veiled threats became necessary. Thus, although fear of political persecution was a potent factor of oppression, the more time passed the less real this fear became. The infamous motive, "We have children, so how can we not comply?" was a ubiquitous excuse that reflected moral ambivalence. People simply preferred not to bother provided they could *arrange* their existence and the existence of their children. They were all experts at *arranging*. Party and police officials were, in fact, the sons and daughters of common Bulgarians. So were military officers, the best paid in the country, and one of the most trustworthy reservoirs of communism's defenders. In virtually every family there was at least one member who was related to the huge apparatus that transmitted power from the top to the bottom. The effort to install adolescent family members within this apparatus was regarded as one of the most fruitful strategies for achieving well-being. The system was in accord with itself. The transmission of power could not be more effective.

Emil was nothing more than a bumper in this transmission, and he was professionally trained to fulfill his function as a bumper. He had no apprehensions or remorse. He was taught to take for granted his collaborators' readiness to serve. But he was not stupid. He just was not smart enough to recuperate what had been washed out of his brain. And, thanks to his secure position, he was hardly willing to do so. He had a nose for anticipating exactly what his superiors expected: a soothing flow of information and a routine that would not disturb the status quo. Since everyone had a well-heated niche in this status quo, the party servants felt strong enough to crush dissenters noiselessly and gracefully whenever a dissenting element appeared here or there.

Emil's reasoning was simple. What might this doctor-turned-journalist expect as a carrot for serving me? Free travel? Professional perks? Certainly nothing could be easier for a secret police officer of his rank. And, as far as I am concerned, I also knew that he could lift all obstacles to my traveling abroad.

Indeed, when I decided to go to the Fourth International Conference on AIDS in Stockholm in June, 1988, I did not hesitate to share my intentions with him. "The passport is not a problem," he said, smiling broadly. "We only need to find the necessary funding." The characteristic *we* in his language meant himself, since he never used the pronoun "I." This also implied the recognition that whatever "I" did was part of *"our"* common game.

On this occasion, I was introduced to the president of the Bulgarian Red Cross, a devoted communist who was over seventy-five years old. An important item on his long curriculum vitae was that he had ruled over the Interior Ministry during part of the tumultuous 1950s, when communist rule was still entrenching itself throughout the country. He blessed Emil's suggestion that the necessary sum of money be allocated for my ticket to Stockholm. The real work was actually done by the head of the Red Cross Foreign Relations Department, with whom Emil was on collegial, even friendly, terms. All these men knew perfectly well their obligations. I was embarrassed that all the clerks or Red Cross activists with whom I had had normal professional contacts could now see me there with Emil. Emil did not bother about that. After all, no leakage about this particular interaction of mine ever occurred, at least to the best of my knowledge.

The only plausible explanation for this is that the Bulgarian Red Cross served as one proxy of the secret police. More importantly, however, people had simply stopped paying attention. Nobody knew who was who or who worked for whom, since everybody worked for somebody. For that matter, the preferable and reasonable attitude was to keep one's mouth shut. There was no community (overt or covert), no current, no group, and no individual that would appreciate the disclosure of someone's links with any given person or agency. There was no moral standard from which to condemn such a person, no instance in which that person could be reported as bad or good.

This is not to say that people had no judgment about right and wrong, about good and evil, or about how the social hierarchy was built. Nor is this an attempt to deny the fact that complex undercurrents of discontent, envy, greed, ridicule, apprehension, disgust, desperation, and expectation did not impress themselves upon people's minds and conversations. Ultimately, however, the mentality of compliance reigned supreme over the efficacy of human deeds.

This was certainly my frame of mind as I undertook my first trip abroad as a journalist. There I was, equipped with an airplane ticket, prepaid hotel accommodation, and a ridiculously small amount of pocket change. From a professional point of view, it was a success; from a personal point of view, it accelerated the revelations unleashed in my soul since my 1981 trip. My admiration of the existential fruits of democratic rule was enhanced, and my apathy toward my own country's regime became full-fledged. I felt committed to no one but my children, my wife, and myself.

After my return, my relations with Emil continued at an even pace: roughly one report every four or five weeks, always followed by a short chat in a bar before I delivered the report. All the empty words and false promises on his part were echoed by the equally empty writings I submitted. My friends circled around me as before; his friends, if he had any, remained his friends.

The state telephone agency called me to change my home number to one ending with 888. Someone had told me that such "easy" numbers were usually assigned to those closely connected to the police.

My grandma passed away in September, 1987. I am sure she would forgive my sin, had she known about it; her devotion to the communist idea was beyond everyday morals. And yet, I am glad she never knew about my infamy, for toward the end of her life my apathy toward communism evolved into unabashed scorn.

When my youngest daughter was born in February, 1988, we needed some formula. Without requesting any payment, Emil supplied a box of a West German Humana brand that could not be found anywhere on the Bulgarian market.

The fifth international AIDS conference was to be held in Montreal in June, 1989, and my trip to Canada was scheduled for June 1. This time it was paid by the Presidium of the Medical Academy. I had such a high profile as an AIDS writer that the academy considered me almost a part of their AIDS-prevention team. Emil took care of the Canadian visa, which was issued in Belgrade and brought by a Foreign Ministry courier (there is no Canadian embassy or consulate in Sofia). Somewhere about the end of May, he delivered my passport in person while we were both attending an international Red Cross meeting in Varna.

During the week preceding this meeting, large groups of ethnic Turks had unleashed antigovernment demonstrations in a few rural areas of the country. When I entered his hotel room, he handed me the passport and fifty U.S. dollars without saying a word. I was at the door when he sighed deeply and wished me a good trip. I knew that the so-called "Turkish events" were unfolding in the vicinity, so I gave him a sympathetic glance in return.

On the night preceding my flight to Montreal via Frankfurt, a hysterical nationalist rally led by the National Committee of the Fatherland Front was held in Sofia, with the Politburo's tacit approval. On the morning of June 1, 1989, I was almost alone at the airport checkpoint. I flew out with a sinking heart. From my hotel room in Frankfurt I called a famous Bulgarian journalist working for Radio Free Europe. A friend of mine had asked me to contact this person and to require publicity on behalf of Dr. Trencheff, who was being held in custody by the Bulgarian police because of his statements against the BCP's anti-Turkish policy. A week later, in Montreal, the media were full of reports about the Tiananmen Square massacre. There was no word about the massacred ethnic Turk human rights marchers in remote Bulgaria.

After my return from Canada I wrote no report for Emil. He summoned me two or three more times, and we talked about the ongoing events without remorse or bitterness: everyone kept his perimeter of neutrality. The subdued tone of our last chat was the only possible expression of mutual sympathy we could afford under the circumstances.

I do not remember when I saw Emil for the last time. It seems strange to me that afterward I used to run into hundreds of remotely known people in the streets of Sofia, but I never met him again. He stopped calling me after November, 1989, and I abandoned his telephone number forever.

PART II

Disillusionment

CHAPTER 6

Euphoria

*Responsibility assumes that we know the alternatives,
that we know how to choose from among them, and
that we use this knowledge to push them aside
through cowardice, opportunism, or ideological fervor.
But I can report what I thought and did, what I
think about these thoughts and actions today, and
why I changed.*

—*Paul K. Feyerabend,* Killing Time

The winter of 1985 was bitterly cold in Bulgaria. On top of that, electricity was rationed. Even in Sofia we spent whole evenings in total darkness. One February day my wife and I hit the icy roads and headed for Varna in our fragile Škoda motorcar. We took the main southbound highway connecting the capital with the Black Sea. Traffic was scarce that day and we enjoyed speed at our discretion. Three times we noticed barriers across the road. The barriers, which looked like those that are usually used at border crossing points, were lifted and deserted.

Dusk fell early and we still had to traverse a mountainous rural district populated by Turks. We knew vaguely that something was going on with the Turkish population in Bulgaria. Rumor had it that the Turks were using every opportunity to retaliate against innocent Bulgarians for the forceful acts of renaming. The only illumination on the narrow, meandering road came from our car's headlights. The villages we drove through were pitch-dark and seemed dead.

Suddenly, the menacing darkness was filled with phlegmatic cow backs swinging in front of my speeding car. I hit the horn and the breaks wildly, but it was too late. The car did a 360-degree turn on the slippery pavement and hit one of the animals from behind. Fortunately, we slid to a stop at the edge of the road, probably saved from going over the edge by the injured cow. I could barely discern a male figure, approaching the car from the passenger side. The man was hiding himself from the glow of our headlights, and it occurred to me that he intended to assault us. I was seized with a nervous stomach cramp but still managed to get the car in gear and force my way through the cattle on the narrow gravel shoulder, risking hitting another innocent animal.

We soon arrived at a village where the pharmacists were a couple of old friends of ours and stopped there to sleep over at their place. After I related (by candlelight) our roadside incident, they provided us with a more detailed account of how the renaming (later notoriously known by the nickname "Revival Process") had been performed in this vicinity.

Men were called up in the army and placed in a well-guarded military camp. Each Turk was surrounded by Bulgarians and was allowed no contact with anyone from his family or with other Turks for reasons of "military security." He then was called by his commanding officer and informed that the Minister of Defense had directed that all Turks in the army had to assume Bulgarian names. He was warned that if he refused he would be court-martialed. The guy was reminded that his family was now alone and might be in need of his help, since they too would be going through this process. The man was then given a list of Bulgarian surnames to choose from and placed under arrest. If he decided not to accept one of the names, he was threatened, abused, or outright beaten. If he persisted, he was escorted to a prison labor camp and kept there until he signed a declaration stating that he had "voluntarily" adopted a new name. Meanwhile, a local official visited his wife and children. The official kindly informed them that their husband and father had just changed his name, and urged them to follow suit. Many family members refused to sign at that point because they lacked the husband's sanction (obligatory in a Turkish family for any important decision whatsoever).

On payday, wives were asked to show their passports. If their names had not been changed, they were not paid. If a woman went to the bank to withdraw money, the same procedure was followed. If she or her children needed medical help, it was denied on the same grounds. It was still possible for a woman to live on savings kept under a pillow or for she and her children to be healthy. Sooner or later, though, she would encounter a passport-control picket and her passport would be branded invalid. From that point on, she could be detained, fined, arrested, and even jailed for "violation of the passport regulations."

There were places where collective resistance to the process was organized. Policemen or special commandos using armored personnel carriers and even light tanks would surround such rebellious villages and the mayor and a few other notables were summoned and talked into signing the declaration, which asked that they "voluntarily" choose a Bulgarian surname. If these men agreed, they were used as model cases for the rest of the villagers. Some of them did not come when they were called and had to be dug out of unlikely hideouts. If they still refused to sign, they ended up in prison camps. Meanwhile, commandos would go from house to house and anything that looked like a traditional Turkish garment was seized, cut up, torn, and trampled in the mud. Also consigned to the mud were books in Turkish (including the Koran). The *shalvari* were stripped unceremoniously from women's bodies. In some places, villagers fled to the woods, hoping the campaign would somehow pass them by. Such ungovernable people were driven back home with fire engines that soaked them with cold water, which sometimes resulted in people freezing to death in the winter cold. The one time that Turks rallied in protest in the Rhodope Mountains region, their leader was run over by an armored personnel carrier, and a woman trying to take pictures was shot dead at point-blank range.

But what about the muftis and imams, I asked? Apparently they were supporting the campaign, my friends answered. It was common knowledge that most Turkish ministers in Bulgaria were former or active party police officers.

I was shocked by these accounts. Most of all, however, I was shocked by my own ignorance. Ironically, about ten years later, worse outrages were committed against Muslims in adjacent Bosnia, followed by the more recent "ethnic cleansing" campaign in Kosovo. Those actions were justified in the same defiant manner as retaliation against the century-long enemy of the "ethnically pure" Slavs and followed the same pattern of *crime committed in darkness.*

However, I should have known that fellow Bulgarian citizens, no matter of what their ethnic origin, were subjected (as a community and as individuals) to a totalitarian depersonalization by their own state, a state, which at the same time enjoyed full international favor and respect. To be sure, I should have known what was going on in my own *small* country, even if I was unable to undertake any action whatsoever. In a country like Bulgaria you do not need sophisticated media coverage to learn what is happening at the other end, which is no more than six hundred kilometers away: word of mouth is a much more powerful tool for dispersing messages.

Well, this is still the smaller part of the problem. What about those who knew? Did they do anything? Now that I had learned, what did I do immediately or in the course of the next couple of years?

What I did in fact do was move on with my own life. My wife and I were concerned about our own physiology. The day after our late-night conversations that touched on the very political nature of life on the Balkans, we drove to Varna to deal with some issues pending after my divorce. We were interested in our sexuality, our housing, and our professional careers. We struggled to obtain Sofia citizenship for me. As I already described, getting an apartment in the capital was impossible without this instrumental formality.

We bought an apartment in June, 1985, and we were sublimely happy when we moved in at the end of the summer, following some renovations I made with the help of a friend.

Two years later, we bought a country house in a mountain village about a hundred kilometers east of Sofia. It was a conscious move to further increase our isolation from the regime.

Only people who have seen the pristine beauty of the Balkan Mountains can really grasp why it was so. A village in these mountains is geographically and socially far from the central politics. The local world was indeed a miniature copy of the same big picture I'm trying to draw in this narrative. Here again, there were the active builders and fighters for communism and the complying peasants. But someone from the capital was regarded with respect and virtually untouchable. So were we. As a matter of fact, we were a kind of a show for the locals: in their tedious quotidian life, our presence was the gossip, the story of the day. We were strangers: unexplained and inexplicable, but also irrelevant as far as their lives were concerned. Hence, there were good conditions for peaceful coexistence. I was nicknamed "The Writer" because, weather permitting, I used to type on my typewriter on the balcony of our house or under the vine tree. My wife and the kids kept their distance by always being polite but never intimate with our neighbors.

Throughout those last five years spent in the country where we still belonged but which we were internally leaving, our country home proved to be the happiest place we ever lived. It had a green yard with lifted vine trees, apple trees, and peach trees. In the summer, we grew tomatoes, onions, cucumbers, and cabbage.

We still own that house, by the way. It is the only object of endless nostalgia we could not part with. It was a part of our former identity. It is now a part of the fading links with our former country.

At that time, the house was an object of desire. We escaped there every chance we could. To find peace and serenity. To get out of the swamp. To breathe fresh air. We emigrated there to be ourselves. We thus transformed reality into a mental process so that we could unveil our emotions only in that remote village and only to our children, our few remaining close friends, and ourselves.

In Sofia, I was meeting regularly with Emil and writing columns and news reports. I was waiting in long lines for bread, butter, milk, or beds. I was seeing people I could not stand. I was being watchful of what I said, wrote, and even thought. In Sofia, I was refused a passport to travel abroad. But my last child was also born there. It was a fake existence wherein we pretended to be what we were not.

Our true existence came into focus only and exclusively in the remote loneliness of the village. The surrounding hills were gorgeous. Oh, how gorgeous they were! In the fall we would pick plums and walnuts and gather wood. There was a cosmic serenity in every single day—especially before sunset, when no human act or existence could matter less because we were above it, uplifted spiritually by the air and the light of that place.

It was indeed the place of our unbearable lightness of being.

During those five years my political self became more and more obsessed with the feeling that I lived in a no-man's-land. Had I belonged to the party, I would have been part of the Revival Process, and, obeying the party discipline, I would not have been able to raise my voice against it. The only means of protest would have possibly been resignation from party membership.

Had I belonged to the repressive apparatus (nonparty members were allowed to be part of it, if certain conditions were met), I would have been directly involved in the torture of unknown fellow citizens.

Had I truly belonged to the Bulgarian *blood*, I would have been proud of this nationalistic frenzy.

Had I belonged to an independent authority, or had I been an authority myself, I would have possessed the means to protest, to oppose, and to fight against the campaign that was legitimized by the existing state laws and, especially, by the recognition given Bulgaria's communist government by democratic countries throughout the world.

But I was nobody. Even those who tried to dispatch information about the atrocities were seldom successful in drawing the attention of any international human rights agency.

Had I been able to challenge other people to found an informal group of fighters against totalitarianism and, thus, had I belonged to such a self-sacrificing community, I would have had a clean conscience today, but only if my body were still intact.

But there were no such people.

Neither was I so reckless as to engage in open antigovernment activities on my own. Before becoming a public dissident, Andrey Sakharov belonged to Russia's top nuclear nomenclature and knew many strategic secrets. Václav Havel belonged to a top layer of the Czech aristocracy. Both were allowed to become single voices of dissidence because of their special status. In contrast, Aleksandr Solzhenitsyn, who was *only* a Nobel laureate and who had no claim to high social standing, was expelled, in due course, from the Soviet land. One had to be protected, to a certain degree at least, by the shield of authority or of public recognition.

I myself belonged to a faceless mass of communism builders struggling for their own useless survival. Even though I belonged to the cream of this crop, it was still a faceless cream. That was the only rational awareness I had at the time of my late-night passage through that godforsaken, dark Balkan village. All of the other above-mentioned options were mingled in an instinctive behavior, the minimal program of which was to preserve the integrity of my own personality.

By the time I started realizing the dimensions of Todor Zhivkov's anti-Turkish policy, the links with my family had already been broken. My father was terminally ill and contact-proof. My mother, still a member of the Communist Party, was in her first year of retirement, and stood awash in the communist propaganda preaching about a prosperous socialist country heading toward its brighter future. She did not want to know what was happening in the villages only a hundred kilometers south of Varna. My grandma, already eighty-eight years old, was feeble, and I was taking care not to incite any controversy in her noble mind with regard to the communist ideology, the communist movement, and the dreamed-of improvement of the Communist Party. Hence, my family, which I used to visit only on obligatory occasions, was not a place where I could gather information about, let alone debate, the issue of the Revival Process. All of my friends in Sofia were preoccupied with existential fears and problems, so the topic of renaming faded easily, all the more so because the press and television kept mute about it. There was no opportunity to cultivate a dissenting position on the issue of the Bulgarian conversion of the Turks, scientifically known as "assimilation."

Nor, as far as I can remember, was I myself eager to become a troublemaker. In the words of a friend: "for the socialist citizen, the absolute power of the state and its ruthlessness are axioms. The only vital point is to know whether this power will in fact be used in concrete circumstances."

Well, was there any other option for handling differently those "concrete circumstances?" Yes, it was the option envisioned by the ethnic Turks themselves. Had I belonged to them, what could I have done?

The majority of them complied and were left alone. They were faceless common people with no urban experience, no political skills, and no authority living among hostile Bulgarian neighbors. And yet, some of them resisted the campaign to the extent of their capacity. This resistance, while powerless to impede or stop the Revival Process, at least preserved their dignity.

There is always an overwhelming temptation to narrate from the viewpoint of the victims' prowess. Seized by courage, which is obviously a less frequent human trait than fear, our eyes and our sense of complicity are magnetized by the brave and repelled by the cowardly. I do not want to fall prey to the same bias. Statistics and testimonies show that the large mass of ethnic Turks complied with the Revival Process and soon social peace was reestablished in the areas they occupied. Of course, social peace is a fairly relative notion under the circumstances, since only the victims can tell what was going on within their souls. I myself was a product of the communist social peace, but the message of this book would not have existed had I not suffered day by day the individual moral price of maintaining that kind of peace.

There was an instrumental difference, though, between Turkish population's compliance with the Revival Process and the Bulgarian citizenry's compliance with communism. Changing your identity defies the very roots of your existence, whereas changing and sustaining the political regime challenges only your political body.

The ambition of the communist ideology was to expand beyond people's political bodies. The living agents of this ideology, the communist fighters and politicians, implemented the ideology's prescriptions to the letter. Their ambition was to reach out to, or to soak in, people's physiology. Communists succeeded in this regard to a great extent because they ruled over a population that confused politics with physiology. Communism was simultaneously thrust upon and yearned for by the people; it induced as much enthrallment as it required oppression to pen people in. The way to communism was forced through society, but communism could not have become so successfully entrenched if it had not met people's basic expectations.

There is, however, a limit beyond which no politics can trespass unpunished. This is the borderline beyond which bravery and cowardice do not matter anymore. The Revival Process in Bulgaria indicates where this borderline might be drawn. While the Bulgarian population, regardless of its ethnic diversity, will remain in history as an ideal example of coherent compliance with communism, Bulgaria's Turkish ethnic minority will be singled out as having resisted forceful identity change. People whose identity was not in danger could find excuses for their compliance. But when the identity was at stake, compliance could only be a sham.

So, *human identity* is perhaps what communists miscalculated they could crush down with impunity, riding their ultimate ambition to rule over the human species down to its individual soul. Because of decades of easy rule over a totally compliant populace, communists had lowered their guard and were already behaving like actors in a mournful comedy, whereby acting according to a preliminary scenario imitated ruling in real society. Their rule had crossed over into a form of mockery.

With the ethnic conversion campaign they unexpectedly engaged in a serious game, where acting became dangerous and cynicism suicidal. The stakes were no longer penny ante; only desperate gamblers would dare continue playing. Zhivkov and his valets were such gamblers. Moreover, they had no room to retreat left. All things considered, the staunch stand by the Turks in Bulgaria was the only group anticommunist response ever staged in that country. That reaction was also *the* factor that profoundly shook the top of the communist pyramid.

I learned the whole story of the Turks' stand by the end of 1989, in those first post-Zhivkov days when I felt at once challenged to participate. Then, suddenly and for the first time, I had been able to reassess the complex picture of my communist experience. I began to realize that there are two ways to save your soul from communism. My Turkish fellow citizens had already tested one: they used all means to strengthen the irrational anchor of their group identity. The other came as an epiphany to me: I could do just the opposite by ridding myself of any constraining group identity, be it national, ethnic, or political.

To be sure, I do not underestimate the complexity of the issue. What I find relevant to my account of communism is the fact that human identity became an issue as a result of communist rule. Communism is an arbitrary system that appeals to people's physiology while scorning their identity. In democratic societies, human identity determines the political rule; in the communist regime, political rule determined what human identity ought to be.

Now, there is an obvious difference in the morality underlying the above two ways of salvation from communism. When group identity is regarded as a legitimate response to an external threat, then everyone is innocent in terms of his or her own identity; hence, the attack upon people's identity has no justification whatsoever. Closing oneself in one's ethnic carapace draws only positive moral judgments, albeit internal to the group. This was the humblest way to resist the communist evil. As far as Bulgarians are concerned, this was also the easiest way to legitimize communism.

By contrast, getting rid of one's national identity in a conscious, forceful way is an ambiguous personal response to any self-alleged involvement in communism. It entails that one identify the political system with the nation this system was thrust upon. I did. The Bulgarian nation embraced communism and lived as one whole with it. Equally true, communism in Bulgaria was tailored to fit the Bulgarian nation to a degree of almost complete fusion.

When I compare my way of resistance to communism (if I was resisting at all) with the way the Turks in Bulgaria opposed it, I experience guilt.

Mine was a multilayered guilt. I felt ashamed about my silence during the course of the Revival Process. I was frustrated by my apathy toward the communist regime. I suddenly realized that I was per force identified with the Bulgarian nationality, whose modern sons and daughters had just committed outrages over their Turkish fellow citizens and were still possessed by the smug feeling of historic righteousness. This evoked sorrow and guilt, because of my belonging. Overcome by guilt, when the November, 1989, events began to shatter the party's inviolability, I turned to the cause of my Turkish fellow citizens who were bereft of identity rights.

Shortly before that, in October, 1989, the last month of Zhivkov's reign, an international ecological forum convened in Sofia. The environmentalist cause was a good pretext for protesting the disastrous ethnic policies of the Bulgarian communists. The abundance of foreign journalists offered an opportunity to voice concerns not only about our badly polluted motherland but also about the more urgent issues of human rights violations, economic decline, and social stagnation. The party police were on red alert. The few Bulgarian "environmentalists" (most of them still active members of the Communist Party), agitated since springtime because of the animosities between the Turks and the party apparatus, organized a series of eco-rallies. Squeezed by "world public opinion" and a power struggle within the highest echelons of the party establishment, communist authorities allowed a rally on the square behind the National Assembly and a public meeting in a small movie theater in downtown Sofia. As many secret police agents as it took to make them look busier than expected infiltrated both events. The people's "spontaneous" protests were led by active communists.

Indeed, all of the leading figures at these particular events sooner or later became enmeshed in politics on the side of the "renovated" Bulgarian Socialist Party (BSP). Only a few came as party outsiders, hoping to gain some political capital for the future. How can I forget Sasho Yordanov, a teacher from Varna, who took the floor at the November 3, 1989, public meeting at the Petar Beron movie theater? He was scared to death as he delivered his written speech. He was sweating and shaking, and he used a rhetoric of complaint rather than one of political logic and anticommunist platform. He raised his voice and declaimed slogans as if he was the voice of all oppressed Bulgarians, but he shrieked out of fear. As a matter of fact, he stood at the rostrum as nothing but himself: a communism-stricken, pathetic individual. Within a month, he joined the founders of the Radical Democratic Party, and, barely a year later, became one of the leaders of the "democratic forces." He was eventually elected president of the Bulgarian National Assembly, but because of his incompetence and suspected behind-the-scenes deals, his star swiftly declined. Today, he is dead as a politician and virtually forgotten.

Nevertheless, the week of the ecologic forum was full of unprecedented events. Top party functionaries later told stories about late-night meetings, clandestine visits to Moscow, and elite Bulgarian army tank regiments being prevented from surrounding Sofia. I am still reluctant to believe any of those stories. The whole fuss was over Zhivkov's ouster and who would grab the power after him.

I have a nostalgic recollection of the night of November 3, 1989. A handful of political outcasts were gathered in a Sofia apartment to see off a visiting Radio Free Europe journalist of Bulgarian origin. As a close friend to one of them, I happened to be there by pure coincidence. Assuming the role of the missing Bulgarian dissidents, these guys pretended to conspire about abolishing the communist dictatorship. As a matter of fact, such a possibility did not occur to any of them at the time. Or, if it did, it was only in the context of aspirations to personal power, like those of Sasho Yordanov.

At that moment, I perceived them as simply obsessed with a vague sense of mission. The Radio Free Europe journalist appeared to me to be like a mother consoling her orphaned children. And they? They were trying to keep up with the sublimity of the moment. After forty-five years of submissive existence under communism, they were nevertheless uplifting themselves by imagining that their existential discontent could be taken as a form of political dissidence. Only a week later, they would claim the status of repressed fighters against communism and, of course, a share of the redistribution of power. Today, these sympathetic personalities, with only one exception, are once again nobodies. My own role was that of an observer. There was no cause to which I was then committed.

At the first anticommunist rally held in Sofia on November 18, 1989, eight days after Zhivkov's fall, most of these newly hatched "dissidents" climbed on the grandstand and spoke the loudest from the rostrum. Our euphoria was staggering. The next day I wrote an enthusiastic essay full of self-accusation, admitting my guilt and the guilt of my fellow Bulgarians for the violence toward the Turkish minority. Two central newspapers refused to publish it. Here is this essay, which I later published in the newspaper I edited:

My great-grandma was the daughter of a French father and an Austrian mother. My great-grandfather was a Macedonian from Thessaloniki, his name was Pauntchev. My grandma married a Banat Bulgarian in Veliko Tarnovo. My father's parents were settlers who came from Edirne in Turkey.

My birth certificate is issued in Varna. It says that I was born to a Bulgarian mother and father. Once, I saw the birth certificate of my classmate Erol, and it said that his mother and father were Turks. It seems that then, in 1946, no one questioned the usefulness of such "exact" information. In my wife's birth certificate there is no more mention of her parents' nationality. And in the birth certificates of our children it is only indicated that their parents have such and such SSN.

My classmate considered himself a Turk.

I CONSIDER MYSELF A BULGARIAN.

But today I, a BULGARIAN journalist, do not want to live in Bulgaria anymore. No guarantees are given in this country that tomorrow some hotshot Bulgarian would not force me to change . . . oh, not my name, no! He would force me to change my feeling of belonging to Bulgaria. He or she will probe deep in my ancestry and will yell: Out! Your blood is not pure.

So, because I do not want to be forced to wander the world with my six Bulgarian children, I prefer take them with me on an airplane and bring them to the civilized world, where everybody will respect my Bulgarian belonging.

But before leaving, I want to declare: I am ashamed that I share a land with buckos who have no respect for Man.

They did not think that in 1972 [the first campaign organized by the communist regime for expatriating Turks from Bulgaria to Turkey] Bulgaria's national interests had been violated.

They did not cry at the bloodletting in the winter of 1985.

They were not appalled that, the summer before last, our motherland brother Turks were forced to join convoys heading south, and they were forced there as numbers, at gunpoint. At the same time, their Bulgarian tormentors rubbed their hands with joy, saying, "we finally got rid of those nasty Turks."

They had never before envisioned defending the national values. The reason is that they themselves were the "national" value: they are people who cannot imagine the world outside their gendarme idea of totalitarian Eastern Europe guarded by the communist Big Brother.

They got scared today, hearing that another value, the Individual, is given priority. They do not know what Individual means at all and even less what Human Rights mean.

All this makes me ashamed of living in my fatherland, together with such fellow citizens who refuse to comply with the equal rights we all have.

Nationalism is no doubt a spider web covering the corners of the junk shop known as the Bulgarian economy. But it has both fervent ideologues and sincere upholders. It is this sincerity that makes my shame still stronger, since I take it as a sign of discouraging backwardness. The poor in spirit are truly blessed, for it is out of the question to ask them for penitence about a guilt they are unable to be aware of.

But my shame will be even more unbearable if I have no proof of the penitence of those Bulgarians who are wealthy in spirit. Today I can only hope such penitence exists. Because what we know is that Turks defended themselves alone! Where were *the caring Bulgarians?*

If some people today are still stirring up nationalist hatred, they are not Muslims, but the Bulgarian chauvinists. Obviously, these chauvinists have not even the consciousness of Christians; so, it is useless to speak of a confrontation on religious grounds. This confrontation arose from nationalist and nomenclature quarters.

The only thing I am not ashamed of and that still chains me to this land is love. My heart appeals not for reconciliation—since nothing was disputed—but for acceptance. The human creations of the totalitarian communism have to recognize the fact that Turks live on this land as well. Turks, people who are dignified, long-suffering, and honest.

My fellow Bulgarians, help me to remain in my native land: join me in my love. No people are more perfect than others and no group of people deserves more love than another. The oppressed, however, merit compassion. And among the oppressed Bulgarian people, Turks were the most oppressed. We owe them our repentance and our love.

This love makes my soul pure. But being part of the ailing soul of Bulgaria, my soul is shrunken and scared. This is not the fear of the soul before a new birth, but the misgiving that Bulgaria's soul is full of hatred.

Meanwhile, two or three consecutive public meetings were held in the same movie theatre famous for the unique ecological protest that occurred ten days before Zhivkov was ousted. After the speeches at these meetings ended, a young Bulgarian lady addressed the audience with an appeal to sign a petition for the release of her husband from jail. Then I heard for the first time his name: Ahmed Dogan. This was the only one of the numerous petitions promoted during this period that I signed. I understood that this man was to be the leader of the pro-Turkish human rights movement. He was set free in early December.

After my pro-Turkish article failed to pass the censure of our would-be democratizing press, the most natural step on my part was to send it to Ahmed Dogan. He called me some days later to express his gratitude, and we met in a Sofia café. I declined his invitation to join the party he was creating at the time, but I accepted intellectually and emotionally that I might somehow be able to help its just cause.

Thus, in April, 1990, when Ahmed Dogan's party was registered for the upcoming elections in June, it was only natural that I did not decline his offer to become an independent candidate for Parliament on their party list and participate in the election campaign of his party, which he called the Movement for Rights and Liberties. It had never occurred to me that I might become a legislator, let alone a politician, but I was so swept up by both the spontaneous challenge of the period and the yearning to redeem my former apathy, that I consented with almost no apprehension. By that time, Ahmed and I became good friends. He provided me with a cause worth working for.

The man-to-man narratives of this intellectual turned politician who had bravely fought personal loneliness and public mistrust from his very appearance on the Balkan political stage, fashioned for me the true story of the Revival Process (1984–89). Moreover, during my two months of campaigning, I met many real victims of the brutal ethnic conversion, and the picture of the events became bold in my consciousness.

Ahmed admitted that until 1984 he had been the same apathetic and rather easygoing kind of intellectual I here described myself to be. But after the merciless renaming campaign unleashed in the fall of 1984 and victoriously wrapped up in the spring of 1985, Ahmed put aside his academic career in philosophy and vowed to save his ethnic fellow countrymen from impending genocide. Bulgarian Communist Party documents from that time account for a "total achievement of the goals of the Revival Process." Ahmed and a handful of desperate companions built up a clandestine cell aimed at "the national liberation of Bulgarian Turks." Two bombing assaults on public transportation agencies and a kidnapping of two teenagers occurred, fragments of which we (Bulgarian citizens) learned only by word of mouth. In front of me, Ahmed claimed responsibility for the bombings only. In May, 1986, a traitor caused the capture of Ahmed and his companions, after which they were tried by a military court and imprisoned for terrorist acts.

A fateful game began between Ahmed and the totalitarian authorities, where the stakes included his life on one hand, and the resistance to assimilation of Turks in Bulgaria, on the other. Saved from expulsion to Turkey by the impertinent intention of the authorities to play "the great national card" with the strong southern neighbor, Ahmed remained alive and in Bulgaria. Although he related the life-threatening dangers he had experienced in the maximum-security prison in Pazardzhik, he never elaborated on his bargain with the party police. But a bargain must have occurred, no doubt about it.

How else could he claim that from inside the prison he established contacts with respectful representatives of the Turkish community and succeeded in persuading them to unleash mass rallies precisely on the eve of the conference on human rights in Paris in 1989? Those rallies were indeed conceived as calm, peaceful marches out of the numerous villages to the district towns, with the marchers chanting and carrying only one slogan: "Give us back our names!" I learned from testifying participants that the marches were confronted by armed force, and several people were killed. The humble population, however, did not exhibit any signs that it would give up, which forced Todor Zhivkov to declare publicly on May 31, 1989, that all Turks living in Bulgaria would be allowed to emigrate to Turkey. At that moment, information about the "Turkish events" in Bulgaria began appearing in the international media. Ahmed Dogan was in jail, and nobody yet knew about his existence.

Emigration was an official euphemism. Bulgarian communists solemnly declared that the Turkish border was open for whoever chose to leave Bulgaria. In reality, however, they implemented a well-conceived plan to expel the entire Turkish minority. Police prepared lists of so-called Turkish travelers, and convoys with their private cars, special buses, and trucks loaded with their belongings were rhythmically directed to the border checkpoints. The National Savings Fiduciary, the only institution in which Bulgarian citizens could deposit their savings, opened special desks to serve the mass withdrawal of personal funds for the trip. Other lines were formed before the police passport departments for the hasty delivery of passports. And Bulgarians began buying the houses of their departing neighbors at ridiculously low prices while selling them cars for transporting their belongings at criminally high rates. It was rumored that this trip would be final and that no return was foreseen. The land stood still in the heat, abandoned by its laborious farmers. Many small factories shut down because they were short of workers. Most families were split, the elderly involved in preparation for departure, the younger people agonizing but staying behind.

In the capital, there were no alarming signs that large rural areas were in turmoil. Life floated in its usual bed. I remember my cousin Angel telling me that it was a good time to sell my obsolete Škoda, and on another occasion asserting that "finally, Bulgaria will be set free from these filthy Turks."

This was the sad end of a five-year period of ethnic cleansing. It was a dress rehearsal for the ethnic-cleansing operations undertaken by the Serbs in the 1990s. It was based on the same nationalistic hatred, rage, and claim of superiority. The only difference is that it did not result in the brutality and mass murders that occurred for a decade throughout the former Yugoslavia. A striking similarity between the two approaches is the almost criminal neglect for the country's economy, which suffered a great deal in Bulgaria and led to a complete economic collapse in Yugoslavia.

The Bulgarian ethnic cleansing occurred behind the Iron Curtain, and was thus shrouded in the obscurity that characterized the whole Cold War era. At that time, nobody cared what was going on in the obscure Balkans. And on top of that, the well-lubricated party and police machine functioned smoothly, undisturbed by dissidents, public unrest, or international indignation. There was no democracy, no foreign press to stick its nose in the internal affairs of a sovereign nation.

By September, about 350,000 Turks had fled from Bulgaria into Turkey. About one-fifth of them came back shortly after Zhivkov decided to shift into reverse gear that same month and reopened the border for the emigrants to return to Bulgaria. At the first post-Zhivkov rally in front of the Alexander Nevski Cathedral on November 18, 1989, large groups of Turks from around the country flanked the cohort of intellectuals mixed here and there with working-class people. These were the social groups that could be driven into genuine euphoria by the fall of Zhivkov. Only one of the speakers even circumstantially addressed the Turkish issue; sadly, in the years to come he turned to a debilitating nationalism and was dismissed from politics.

My emotional reactions in that initial period determined my attitudes and choices. I was finally able to act with some freedom. For the first time in my life I was not pressed, directed, observed, restricted, or forced to behave hypocritically. I was *not obliged* to participate. I was *not obliged* to defend the departing communism, either.

So, if I must believe in the rightness of my emotions, I cannot be at ease with the conclusions to which they led me. These conclusions were that I experienced no sympathy toward my fellow Bulgarians or myself, while I was swept away by compassion toward my Turkish fellow citizens. There was widespread evidence that the latter, as a group, had suffered under communism, while there was accruing evidence that the former (again, as a whole) had rather benefited from it. The Turkish minority contributed to the fall of the dictator; we of the Bulgarian majority had sustained dictatorship.

The fall of 1989 has to be regarded as both a turning point for the communist countries and as a watershed for every single communist citizen. The moment of transition turned into a step toward a cure from the brainwashing. My mother and my cousin Angel remained communists. They and their closest friends went on siding with the would-be reformed Communist-turned-Socialist Party. I myself opted for antinationalism (which is just a humanitarian face of anticommunism, as far as I am concerned). My closest friends chose different versions of anticommunism, though none of them translated it into such a staunch denial of the nationalistic ideologies as I did. Those who hesitated to cut their links with communism were not my friends anymore.

What was Ahmed's option? He chose anticommunism, of course. But he also aspired to be a political leader. In Balkan politics this means to regress inevitably into a caricature of the political principles that brought you to the scene. His swift success instantly became his defeat: by achieving the human rights goals of the Turkish ethnic movement, he lost the political basis that justified his stay in politics. In order to construct a new platform, Ahmed had to forcefully embrace additional principles relevant to the chaotic post-Zhivkov period, lest he lose his electorate, pure and simple. Continuing to represent an ethnic party would only transform him into an ethnocentrist—a very dangerous position in the Balkans—and would enhance the ethnic confrontation that split Bulgarians and Turks, instead of allowing it to fade gradually away.

But there was something else, something fatefully interwoven with the omnipotent communist system, which overpowered Ahmed's choice. His case, all speculation involved notwithstanding, followed a *pattern* that determined the moves and strategies of most postcommunist politicians throughout Eastern Europe. This was the pattern of their political survival. The rule was quite simple: follow the pattern or die! Many of them "died" with a vengeance, hence, the mess in East European politics in the 1990s. The golden standard of this pattern was to have had links with the party police and to possess information about something top secret, either of a political or social nature.

No matter how disciplined and coherent the party police may have seemed, there was a wild struggle for power going on inside its basements and high floors as well. Police bosses were the real strongmen behind the regime. The rise of such an ungovernable figure as Ahmed could be dealt with in two ways: physical annihilation or spiritual purchase. Murder is a sentence reserved for medium personalities whose disappearance will do only limited harm and will soon be veiled. Killing leaders whose authority over large groups of people is unquestionable creates more problems than advantages. Therefore, buying them is as much a challenge as a far-reaching political success. Those who had access to Ahmed in his prison cell were not simple-minded servants. On the contrary, he was visited by, or allowed to correspond with, top party and police functionaries who were the perfect regime insiders. Some of them sided with Zhivkov, but some of them were shrewd enough to expect that the dictator's years were numbered. Zhivkov alone was well-stained with Turkish blood, and this was not only due to the fact that he was the dictator: everyone at the top of the communist heap sensed that the Revival Process was not the usual schmoozing between comrades that resulted in issuing another nonsensical decree. It was a matter for which liability would one day be demanded. For those who despised Zhivkov, Ahmed Dogan offered an excellent opportunity to undermine the secretary general's impunity by eroding his power and claiming anticommunist dividends in due course.

The other benefit of keeping close with Ahmed had to do with blackmailing Turkey. Ankara had never cared much for Bulgarian Turks themselves, but the support declared for a Turkish ethnic leader in hostile Bulgaria could be used as a trump card in other Balkan political conflicts, as well as in the attempts to improve the Turkish government's infamous human rights record. Equally important was the possibility that an eventual top figure in post-Zhivkov Bulgaria might have links with the ruling Turkish political upper crust. Thus, the executors of the Revival Process were, in their turn, eager to imply that if Turkey failed to accept the expelled Bulgarian Turks, it could never benefit from Ahmed alive. Moreover, the Bulgarian Turkish community could be more easily manipulated when their recognized leader was in jail.

One may, of course, trace several other lines of political calculations that intersect with this man. Let me restrict myself, however, to the observation that he himself could not emerge unscathed. He could not start a political career from scratch. He knew all too well those who owed him something, as well as those to whom he owed his life.

The fact is that although fellow prisoners twice attacked him with a knife, Ahmed survived unharmed and was freed before the release of other political prisoners. He was left to found a party that was frantically opposed both by executors of the Revival Process and sincere Bulgarian nationalists. And he registered this party in defiance of Bulgarian law that clearly prohibited any political organization based on ethnic grounds. Even the newly elected Constitutional Court did not succeed in overruling the illegality of his party. On the other hand, he adopted the posture of an untouchable new leader and was indeed successful in manipulating people from the whole political spectrum in achieving his political agenda. But although he was designed to lead the forces entitled by conscience and by law to punish those who conceived and executed the Revival Process, he remained mute on this matter. He had always escaped my direct questions in this regard, and he did not step up and ask for righteous revenge for our humiliated Turkish fellow citizens. As far as I am concerned, he failed to meet many moderate Bulgarians' expectations, mine included, for an effective anticommunist leadership that might fully correspond to the power he has wielded since the first post-Zhivkov elections.

This puzzle was still missing a number of its pieces at the time of the 1990 election campaign. Nevertheless, it was the happiest time of my life in Bulgaria. I truly believed that liberation had come, unexpectedly but definitively. Now, all we had to do was clear the way for the *good* people to come into power. How truly ridiculous! But that was the holy truth: it seemed to me that there were enough fellow Bulgarians not stained with communism to constitute a group of *good* (i.e., clean and democratically minded) people to provide leadership.

One must keep in mind that I thought of myself as one of these people. I had not yet realized my own contamination with communism, which I am exposing throughout this book. My enthusiasm was my excuse for being involved in the democratization process as a politician, despite the fact that I had neither the experience nor the intention to become one. To cut the hydra of nationalism seemed to me *the* noble cause that would enable me to rid myself of my remorse and to contribute to the renovation of society. After this was achieved, I thought, I would withdraw to my writing and leave the process in the hands of professional politicians. The momentum was so powerful that as many intellectuals as there were in the country (from the brainwashed to the infantile) they all engaged in politics, regarding it as their humanistic and civic obligation.

Emotions overwhelmed reason. Emotions allegedly are the best compass for distinguishing good from evil and siding with humanistic causes. Ultimately, they are the basic motive of intellectuals (or of all other people, for that matter) not to withdraw from the camp of liberals and leftists. But emotions cannot be an instrument for achieving political success. Reason is what renders you victorious in politics, since reason manages knowledge, experience, diplomacy, and will.

With regard to the communist legacy that happened to be available in the transitional period I am talking about, I realize today that several decades of communist brainwashing had succeeded in damaging our reason but had failed to scrap the integrity of our emotions. My conclusion is that emotions were not (or were less) susceptible to this particular kind of manipulation, while reason failed to resist it.

Therefore, swept up by righteous emotions, most honest people in Eastern Europe imagined that they had accomplished an anticommunist revolution. In addition, they deluded themselves into thinking that nothing
more than honesty and noble humanism was required for this "revolution"
to succeed. However, a *rational* assessment of the disposition of forces was
tragically lacking. It soon became evident that communists were the only
trained and experienced politicians available. For the realization of this,
Eastern European liberal-minded humanists paid the price of being led by
their noses by agile, self-styled would-be reformers who swiftly sniffed the
political dividends resulting from an anticommunist engagement. Even if
some of these humanistically minded liberals had sincerely joined the fledg-
ling democratic parties, their unprofessional performance in politics cost
them dearly and, worse yet, compromised the success of those parties.

All this emotional uplift I now call euphoria. As a rule, when one is
euphoric, petty things do not matter. You are swept along by joy, and you
fail to realize that the complex picture is not as glorious as it seems to your
open heart. But who is seized by euphoria? Usually those who experience
victory as a miracle, and rarely those who have themselves worked as mules
before the happy events come to life. All this provides sad evidence for my
theory that we, the able people of the Eastern European camp, were not
adequately prepared to meet the so-called fall of communism. And we did
not prepare the "fall" either. We were simply catapulted from a state of
isolated apathy into a state of collective euphoria. Rationality escaped us
during this parabolic flight.

The spring, 1990, electoral campaign was an ideal occasion to reinforce
my euphoria. Everything was new: the encounters with people who seemed
exotic to me; the sympathetic awkwardness of all these newborn politicians, coordinators, bodyguards, and local activists; the rallies held on village squares, long-abandoned provincial stadiums, or right on the field
behind the last house of the village; the press conferences for which we
flew back to Sofia; our dream of launching a newspaper for the Movement.
One special touch of freedom was that the police did not seem to care
much about this agitation. The communists and their servants had been
scared by the overwhelming emotions and were hiding in a wait-and-see
mode. Watching how police troops were deployed to protect our rallies
instead of chasing them away was an entirely novel experience.

I spoke at these rallies with the vocabulary of a staunch anticommunist,
keeping in line with the general mood. The public yelled frenetically after
every slogan directed at the executors of the Revival Process, and at the

very idea that they would finally be cornered, with Todor Zhivkov on top
of the list. What I spoke came from the bottom of my heart, and breaking
my former silence made me feel relieved. Every day we visited at least five
villages, and late in the night we ended up in the last village's pub in the
company of local people who spoke their hearts to us over a glass of wine
or beer. During that month and a half, I learned a great deal about my
Turkish fellow citizens and got to know my friend Ahmed better.

I trusted him. Ahmed Dogan was a born leader. He also combined visceral
anticommunism with rational political will. His electorate received him
like an apostle. He surpassed all his disciples in his brightness and political
acumen. For me, he surpassed the other freshmen in Bulgarian politics
aspiring to monopolize the disentanglement of the communist regime in
two crucial respects: he was not swept away by emotions, and he was not
possessed by the perverse ambitions of an adult child long kept from power.
He was, however, vulnerable in this particular regard: he did not have a clue
about our country's democratic perspective.

As far as I am concerned, there is no better example for the reciprocity
between the communist regime and the communism-stricken population than
Ahmed Dogan. First of all, his natural talent as a politician was absolutely

Ahmed Dogan (far left) *and me at a rally promoting the reclaiming of
Turkish names and restoration of the Bulgarian Turks' human rights.
Sofia, January, 1990. (Author's collection.)*

buried in totalitarian times until a shocking provocation suddenly woke him up. Secondly, when finally awakened, he could only pester the communist authorities for a short while since anticommunist resistance was not ubiquitous. Thirdly, while imprisoned in the communist penitentiary, he was compelled to participate in corrupt power bargains that restricted the full moral authority he needed for a healthy political victory upon his release. Finally, he had no strategy. He was forced to fight for the rehabilitation of the disfranchised, a cause he fought for with fury and fervor. He could not make out an agenda for the construction of a pristine postcommunist society.

After forty-five years of communist rule, Bulgarian society had not created an alternative to communism. Today, the whole world is confronted with the lack of such an alternative. Who is responsible for this state of affairs? All of us or only some of us? All of us or nobody? The so-called political forces or the nameless actors? The dictators or the oppressed? Some suspected world conspiracy or the nations themselves? The owners of the world money supply or the dispossessed?

Am *I* personally responsible?

Ahmed Dogan (third from left), Yunal Lyutfi, and me campaigning at a rally in Kurdzhali, the stronghold of the Movement for Rights and Liberties (MRL), during the first postcommunist elections in June, 1990. In 2002, Ahmed is still the leader of the MRL, and Yunal is serving his second term as vice president of the National Assembly. A good friend of mine, Yunal was my schoolmate at the French language school in Varna during 1961–63; he was officially identified as a collaborator with the SS from 1965–92. (Author's collection.)

Acting in my capacity of editor in chief of Rights and Liberties, *the weekly newspaper of the Movement for Rights and Liberties, I am speaking here at a seminar on ethnic problems organized by Bulgarian nationalists (who had three small parties at the time). Sofia, April, 1991. (Author's collection.)*

CHAPTER 7

Deflation

Posterity is always more given to assigning the blame
for failure to individuals than to circumstances.

—*Henry Kissinger,* Diplomacy

I will refrain from taking sides in the endless debate about who really loses a war (generals or soldiers) although the temptation is certainly there. So many experts on Eastern European communism have already distributed the victory cake to the eminent dissidents while parceling out the blame to communism's chieftains. Jumping to conclusions has always been sustained by wishful thinking.

In real life, people function and make judgments based exclusively on the knowledge and information available to them. I was one of these real people under communism. I was part of a population that was left with a limited number of choices, if any at all. And I had suddenly realized that democracy was no longer a choice for my lifetime. We had lost the battle long before it started. Our long-dreamed democracy never came about.

I suddenly had a new choice: I could quit!

I had failed both to keep the family continuity bequeathed by my grandma's spirit and to pursue my career. Moreover, I had detached myself from our society's essential aspirations: nationalism, petit bourgeois happiness, and communist conformity. The big question was: what changes could we expect? Would we become new, better, happier, or mightier? Did the departure itself represent *a* change? When you have lived for so long in a sleepy railway station with almost no trains dropping by, and suddenly you notice express trains whirling past, seducing you with their speed and unknown destinations, is that a change in yourself? How could I change the fact that I was raised in a communist family or that I had had six children with three wives, and they all were somehow related to my place in the world?

I have a vivid recollection of December 22, 1989. Behind me were forty days of euphoric delusions that we were kicking communism away and that the whole democratic world had joined in to help *our* cause. That chilly December day I watched Bulgarian National Television broadcasting live from Bucharest the pathetic struggle "against" communism in neighboring Romania. Someone at the studio in Sofia provided a simultaneous translation from Romanian. This show was allegedly run without a scenario. There was only one camera shooting from a studio where electricity went on and off intermittently. Unshaved men in uniforms or wearing jackets over T-shirts appeared before the camera to tell about the battle outside the TV tower or to provide the latest information about Ceauşescu's whereabouts, or simply to raise a hand in a V-salute. The anchorman was a beardless fat man who sat in the midst of half-burnt candles. When the current went out, he managed to fire up a portable generator, so that within a minute or so, the picture reappeared on the screen, each time more pathetic and desperate than the preceding one. He was able to convey the feeling that a handful of people were barricaded inside the television studio, while in the streets outside a deadly skirmish prevented free movement. There were no windows, and the noise of small-arms fire and distant explosions could be heard over the broadcaster's voice.

The red thread of this happening was the follow-up of Nicolae and Elena Ceauşescu, who had fled by helicopter from the roof of the central party building in an allegedly unknown direction. Were they still in Romania? Would they soon land somewhere? Who was with them? Was the Securitate at their heels, or would some unknown fighters for democracy ambush them since they could not stay in the air forever? The broadcaster asked some of these questions, while others occurred subconsciously in my mind. On December 17, 1989, the Romanian army and police attacked demonstrators supporting Pastor László Tokos in Timişoara, a city of two hundred thousand in the western part of the country. Hundreds of civilians were reportedly killed. László Tokos was the spontaneous leader of a pro-Hungarian nationalist movement used as a platform for a peaceful anticommunist protest. The Ceauşescus allegedly ordered the massacre in Timişoara. No one knew exactly. Hardly anyone will ever know, since documents were destroyed and witnesses kept silent and no trial has been set to prosecute those events.

I paid little attention to the fact that virtually no one had mentioned the existence of an organized force, or camp, or front in opposition to the regime. Nevertheless, the notorious couple was fleeing from something. The implication, of course, was that they were fleeing from the popular anger that spilled over from Timişoara onto the streets of Bucharest. Who had armed the people? Who led the attack against the party headquarters? What about Ceauşescu's bodyguards and the whole gang of Securitate personnel?

A "revolution" unfolded before my eyes as the miraculous TV "eye" witnessed its "spontaneity," reflected its chaos, and provided us the soothing feeling that we had somehow participated in it. There was the bad guy who had tried to escape. There were the good guys who had to win. And there were the nameless riflemen who shot in all directions to establish justice. It was like an action movie in every respect, except that I (the watcher turned participant) had my own sublime bias and did not require any logic from the scenario. I felt certain that communism was on the chopping block and I really did not care who was brandishing the cleaver.

At one point, there was a scuffle in the lower portion of the studio. Then the camera stopped rattling and focused on a group of men talking in hushed voices amidst the hustle and bustle. After a few seconds, they turned their faces to the left, where a short man with a Leninesque beret on his head emerged. He was unshaven and wore no makeup. In fact, he had just charged in from the battle raging outside. The news anchor announced that the man had fresh news about the Ceauşescus. Two guys with Kalashnikovs in hand flanked the man with the *casquette,* who was introduced as Ion Iliescu. The news was that the couple's helicopter had landed somewhere in the middle of Romania and an armored Mercedes had taken them away. A car chase was under way. Beyond that, the translation worsened so that I could not grasp where the Mercedes was headed or exactly who was chasing it. Somehow, I had caught the name Iliescu, even though he appeared only incidentally on the screen and with nothing to distinguish him from the other combatants.

The revolutionary confusion continued for quite some time. I turned the TV off, or perhaps the broadcast ended. I do not remember exactly. On Christmas Day, it was announced that Ceaușescu and his wife had been shot dead. Within a short interval, perhaps several days after New Year's Eve, Bulgarian TV rebroadcast a one-hour Romanian video graphically depicting how the precipitous trial of the Ceaușescus and their killing actually occurred. There were three actors in the video: Nicolae, Elena, and a baritone voice. The voice asked questions and argued with the two helpless victims. Popular nemesis was implied to be the ultimate justification of the verdict's righteousness. In the end, the voice ordered the shooting and the couple fell dead. They deserved it.

Later, the whole world saw this video, which provided further evidence that speculation about the fall of communism was based on more than jokes and idle chatter. These men took their job seriously. Obviously, the fall of communism was so desperately expected that no one had bothered to explain to the public who the serious players really were.

Shortly after the broadcast, Ion Iliescu was declared leader of the postcommunist forces in Romania. We learned belatedly, and by chance, that he had been an ideology secretary in the Romanian Politburo under Ceaușescu. In the summer of 1990, I saw a brief announcement in a fringe newspaper that said the military prosecutor with the baritone voice who had interrogated Ceaușescu and his wife and ordered their execution had committed suicide after being haunted by insurmountable remorse. He was a general from the Securitate. In 2000, Iliescu became Romania's prime minister, leading a government dominated by the Communist Party.

In my memory, the baritone voice will forever remain a metaphor of the *invisible* forces that hatched a plot against each other. With incomparable bigotry, however, they succeeded in presenting this very conspiracy as a spontaneous people's uprising. With a similar invisibility, the leading governments of the great democratic countries stood by and waited while the communists dethroned and eroded one another, leaving the alleged democratic forces adrift.

I was on my first visit to the United States in the middle of June, 1990, when the North American media offered their account of the ten thousand miners called by Ion Iliescu to bludgeon the demonstrating intelligentsia in the streets and squares of Bucharest. This was the same "accidental man" from the Christmas, 1989, broadcast who had already planted himself on the top of "postcommunist" Romania. The miners came with their clubs and beat innocent people, yet this was not reported as a violation of human rights. Analogies were never drawn between the first anniversary of the Tiananmen Square massacre and the breaking of human skulls and limbs in Bucharest.

In late August, 1990, I was in my cottage 120 kilometers from Sofia when Bulgarian television showed the big fire set on a hot summer evening on the Central Party House, right in the heart of the Bulgarian capital. A huge stone building erected during the Stalin years to evoke might and eternity, the Central Party House served as the BCP headquarters and archive for the party's records. During the Zhivkov regime, it had been the pinnacle of the country's pyramid. The real operative management of the country had been executed from the Central Party House. The Council of Ministers, which was supposed to represent the legal locus of executive power, used to be in a building facing the north side of the Party House. Unlike the Eastern Orthodox churches, however, the front of the Party House faced westward, and there was a five-pointed ruby star atop the western facade. Facing the south side of the Central Party House was the Bulgarian National Bank, and behind it, slightly to the east, was the Ministry of Defense. Between the latter two, the mausoleum housing Georgi Dimitrov's mummy stood defiantly in front of the Tsar's Palace (after 1948 it became the National Art Gallery). The entire complex was linked with underground tunnels and bomb shelters. A chain of service buildings lining the boulevard south of the Party House wrapped up the whole party space. Military parades and popular demonstrations of gratitude to the mother party took place on solemn occasions on the yellow cobblestone square formed by the party space.

I watched as flames and black smoke spewed out of the windows and gathered ominously around the open gate on the eastern facade of the Central Party House. A full hour reportedly passed after the blaze erupted before any firefighters appeared on the scene. An ecstatic crowd of people (called *lumpens* the next day by the still party-controlled "free" press) gathered outside and moved in and out of the burning building. Tons of paper flew from the windows as the crowd seized sheets, folders, and books, and tore them apart before consigning them to the flames. Firefighters slowly set up their hoses and ladders, and uniformed policemen emerged. No line of control formed, however, and it seemed as though people were simultaneously maintaining and fighting the fire. Sometime near dawn, the fire began to die down by itself.

This fire was a portentous symbol. At the most trivial level, it was enthusiastically regarded as an appealing emblem of the ongoing "people's revolution" that allegedly toppled Eastern European communism. However, we must quickly discard that notion, since evidence sifted from the ashes shows that the party people set the fire themselves. It started inside the building, and only after it had grown brisk enough did an invisible hand open the gates to allow the crowd outside to enter. Witnesses testified that police acted without coordination or purpose. For several hours, no focused attempt was made to fight the fire or to save any of the materials in the blazing offices. During the next few days, party officials, who groundlessly accused the democratic coalition of having deliberately instigated an attack on the Central Party House, drummed up a hysterical campaign. A great deal of the party's records perished in the flames. At the same time, the fire coincided with the first days in office of newly elected Pres. Zhelyu Zhelev, the leader of the democratic coalition. The official investigation, which began a month after the incident, was still under way at the time this was written.

To grasp the symbolic sentiment behind this August event in Bulgaria, one must keep in mind that Eastern Europeans, and Balkan people in particular, are less myth-oriented than the Western, and in particular, North American public. Instead, they tend to assign special meaning to material symbols like stars, mausoleums, flag emblems, tombs, monuments, names, even the geographical orientation of buildings. In this regard, a great deal of energy was wasted during the initial period after Zhivkov's fall on changing the symbols of BCP authority. Countless speeches were delivered at rallies and in the National Assembly over the design of the state coat of arms, the fate of Dimitrov's mausoleum (which was demolished in late 1999), the removal of the five-pointed ruby star from the top of the Party House, and so on. Even the persona of Zhivkov himself was evoked as a symbol, and a special debate took place in the legislature on whether it was appropriate to pay him a visit in his posh Boyana villa where he had secluded himself with his granddaughter.

In July, 1990, when the newly elected Great National Assembly opened its session (with a communist majority), a popular movement aimed at changing the symbolic codes all around the country was organized. Self-respecting intellectuals engaged in a logorrhea for replacing public signs with little significance, all based on the misguided belief that such a change would somehow trigger a change in the real power structure. This movement set up camps in the middle of major Bulgarian towns where people slept under canvas during the night and took part in a variety of protest activities during the day. One of these so-called Cities of Truth was established near the Party House, on the yellow cobblestone central square. It was this City of Truth that was assaulted by police the day after the Central Party House fire. Some of its "citizens" were arrested for suspected arson but were soon released for lack of evidence.

All this agitation was much ado about nothing. Party members started the fire for two very practical reasons: to destroy compromising party records, and so they could accuse prodemocracy organizations of illegal violence. Both motives produced long-lasting effects. A third possible consequence, namely that the event would be regarded by the world as a revolutionary deed, did not preoccupy post-Zhivkov party strategists. They were perfectly aware of how empty all the revolutionary phraseology was and how it would never fully impact those who would inherit the power of the former dictator. They were also aware that their political base was far from being even superficially eroded and that a little self-inflicted violence would garner future political dividends. Those who best knew the inflated price of symbols could not have cared less about giving away yesterday's fetishes while preserving control of the real levers of power.

However, the ultimate symbolism of the Central Party House arson is its ambiguity. There it was, the whole Eastern European camp set ablaze by an intangible force, while people of undetermined color, shape, and interests, bustled about with little or no sense of how to extinguish the horror. No front, no loyalty to any political group or philosophy, no borderline between communists and anticommunists (just a throng of brainwashed individuals with no commitment to revenge or redemption).

The failure of the self-styled democratic forces to square their accounts with the former Zhivkov servants for this arson was a strong signal for me that my euphoria had no silver lining. Reality proved time and again that I was disoriented, since the winning side was, in fact, a "dynamic" coalition of communist turncoats. For a little while, I refused to admit this to others or myself. However, when I did, I realized that I had gone through my ultimate change. No, I did not become a cynic, but my mind was definitely and irrevocably cleared of any illusions about honest politics, especially, about the final dismissal of communism.

The bulk of intellectuals I knew from communist times joined either the nationalist camp or the camp seeking Communist Party reform. The latter was equivocally relabeled "socialist" and implied that the violation of human rights constituted the only significant difference between dictatorial communism and democratic socialism. Those intellectuals who had been fully isolated by the communist regime and were now seizing an opportunity to satisfy their insatiable hunger for power embodied another characteristic metamorphosis. All of them strove to lead the camp of the anticommunist forces without bothering to conceal their personal frustration as a motive. Some of them appeared pathetic in their rhetorical impotence, but others were cynical enough to grab the utmost power available and manipulate it cruelly on behalf of their personal ambitions. Their creed was vengeful: "They destroyed our lives; now it's our turn to destroy theirs."

While there were some who were openly brutal in their quest for power, many young intellectuals (most of them from privileged communist families) adopted a more sophisticated strategy. The crux of this strategy was to preserve the middle-ground power channels from newcomers who were regarded as intruders with unpredictable orientations. The latter included genuine anticommunists, anarchists, and artists—even scholars who lacked any political fervor but were simply swept into action by the common euphoria. The most vocal team of those young sons and daughters of top-level communist functionaries (including acting members of the BCP Central Committee) disguised themselves as sociologists and philosophers. In this capacity, they occupied the mainstream intellectual media and began to preach abstract postmodern explanations of democratizing communism. They even went so far as to justify why communists should remain in power. Nevertheless, the major task of those intellectuals was to maintain the invisible party grip on the burgeoning pluralist groups, clubs, and associations of liberated intellectuals.

My attempts to play a role in these events offered innumerable occasions to deal with such people. My first endeavor after Zhivkov's fall was to initiate a group of fellow reporters to found a club of independent journalists. The sociology of the emerging club deserves a whole study of its own, but for the purposes of this book I will single out only Yuri Aslauov, whose father was a retired high-ranking party boss. Smart, well read, and skeptical, Yuri showed up as a sociologist, who, before November 10, 1989, had been linked with the Bulgarian Trade Union's headquarters.

At the very beginning, I gathered a number of colleagues and we met several times in my apartment until we found a room at the university for our meetings. Everything went so spontaneously. No agenda, no plans, no strategies (just the enthusiasm of finally being free to decide something for ourselves). In fact, everything went spontaneously right up until the day we had to construct our bylaws and apply for registration as an official organization. At that point, I was told that a similar group was forming in Sofia and that it was worth pooling our efforts and interests. I must say, of course, that I was regarded as one who had conducted his professional life with rare independence; I was a nonaligned, unassociated, and suspiciously resourceful journalist. In this sense, my authority as a spotless person was largely recognized. Moreover, it was exactly this neutral position of mine that made me look dangerous to the metamorphosing party establishment.

So, I established contact with the other group who listed young journalists mainly from the police-watched Sofia Press, the agency authorized to export news from Bulgaria in editions translated into several languages. I was not very happy about cooperating with people I had not chosen myself, and I confess that my choice was based partly on my intuition and partly on my personal criteria for fairness, professionalism, and reliability. Once I believe in the righteousness of my undertaking, however, I am neither cunning nor able to protect myself.

The informal leader of the other group was Yuri. We liked each other, so there were no personal obstacles to cooperation. He played the role of a well-informed and well-connected person and made the necessary arrangements for the material base of our budding organization. When elections for president took place, he and I were obvious candidates. He won by a small margin.

At that time, mid-January, 1990, the Bulgarian Union of Journalists was among the first professional organizations in the country to schedule a congress with the purpose of electing noncommunist leaders and changing its bylaws in accordance with the spirit of the time. The incumbent president was a notorious communist, and the entire governing body was composed in the communist past. A well-known pen-brother, Stephan Prodev, himself a communist, was not even a member of the union because of his opposition to its communist leadership and his alleged involvement in the first anti-Zhivkov ecological movement in 1988.

On the eve of this congress, our club was regarded as the main opposition force outside the union, and we had to fight for admission to the congress, as auditors only. Admission was granted for twenty persons thanks to Yuri's connections with one of the union vice presidents, a journalist positioned in the top hierarchy of the Bulgarian Trade Union. We got twenty passes, but it was again Yuri who took care to distribute them, even though no one had bothered to make a list of our delegates. On the opening day of the union's congress, Yuri proudly told me that Stephan Prodev had been guaranteed access to the congress with one of our delegate passes.

I considered this a matter of course and even felt glad that such a hopeful personality had been given the chance to fight for our cause, a cause dedicated to nothing short of the full dismantling of the union and the free reunification of journalists according to their choices and interests.

A hot debate exploded and we soon found ourselves fully engaged. Prodev took the floor and delivered a moderate speech seeking a compromise between the two extremes (dismantling the union or preserving it in its present form). Several hours later, I suddenly understood the whole intrigue. When the election period began, a woman in the middle of the hall stood up and nominated Prodev for president. She was an unpredictable person, but I knew her only as a formerly repressed translator from the BTA staff and had no reason to suspect her of being involved in any wrongful machinations. More nominations were proposed than expected, so the election progressed slowly and chaotically, sparkling all the while with blistering debates. Finally, Prodev and Yuri's Trade Union connection were the two candidates left for the final vote. Stephan Prodev was elected by a substantial majority.

However, this was only half of the big intrigue. I did not know Prodev personally, although I remembered him publishing an unusually critical article of mine in the communist intellectual newspaper he used to edit before his so-called dissident period. In short, I had little reason to disapprove of his election. I was just upset by the way our feeble "independent" organization had been used to promote him to the top. Only two months later, the same "dissident" Prodev was appointed editor in chief of the notorious central organ of the BCP *Rabotnitchesko Delo* *(Workers' Deed)*, which he immediately renamed *Duma (Word)*, the publication of the turncoat BSP. Within three months, he became a communist MP and turned into the most vehement adversary of democratic forces in the country.

After all of this happened, I started to have reservations about Yuri's real allegiances. But I could only suspect him in the absence of any proof, since his behavior was ostensibly critical, liberal, and (on the surface, at least) independent. Nonetheless, he joined an offshoot of the reformed Communist Party and then resigned. He was later appointed editor in chief of a moderate newspaper, which was allegedly funded by laundered communist money. Finally, he ended up as a poll analyst for the newly established Institute for the Study of Public Opinion. That institute consisted of the same young Komsomol-grown sociologists who then claimed neutrality.

Thousands of similar examples (regardless of the level or the people involved) demonstrate the same basic pattern of profiting from the naïveté and disturbing lack of pragmatism in honest intellectuals, of obliterating all roads leading from the outskirts to the key positions of the power pyramid.

Still, at least some honest intellectuals possessed the guts and skill to infiltrate the top by using independent roads. Their disappointment and ultimate resignation from postcommunist East European politics offers the strongest evidence of the impotence of any democratic alternative to a communist establishment that is well-entrenched, professionally mobilized, and viscerally supported by the electorate. I had the privilege to be close friends with one such rare bird in Bulgaria and to follow up his after-Zhivkov political career.

Even though his father had been a member of the Communist Party, my dear friend Dr. Boyko Proytchev was a unique example of an intellectual who had no inclination whatsoever to view Bulgarian affairs from a communist standpoint. Alternatively, he regarded Bulgaria from the perspective of her nationalistic tradition, born and raised in the bosom of the Bulgarian bourgeoisie at the turn of this century. Boyko was a royalist at heart, and he was convinced that a bourgeois republican government under a paternalistic king would be the best political state for this peace-seeking Balkan country. No matter the slight old-fashioned touch that his political views conveyed (and of which he was aware), Boyko was a believer in national intellectual values whose natural evolution had been abruptly cut down when the communists assumed power. Thus, he rejected communism as an ideology and political regime that were foreign to this nation. At the same time, he fantasized about substituting it with a political ideology deprived of any practical utility under the circumstances. In both his predilections, Boyko mistook intellectual values for national values. He was blind to the visceral support communism enjoyed with the large population, and this rendered his elitist stance something of a castle-building enterprise. Ironically, I have always had a great deal of respect for and empathy with castle-building philosophers.

I am making the above assessment of Boyko's political orientations today, but after I met him in 1987, I simply yielded to his vehement anticommunism. We both had no clear ideas about the way communism should be abolished, and especially about its prospective alternatives, but the opportunity to share masochistically our disgust for the totalitarian regime helped build a solid bond between us. I owe a great deal of my disillusionment with real communism to Boyko. While my apathy produced an ambiguous, and to some extent compromising, attitude vis-à-vis my living

conditions and political neutrality, Boyko was clearly subversive and prepared to act against the regime.

But with whom? That was the question we used to discuss late into the
night, and our lack of potential disciples caused us both frustration. Boyko
was married but had no children. He told me unequivocally that this was
a conscious contract between his wife and himself. They were both pessi-
mistic about the future of Bulgaria, the communist camp, and the whole
of mankind. In addition to that, Boyko's thinking was not guided by any
humanistic motives; I would say that his misanthropy prevailed over his
compassion for the suffering human race. Although his was a rather rational indifference toward people, born of frustration and desperation, it was
one of the clues to the complexity of his motives and reactions.

Boyko listened devoutly to the BBC and Radio Free Europe in Bulgarian and maintained some contacts with the Bulgarian royal family in
Madrid, the American chargé d'affaires in Sofia, and with a classmate of
his, Dr. Konstantin Trencheff. The latter was also married but childless and
(according to Boyko's accounts) despised and hated communists. Dr.
Trencheff's father was also recognized as an Active Fighter against Fascism
and Capitalism. The role of these contacts amounted by and large to mani-
festing a presence as an anticommunist citizen rather than to some con-
spiratorial activity. However, they proved helpful once the opportunity of
passing from visceral hatred to political struggle had emerged.

When the Turkish events of 1989 began and Zhivkov's regime seemed
somewhat shaken, Dr. Trencheff risked several unequivocal statements de-
nouncing the human rights violations against the Turkish minority. He was
second to Zhelyu Zhelev in giving interviews to the BBC and Radio Free
Europe, where Zhivkov's policy was frequently criticized. Dr. Trencheff was
promptly taken into custody by the Sofia police and spent the summer of
1989 in jail, without any formal charges being raised against him. The day
after the communists conducted their palace coup against Todor Zhivkov,
and the country's democratic hopes rose dramatically, Boyko and Dr.
Trencheff engaged in the emerging democratic coalition. Their strategy was
based on the decommunization of the Bulgarian Trade Union. Following
the model of Lech Walesa's Solidarnosz in Poland, Dr. Trencheff had already
set up a dissident trade union in the winter of 1989. He named it Podkrepa
(Support) and applied for its legal registration on the premise that Bulgarian
law did not foreclose the establishment of alternative labor organizations.
Since the BCP and its chief stood above the law, they never authorized Dr.
Trencheff's trade union and denigrated the self-proclaimed leader. Thus,

until November, 1989, a dozen marginal people represented Podkrepa, and its "headquarters" was Dr. Trencheff's apartment in Stara Zagora. After Zhivkov's fall, the two physicians poured all their energy into structuring the new organization, making it broad-based and national, and legalizing its existence. Their ultimate goal was for Podkrepa to absorb the mass of the communist unions, and to become *the* modern, democratic organization of Bulgarian workers, following the example of Solidarnosz.

Although contradictory in its goal, theirs was an intelligent strategy, since such an organization would quickly gain mass support based on something tangible for the electorate (the defense of their professional rights and freedoms). By attacking the nonpluralist character of the communist trade unions, they were in fact headed for another form of monopolism. At the same time, it was difficult to anticipate that the mushrooming political parties would be able to advance any winning political platform capable of attracting major support. Amidst the post-Zhivkov political chaos in the country, it mattered very little that trade unions were not, by definition, political organizations (i.e., eligible for the legislature or the government). To Dr. Trencheff, Podkrepa was merely a vehicle for achieving his political ambitions, a vehicle fueled by sheer anticommunism and a personal thirst for power.

For a certain amount of time, this strategy proved successful. Owing to the extremes of his anticommunism, Dr. Trencheff was admired and supported by many. He did not commit the mistake of running for MP or for any other office, he just built his organization carefully, making certain he was its undisputed leader. My dear friend Boyko was appointed his personal political adviser. He became Dr. Trencheff's right arm. "The Doctor's" popularity was gradually declining after his failure to promote a viable democratic alternative to the popular communism of the redressed BCP. Boyko and his friend stood in opposition to the communists and to the new democratic right as well. To a certain extent, they fought for politics based on morality, or for "honesty in politics." They claimed to offer a long-term strategy for communist cleansing in the country, one based on moderate royalism, populist trade unionism, and bourgeois morality. At no time did Boyko express a belief that communism would be overthrown immediately, or that communism would not withstand the unfocused "revolution" of the early 1990s. Instead, he opted for a slow, evolutionary substitution of the communist establishment, first by experts and then by mature middle-class politicians. During the period I am talking about, though, the country was desperately short of such politicians.

During the first months after the palace coup (and probably up to the second election held in October, 1991), to be a politician in Bulgaria meant to stay out on the streets and face the crowds courageously. These were the months of personal revenge. Yesterday's powerful communists went into hiding, barricading themselves behind the walls of their houses and police departments. Boyko confided that he was extremely pleased to see and feel how communist big shots bent over backward to please him, hoping to win his good graces. And he was especially appalled by the venality of human nature when it came to obtaining power, privileges, and popularity. Dr. Trencheff's organization was crucial in building a winning electoral strategy, in appointing ministers, even in propelling draft-laws with the legislature, and a great many people waited in front of their doors seeking favor and support. Dozens of press conferences were organized daily, and they were a major source of anticommunist rhetoric. People felt as if they had just been released from jail and they wanted to sell the public their personal methods for saving the country. Democracy was on sale and the prices were falling fast.

Boyko almost completely disappeared from the quiet circle of friends who used to gather for wine and talk. He was in his element. From early morning until late in the evening he met with "important" contacts or with common people. He traveled around the country, visited foreign embassies, and attended cocktail parties. Cocktail parties became one of the chief means of democratizing the country. On one hand, they provided an anticipated luster (mistaken for legitimacy) to the new political hustle; on the other, they were the best opportunity to talk to the extremely busy, newly hatched political guys. Boyko had become just such a new guy.

I can testify that he was busy. I hardly ever had a chance to see him, even when I called him for behind-the-scenes information, which I sometimes needed for my political commentaries. My wife noticed that he had become high-minded, aloof, and exhausted. He often behaved as a fugitive. But in the euphoria, he still radiated satisfaction and optimism. He would come late at night to tell us about the latest husking, or about how much he had enjoyed the fire at the Central Party House, or about the forthcoming hunger strike by MPs from the democratic union aimed at disbanding the communist-laden Parliament, or simply to share with us the happy thought that *we would get them shortly.* It was only later, when every smart politician realized that it would not be so easy to get them shortly, if at all, that he began to avoid our company and retreat into an increasing public loneliness.

What Boyko complained of most was the complete lack of rules. "You can't trust anybody except yourself," he used to say, although he trusted his boss and friend, Dr. Trencheff. In fact, there was only one rule to which they both strictly adhered: pick out the disguised communists and under no circumstances strike a deal with them. This served as a kind of admirable moral watershed. Beyond that, no other morality was robust enough to withstand the intricacies of everyday political bargaining.

Resources were simply insufficient to pursue a struggle against an experienced and pitiless adversary. Coalitions fell apart, promising figures betrayed their disciples, bribes and perks corrupted the newcomers, the electorate oscillated from side to side, and living conditions deteriorated. Political reality turned out to be very different from political dreams and prejudices. No front against the communists emerged. After Dr. Trencheff and Boyko began to realize their isolation, they gradually lost their scruples, and with them both the momentum of their initial euphoria and their moral leadership. In their deflation, they had but two choices: to yield to the immoral realm or to withdraw. The boss chose to yield. Boyko resigned.

By 1992, there was nothing left of our hopeful, highly optimistic euphoria from the "revolutionary" year 1989. A general collapse of values replaced the hopes for a change. Pragmatism took the place of concepts. The prevailing feeling was that we had been deceived, deceived by ourselves. Boyko got it partly right when he said that the whole construct of moral politics to which we had adhered, was wrong, useless. Politics is practical action, not theory or wishful thinking. And practical action needs to succeed no matter what, because what is at stake is power.

By blaming the circumstances, we failed as individuals. I retreated into my former apathy and applied for immigration to Canada. Boyko retreated into lonely reflection about Bulgaria's lost glory and eroded national pride. His wife immigrated to the United States in 1991, where she is now practicing medicine. The wife of his boss and friend, Dr. Trencheff, reached the United States even earlier and is now a licensed nurse in a New York public hospital. Neither couple has divorced.

We all belong to a broken generation. *Sauve qui peut* is our logical alternative after so many years of brainwashing, anticipation, apprehension, and deceit.

CHAPTER 8

Nostalgia

You cannot be a communist and a free man.

—*Milovan Djilas*

Before stopping at the Varna terminal, the train makes a large curve and, despite their precursory deceleration, the wheels always whistle. I listen to this heartbreaking whistle as I stand by the open door of the wagon, ready to jump off on the platform. As a rule, it is always half dawn when the train goes silent. Then I hear the herring gulls' squawk, the song of my earliest childhood. Everywhere else around the world, birds' squawking or even mellifluous singing wakes me before daybreak, but never in Varna, where strangers complain about the ugly morning sounds of my soothing herring gulls.

The clock tower atop the shabby nineteenth-century railway station is barely brushed by a first pink-yellow ray when I arrive on a summer morning, or reposes in a predawn ink-blue sky if my arrival is in winter. But the air is always sea fresh. Varna has been my point of departure. Now it is the mirage of return.

A popular poem by a tender Bulgarian poet from the late nineteenth century, this nation's equivalent of Robert Burns, portrays the quintessential return in a line that reads, "Coming back to father's house." With regard to myself, alas, this is irrelevant. Not because we had no cherry tree in the backyard, nor because my father lacked a house of his own, but because something alienated my soul from my father. I just do not get emotional about him. Neither he nor I bear any guilt about this. Our natural link was either disrupted by communism or it never materialized.

When my plane takes off from the Varna airport, I see the graveyard where my grandma's remains lie. She had always seen me off on my journeys, and that is why my return is a comeback to grandma's tomb.

Before the plane lands, I watch the lake on the south side of the runway and hope to glimpse for a brief moment the treeless graveyard. Most often I fail, but I know that she is there. I want her to meet me and ask me what new has come out of my broken life. For her, communism was a project full of hopes, a project in which she had never really participated. For my father, communism was no project, although he yielded entirely to the ordinance for turning it into a project. And that made all the difference.

As a dream, communism is quite an endeavor; as a reality, communism is nothing but coercion. Both dream and coercion are, of course, part of human nature. I find no contradiction in claiming that both communism and anticommunism reflect human nature. The former fits one kind of instincts, while the latter is born from another range of impulses. The point is to admit that people warrant the difference. In one kind of people, communist instincts prevail to the extent of inhibiting all other aspirations; in another kind, the striving for freedom and justice takes over the egalitarian neglect for individual values.

I know that wherever I may find myself in the world, I will quickly meet people from both realms gazing suspiciously at one another. It does not matter that all these people are washed in a sea of claims that history is made, led, created, constructed, and even written by some specially designated representatives of mankind. These "subjects of history" will always know it is *their* obscure lives that determine how society works.

I know that if I ever leap off the train at the Varna railway station again, I will be diving into a context of animosities. Real communism in Bulgaria had clearly distinguished two categories: its visceral supporters and its rational detractors. They still know each other all too well and have no pity for one another.

I am as sure of this judgment as a Westerner is ready to give in to the claims of victimization uttered fervently by experts on communism. Had I already become a Westerner myself, I would leap out of the chartered airplane into the summer midnight charm of the remote town of Varna and would walk down the meandering small streets toward the sea. I would listen to the people talking, singing their songs, or drinking noisily in their tiny yards lit by an outdoor lamp, at a table under leafy trellised vines. I would have a drink in one of the numerous tiny bars in the quiet neighborhoods or along the main street. I would remember how, on a September afternoon in 1992, an air-conditioned bus crossed for the last time in this man's life this same town, cutting off all hope for his return forever. *Lasciate ogni speranza* was not just a cultural icon in his mind, but also a watershed imperative in his real, fleshly life. The difference, though, was that he thought he had exchanged a hell for a paradise, in contrast to those of Dante's *uomini,* who left earth only to enter purgatory, or the lasting inferno.

Yet if the dusty beauty of this hell stabbed the man's soul, it caused a mellow pain. Fig trees peep over wooden fences into the narrow cul-de-sacs. Garage gates stand wide open, their wooden arrows inviting to a workshop's coolness now turned into a primitive coffee bar. The man's former schoolyard is deserted, the façade of the old school molting with dry plaster. The park is evergreen, the sea ever emerald, and the sky ever blue. White toy ships are sprinkled around the bay. Time's ripples stand still under the sun, the only perceptible movement being the man's farewell, the parting that occurred deep inside his brain.

Had I not been a regular on these streets, I would indeed have stopped my imagination somewhere between the gold-yellow beach and the light-house keeping watch on the bay to the south. I would tell everybody that I had found a paradise on earth. Even though this were a sheer exaggeration, people would believe my words since it is always soothing to imagine that earth is not deprived of paradises.

In July, 1998, I did indeed jump off the train at the Varna railway station. It was a hot summer noon, and I was coming back for a visit—this time as a Westerner. My ten-year-old daughter, Bistra, a Canadian citizen, an English speaker, and a stranger to the city, accompanied me in my aching homesickness. What I found and saw was far from the sweet pictures drawn by my imagination. I found people inflamed against each other. Both warring sides have been frustrated: communism's backers because they were losing their existential paradise, and communism's detractors because they were not seeing the establishment of the new social paradise.

Lamentably, the blueprints for a new social order are still nowhere to be found, while the experience of a certain existential security under the communist rulers is still vivid in people's memories. Bulgarians are not daydreamers; or, more precisely, they only fantasize after a hearty dinner. They are not gamblers either; or, if someone behaves like one, it raises suspicions about the individual's soundness of mind. Above all, Bulgarian folks are highly cautious before standing up for a cause if the material profit is not plainly in sight. "Bread and wine for all" was clearly written all over the communist flag, and the communist system was cast painlessly over them as easily as one might spread out a tablecloth for dinner guests. Now, for much the same reason, many Bulgarians—and many Balkan people, for that matter—are still feeling nostalgic about communism. They no longer see food and lodging for all on the banner of democracy, but *freedom for all and prosperity for some,* with neither prosperity nor freedom offering tangible returns. In this sense, the communist brainwashing acquires a more complex meaning. It had not only cleansed the critical faculties of people vis-à-vis the totalitarian character of the regime, but it had washed away the building blocks for an alternative project of a noncommunist society.

Incidentally, what else did we, the detractors of totalitarianism, do beyond our quarrel with the communists? As far as I am concerned, I appear now to have been a proponent of *"distancing,"* perhaps only a more subtle way of saying "apathy." To distance myself from this demeaning environment involved a kind of existential philosophy. Having grown up in such a patriotic spiritual climate, I at first rejected the alternative to flee the country. To remain required a flexible bargain that would provide at least some emotional and intellectual comfort amidst the common blank of communist living. The bargain was this: I consciously yielded to a way of life overseen by the omnipotent but deficient-in-imagination communists; that is, I fulfilled my duties as a citizen, regardless of how dull and aimless I found them to be, and I did not openly utter my discontent. In return, I was not harassed in my private undertakings, which were preemptively apolitical and asocial. I was an escapist par excellence.

Escapists abound in most intellectual classes in the world. Under communism, however, escapism was not a viable modus vivendi, because communism's repulsive nature demanded that the regime be fought. Healthy behavior in an ill society was unacceptable as it actually helped the evil thrive.

My own small measure of happiness depended on finding all kinds of occasions simply to ignore the surroundings and indulge in meditation, self-perfection, and return to nature. Ordinary life was depressing. Intellectual talks at tea, philosophizing over abstract spiritual concepts, and imitating social importance by gathering with other disgruntled members of the intelligentsia were means of assigning some acceptable meaning to our (by definition) *extraordinary* life. I do not contend that I was idle, dumb, or criminal altogether, but under the circumstances my detachment must have been as suspicious as it was socially irrelevant, and to some degree pernicious.

Nevertheless, something extraordinary happened with my life at one point. In the late summer of 1982 I met a young woman. She was an English teacher. In a matter of days, she became the most extraordinary woman of my life.

When she first saw me, I was thirty-six years of age and she was twenty-four. When I first saw her, she was a nonchalant, charming, fragile divorcee, the mother of a two-year-old son, while I was a solid professor, the father of four wonderful children, and a purportedly good husband. The gray sky of communist politics covered our lives—forever, or so we thought. The underground of thick, parochial mores infiltrated our bodies.

Does it take special courage to plunge into a love story under these circumstances? I still do not know. I leave it to our children to judge. Wish it or not, there happened a love story that also shaped their lives.

To be sure, it all started in the most innocent way. We had been independently hired as translators for an international medical conference held in a seaside hotel near Varna. Those four days changed our lives and the lives of many other people.

At the end of the first day, I invited her to join me for a cup of coffee in the hotel bar. She told me she was thrilled to see me around. The coffee tasted of clove and bitter almonds. I looked at the bottom of my cup and saw a thick, even, dark-brown deposit with no indication of fateful events to come.

On the second day, she asked me to drive her home after work. I did so gladly, noticing again that she had big, green eyes and a joyous, roundish hip. Maybe I told her this. Maybe not. Our consciousness is utterly unaware of any signs of forthcoming fire. An incidental woman, still a complete stranger, can have no meaning in a man's orderly life. Or can she? Can memory tell at what fatal second the spark was lit over the stack of flammable hay in our souls?

The conference participants were taken by bus to a farm for apple picking on the third day. An early October afternoon in a Balkan orchard seems to be a perfect stage for a man and a woman to talk of love. Or even to make love had they been left on their own. But we could be together only in the crowd, so we talked about literature, teaching, and family matters. After the apple picking there was a cocktail party at sunset in a small restaurant overlooking the lake. She was sipping chilled white wine from a crystal glass; I was holding a mug of icy beer and entertaining a small group of foreigners. Again, she looked at this interesting professor of anatomy anticipating no future with him, perhaps only sensing her momentous female power in the flirtation: the power of female modesty in a male-dominated culture where no one really knows who makes decisions for a date or intercourse or marriage. . . .

By the evening of the fourth day, my epiphany was that I did not want this charming conference to end. There was this woman with the smiling green eyes. The new relationship seemed just about to die. I loathed the separation, since, as one of my colleagues used to repeat, any separation is a minor death. Was it actually a separation? Why did I think of it as a separation? Life would move on to its usual course, and, amidst the general course of events, this would be just an episode, an insignificant encounter of a man and a woman—perfect strangers in an estranged society dominated by political and material concerns. It looked like an episode, indeed.

However, after a week or so, I saw the young English teacher on campus and impulsively invited her home for dinner. I was proud of my family and, no doubt, I craved to show off as a caring father and loving husband. I was doing exactly the opposite of what I had to, I suppose. There was, alas, no one around to warn me that this was the distant thunder of an upcoming shake-up.

There is no better phrase to express what fell upon me a couple of days later but the French *coup de foudre.* I fell in love. She fell in love, too. Nothing was premeditated. We had no plans for a future. Or for *the* future. We simply ran into one another and plunged into our autumn of secret dating. We had sex in an empty hotel closed for the off-season: a classmate of mine who happened to be the manager provided the key. This was a car love; our only reliable intimate space was my small Škoda car. The advantage of a love car is that it is mobile.

Movement was critical. It took everyone by surprise, myself most of all. I gave up my professorship and we moved to Sofia. There was the nearly two-year struggle for divorce before I finally obtained a settlement. Meanwhile, I had become a freelance journalist, she an English professor in Sofia University. My kids stayed in Varna. Only her son lived with us. Then, three years later she wanted us to have a child of our own.

That is how we laid the foundation of our ivory tower. We tried to live happily in it, anticipating no changes whatsoever until death do us part. Life ruled differently, however.

To choose an ivory tower instead of resorting to insane drinking was largely a matter of temperament. Indulging in promiscuous sex was yet another obsessive preoccupation hypertrophied because of social idleness. The beauty of our motherland's sceneries was also a source of escape, which elevated somewhat our individual sense of purity. To climb alone the high mountain and to contemplate the heavens in sublime loneliness meant to appreciate the spiritual strength of God and to spit contemptuously over the political crap below. Every individual form of protest that reached the public unsanctioned evoked unwarranted admiration. More realistically, these "protests" were simply allowed to pass unsanctioned because of their obvious harmlessness to the regime. In fact, they mistakenly increased the ivory tower mentality instead of uniting us all in a self-sacrificing front against the common foe.

Aimed at criticizing the pawns of the regime, or in most cases just abstract artistry, creativity also became a vehicle for escape. In my case, medicine (more specifically, medical research) was believed to shield my personality from involvement with social issues by virtue of its apolitical neutrality. But I also played the role of the local patron with actors and painters, not in terms of funding, of course, but in terms of "creating an ambiance" for their offstage social performances. Many among them were my friends. Now, when viewed from a distance, our group appears to me a colorful medley of snobs, unfulfilled stars, bons vivants, provincial geniuses, and bitter lame ducks. We adopted the bohemian posture as art, and the artistic products of our deep discontent as a form of social revolt. It was fun, and it helped us forget communist reality.

We actually pretended to be genuine and integral. The truth is, we were artificial and fragmented. Those among us who saw through the pretence felt truly frustrated. Most of us, however, preferred to float along the surface, and ended up believing that this artifactual creativity was a sublime emanation of the chained human spirit.

Despite these vain strains of a lost generation, and in contradiction to my present irony, I fancied my 1998 visit to Bulgaria as a comeback in the middle of the same warming aloofness. The nostalgia that evoked memories of the evergreen park, the ever-emerald sea, and the ever-blue sky caused a lump in my throat when I walked down the platform of the Varna railway station. And it will cause a lump in my throat every time I remember Bulgaria.

I wish everything could start anew. I wish we (the same country that I used to call mine, that is, and I) could be reborn and reshaped into another type of society. I wish that communism had been nothing but a historical artifact. Lamentably, communism is *the* fact of history, while we—its prisoners, supporters, and sometimes detractors—are the artifacts.

The desire to detach ourselves physically from communism had first seriously crossed my wife's and my mind in 1990, when we were vacationing at the Black Sea. It was September, the season when the sea deposits its summer fatigue under a still unfragmented, endearing sun. Along with a couple of British journalists, friends who had shared with us the frenzy of the first post-Zhivkov year, we were almost the only dwellers at a luxurious seaside hotel that had been restricted to the privileged families of Politburo members. We were "rich and free," although I could not envision wealth and freedom extending into the foreseeable future with any impunity or, at the very least, painful tradeoffs. Despite our soaring mood and apparently inexhaustible resources for a useful life, my soul was not free of anxiety.

The officially sanctioned disentanglement from the totalitarian communist system had begun nearly a year earlier, in 1989. We had never before thought seriously about quitting. The reason for this was that we had never before seen communism as an organism, a being, a historic character. However, after having been given time to observe communism from the periphery, we were thunderstruck by its actual, enormous presence.

I became obsessed with the desire to disentangle myself from its powerful hug. My wife was equally engaged in the process, and we both never had the smallest doubt that our children's free development was possible only outside the communist body. The ivory tower that had been possible to maintain under communism, was no longer a viable alternative. We could no longer delude ourselves into thinking that we could adequately distance our family anywhere in Bulgaria. It suddenly became clear to me that our family's prosperity should be sought out in another land. Today, however, my concern is not with the rectitude of my family's considerations, which are self-evident, but with the revealing impact of the postdictatorial era of Eastern European communism on our individual fortunes.

We immediately realized that the decision we faced was neither trivial nor profane. We walked down the dear streets of our native town filled with the anticipation of nostalgia that we knew would invade our hearts after we left it for the last time. We wanted to reconsider for one last time our deepest knowledge of what we were about to leave behind, since we had only a glimmer of information about what we were heading into.

Expectations drive our moves; routine, laden with memories, anchors us. Someone had cast our anchor on this beautiful soil, and expectations should largely exceed routine if our resolve to weigh anchor was to succeed. The dilemma might seem expendable to people of the New World, but it is unavoidable, even indispensable, for those born in old Europe. Departure is dramatic, and it is experienced as a loss. Return is problematic, so one usually quits for good. Attachment to the native land is part of one's identity; therefore, any displacement is regarded as at least a partial loss of identity. Only in the light of this cultural context can one fully realize the disruptive force of communism.

After bidding farewell to Varna, on our way back to Sofia we stopped off at the place we fancied was void of communism: our old peasant house, still kept erect at the bottom of the green yard. If we had ever been truly happy in our communist years, it was in its remote yard. If we are ever asked to give a name to our own ivory tower, we would not hesitate for a second to answer that this yard and its superb view of the surrounding peaks was its physical embodiment. Here, in privileged isolation, we enjoyed the presence of the people we truly loved: our children and our intimate friends. Here we beheld the ecstasy of nature, the silence full of fertile animation, the flowing line of masterly superposed reminiscences, the unfragmented colors of the rolling sun replaced late in the evenings by a black-purple sky sprinkled with stars. Here we read the books that elevated our characters above any communist context. Here I listened to Wagnerian operas in the company of a friend of mine who was a connoisseur of this composer's musical philosophy and a devout follower of Rudolf Steiner's theosophy. Here another friend, a secret follower of the Bulgarian White Brotherhood, initiated us in the mysteries of astrology.

Finally, it was here that we felt our physiology stripped of communism, although on a rational level we spent hours analyzing our moving bargain with it. On one hand, this place recharged our social batteries, exhausted from our forceful compliance with communism. On the other, it fueled our intellectual reluctance to extend this compliance into our whole lifetime. Trapped by communism, we had found a room of unbelievable luster to feed our intellectual hedonism. Now, I realize that we overappreciated this place because we had made it inaccessible to communism by virtue of our imagination. But beyond any rationality, our affinity for this corner of perfect vibrations was a strong argument for staying in Bulgaria and living through the whole agony of democracy in *her* wishful attempt to knock down communism's robust body.

We returned to Sofia with mixed feelings, burdened with a task of ultimate importance: to assess the short-term chance democracy had of prevailing over communism. The difference between our former compliance with communism and our present disentanglement from it was essential. In both cases, communism was there, but in our past we had been embedded in it and, whether we wished it or not, we felt we were part of its body. Now, by contrast, we were detached and able to observe it from outside, even under the microscope. The truth is, its sticky vitality and endurance stupefied us.

Awash in so many memories, rooted patriotically in the proud past of our land, and having suffered through the diminishing presence of totalitarian communism, we stood perplexed before the huge presence of Another Communism in it. We faced a real, nonenhanced communism within a much-unexpected context. This was a communism that aspired to remain forever, to command and determine destinies and orientations stemming from the very mentality of our fellow citizens.

Having spent all forty-five years of my existence within the totalitarian bed of Soviet-style communism, I imagined its end as a momentous act of evaporation, of sublimation without traces. Having never lived before in a free society, I indulged myself in dreams of what all of us had long waited for: freedom, market competition, and private initiative.

As far as many of us were concerned, the totalitarian communist body was decapitated suddenly, although with an acceptable historic logic. When this happened, we could not have expected another body to emerge from beneath the stripped totalitarian clothing, only to sprout a new head in the same manner a hydra would resist extermination. We should have. Again facing another aspect of the communist brainwashing, I must say that had I not been self-fed with the above illusions, I would have been well equipped to face this new body, and could have avoided galvanizing my resolve to flee the creature.

I regret today that we emptied our ivory tower of any practical analysis of communism, giving in to the pleasure of hating it without dissecting it. Consequently, we were convinced that communism would fall apart by itself, since we believed it was eroding from within. It was, unfortunately, only rust (economic rust) that we mistook for chronic erosion. Our slow epiphany was in seeing that the so-called centrally planned economy was only the cheap clothing that garbed the communist body. Its tenacious interior consisted of living "common" people guided by a rigid mentality fit into the precept of communist social theory. Thus, our ivory tower became a monument to my personal failure. As such, it now seemed easier to give up its natural beauty and to rely on expectations.

As the editor of a newspaper that had never been regarded with indifference or moderation (it was either fully rejected or fully accepted) and as an industrious member of the journalistic community, I had the chance to live and operate in the very center of the post-Zhivkov turmoil. It was actually post-Gorbachev turmoil, because everybody was aware that Mikhail Gorbachev had lost his grip over the formerly consolidated socialist camp. He was losing the absolutely required grip on power in his own capital, too. There is no doubt that the flagging spirit on our side of the Iron Curtain began with Gorbachev, and because of Gorbachev, and that the system as a whole was falling apart.

Upon our return to Sofia, I was concerned about the people's enduring ability to cope. What part of the communist body was due to the Balkan mentality and what part of it was related to some genuine features that might be defined as a communist mentality? Or did they overlap? When I say that I was in the center of the post-Zhivkov turmoil, I mean that I was an observer of both the everyday works of the National Assembly and the behind-the-scenes political trade that characterized this work. After Zhivkov and his Central Committee lost control over the Council of Ministers, the latter was submitted to the authority of the legislature. The newly established presidency was regarded as a conciliatory, peacekeeping institution. Thus, all real and potential power in Bulgarian politics was concentrated within the National Assembly. In theory, this was a correct interpretation of the badly needed democracy. In practice, however, the degree of real democracy depended on the freshly elected parliamentarians' individual attitudes toward democracy.

Except for the communist MPs, representatives of the democratic alliance fell within this shrine of national power for the first time in their lives, and, to be sure, did so unexpectedly. None were trained or experienced politicians. They were former university professors, teachers, lawyers, doctors, engineers, poets, TV anchors, journalists, and economists. Here and there one might run across a worker who had actually left the factory in Zhivkov times, claiming dissident activities, but those types felt rather like a cat in a strange garret.

It is a pattern in post-Ottoman Bulgarian politics that one comes into power out of poverty. It is the easiest way to become wealthy. Power generates money, not vice versa. Obeying this pattern by natural instinct, our "democratic" hopes mastered swiftly the rules of the primitive power game. First came the small perks: the use of limousines (those left by the Zhivkov gang), hotel accommodations, special food supplies, and reserved places in elegant restaurants and the former party residences, or resort facilities at special MP rates. The serving personnel all around were the same, with the same habits and expectations; the bodyguards came from the same police department. The supply agencies could not be set anew, of course. In other words, the new people could not change the office of power. But high offices did change the small people.

It did not take long for the new people's representatives to acquire a prompt awareness of the utility of good relations with the omnipresent and omnipotent communist bureaucrats. The difference between the hotel maid or the bodyguard and the ministry clerk was only in the extent of the services they could provide; otherwise, their main skill was to serve.

Moving up through the hierarchy from the legislature to the pinnacle of executive power, where real money seemed within easy reach, required lobbying, agile networking with the useful people, and the steering of old acquaintances and contacts. There are hundreds of examples of yesterday's obscure provincial GPs or accountants or schoolteachers joining the democratic wave, strengthened miraculously by some remote kinship connections. Through participation in marginal committees, agencies, or interest groups, they crawled up to influential ministry posts. To be sure, the set of so-called economic ministries (finance, industry, economic recovery) and the privatization agency became the main targets of aspiration. And, of course, the old golden egg of Bulgarian politics, and of every poor country, for that matter—the ambassador's institution—was immediately besieged by people swearing utmost fidelity to the principles of anticommunism. Such principles were still not invented, but fidelity and anticommunism were the required golden key words that opened long-dreamed-about gates. In fact, democracy was carelessly identified as being nothing more than anticommunism. As for the two most powerful ministries—defense and the interior—they remained the strongholds of former BCP apparatchiks despite the desperate attempts of several democratic "strong men" to gain control of them. It was pure chance in Bulgaria that the top people in those ministries were moderates who prioritized professionalism over the political market. Thus, even if some dramatic changes of ministers and pathetic attempts at reform occurred, those two ministries kept far away from hot politics and their professional foundations remained firm.

I found it fascinating to follow up on the individual evolution within the heavily delineated scale of a great variety of people. The smartest were, as a rule, not the most loyal to the democratic movement, and vice versa. Genuine activists (even in those cases where they were smart) lost ground and political credibility as the process of power redistribution advanced during the hot post-Zhivkov period. I do not have sufficient evidence to claim that this period saw the birth of a new political class in Bulgaria. For me, as an observer of this chaotic movement, it seemed more like a reorientation of individuals who did not belong to a solid political background. Even communists, the real locus of power in Bulgaria, purged themselves from the old red guard and strained to reemerge with a fresh, pejoratively named, pink face.

To my greatest astonishment, morality became the crucial weapon of political confrontation. It poured on the new legislative body like a tropical rain, soaking every sensible effort for a political debate with intrigue, blackmail, and bribery. The central source of this moral dark cloud was the secret police. The first indication of the approaching tempest came as rumors that the interior minister in the 1990 communist government (a communist and long-term chief of the general staff of the Bulgarian army under Zhivkov) ordered a purge of the secret police files. One will never be able to establish with precision whether these rumors were part of a strategic plan to wreak havoc or just a routine information leak. The framework of plainclothes agents, informers within and outside of the Communist Party, and kinship links was so dense that regardless of their color (to contrast the communists who kept their traditional red, the self-made anticommunist groups called themselves "the blues" after the flag they raised at rallies) people still interacted after the old inertia.

Rumors spread with increasing speed, began filling the newspaper columns, and even penetrated the debates of the National Assembly itself. The blue MPs saw in the minister's move an attempt to cleanse the past of certain democratic rising stars. In this way, the Union of Democratic Forces (UDF) could become infiltrated with people loyal to the communists, or even worse, with people who would fear disclosure of their former collaboration with Zhivkov's police. It is certain that no one believed the files had been destroyed.

The blackmail began with blue MPs threatening some of their fellow partisans with "opening the file" in situations where a designated individual became too autonomous or disobedient, or simply broke the "unity" of the democratic forces. Because of the vast heterogeneity of this political coalition, such cases were the rule rather than the exception. So, in the very beginning, in an effort to maintain at least some solidarity, the UDF leaders too often resorted to file blackmail. This proved effective in most cases. Even President Zhelev took the liberty to officially blackmail Petar Beron, a rather unpredictable high-ranking member of the UDF, in an effort to cool his aspirations for the prime minister's office.

File blackmail became a means of verbal terrorism. Most people lived in fear of their files being publicly disclosed. Thus, even the *suspicion* that something negative might be found in a file was taken as serious evidence. Ghost files circulated among the main political actors. The ridicule achieved such absurd extremes as to "measure" which of the ghost files revealed more collaboration. "You are more compromised than I am," the blue MPs often yelled at each other.

As for the cunning communist legislators and still efficient apparatchiks, they rarely took part in such debasing affairs. Nevertheless, there is ample evidence that they pulled the strings via trusted police officials. There was always *someone* who was *ready* to show a file, or to send a file to a news-paper. In some cases this actually occurred, although one never knew the real source of the leak. With the unfolding of the file war, police commanders and even smaller fry, took illegal possession of *authentic* files and truly blackmailed elected or appointed high-ranking officials in ministries, committees, agencies, and so on. In such cases, files were not merely abstract political weapons, but valuable trump cards for achieving concrete financial goals (in the long run, everything amounted to getting rich as quickly and as painlessly as possible). The communists pursued a double objective. On one hand, they aimed at compromising and thus getting rid of strong people in the blue cohort, that is, people who were truly becoming new politicians. On the other hand, they wanted to shake the entire democratic movement by infesting it with uncertainty and suspicion, and by fragmenting it into weak fractions. They achieved both objectives.

At this point, I realized the long-term ubiquity of the communist secret police. Having personal knowledge of the ways in which people became wrapped up in its tentacles, I laughed aside all the dramatic stories and "revelations" that appeared day after day at the very center of the political struggle. It was absolutely clear to me (just as it must have been clear to the main actors in the show) that, with very few exceptions (President Zhelev being an obvious one), everyone was more or less caught in the party police net. Now the long and diligently piled up draught was taken out of the freezer and manufactured into an expensive commodity for legitimate political violence.

The plot was ingeniously simple. The Communist Party leaders anticipated that their totalitarian rule would one day fade away. The problem they needed to solve was how to regain it. Two alternatives were envisioned: either radical replacement or soft succession. Of these two, long-term preparations were made to ensure a peaceful succession. What this meant in practical terms was that all possible noncommunist or rugged anticommunist opposition was either to be eradicated or rendered vulnerable by turning its active members into stooges.

Indeed, when a green light was given to people with anticommunist sentiments to form an anticommunist, presumably democratic, alternative, the Communist Party strategists knew that most of those people were doomed to become stooges. Everyone who aspired to become an authority in the new "postcommunist" times was supposed to do so on the condition of *purity*. Their credibility was evaluated (by the electorate) exclusively on the degree to which they were able to demonstrate they had *not* collaborated with the communist regime. Noncollaboration was the moral passport a candidate needed in order to enter the new political fray on the side of the anticommunist, blue alternative.

To be sure, demonstration of noncollaboration consisted largely in claiming it, because no one was able to provide evidence. Claims were a good thing, especially in the form of an inspiring and self-elevating rhetoric, as it was during the rally period of postcommunist inebriation. Therefore, at first such claims were light-heartedly granted credibility. But when the political fistfight involved the occupants of the velvet offices, a malicious campaign ensued. It required proof for the claims, or, more often, resulted in insinuations that the proof that existed proved the falsity of the claims. No one was left innocent, because people felt free to accuse everybody else, even though the so-called proof was available only in their imagination. After someone unleashed this competition in corruption in the beginning, the process was soon progressing by its own logic.

The notorious interior minister asked for a pistol so he could shoot himself while standing at the rostrum of the National Assembly instead of handing in his long-awaited resignation. A rabid lawyer from the democratic movement declared in print that he would personally hang all former communists who tried to disqualify him as a genuine democrat. An obsessed poet from the hard anticommunist string publicly accused the president, loudly exclaiming that the latter had betrayed the UDF by using files to discredit unhandy MPs. And a high-ranking police official declared in an interview with a small turncoat newspaper that he possessed material evidence that Ahmed Dogan personally delivered a secret list of Bulgaria's top counter-intelligence agents to the Turkish embassy.

What better result could former communists expect of their efficient strategy to prevent communism from being smoothly replaced? They all stood by, including the eighty-year-old former dictator high in his mountain retreat, and enjoyed the chaos. Of course, their integrity was also at stake, and many signs showed that the processes of rearrangement and filtration were seriously initiated within the communist body.

The Bulgarian National Assembly in those months resembled a Middle-East marketplace where everyone made bargains about everything with everybody. Blue and red dissolved into a strategy for personal survival, with red being stronger, as usual. The issue of files gradually gave way to the rhetoric of extremism: Those who still held onto their democratic affiliation were accused of extremism with respect to the majority, who supported a moderate middle way.

The replacement of totalitarian communism by Western-style democracy proved an impossible alternative. During the lifetime of Eastern European regimes, this kind of alternative was envisioned only by a small group of liberally minded Western intellectuals and by naïve Eastern European intelligentsia, as evidenced in this memoir. After the fall of the regimes, it was undermined by the support the largest part of the population provided to the communist succession and evolved into an Eastern-style egalitarian socialism. The people thus supported a reformed communism consisting of a strong government, controlled economy, and welfare provisions exercised by a socialist party, as opposed to the former authoritarian dictatorship. The people simply were not ready to back free initiatives, a market economy, and the reduction of welfare benefits.

Bulgarians seemed to be afraid of democracy. They were so well accustomed to the modest benefits granted by the communist state that they hardly aspired to anything more. They were also so well conditioned to work in a take-it-easy fashion and to receive salaries as a gift for their obedience, that the mere idea of competition and effort was resentfully interpreted as a new condition of fearful loneliness. People were scared that the state might abandon them to their own resources.

All the drawbacks of this mentality, in combination with the genuine slowness of the Balkan people, showed up during the transition period that I had the chance to observe. The intelligentsia's inability to take hold of power and to exercise it for the benefit of the people doomed efforts to establish democratic rule. The paradox is that the application of democratic principles, namely free elections, worked against the establishment of true democracy. A population that was not ready for democracy voted democratically for the communist status quo. For that matter, a multi party legislature could not impose true democratic law because of the overwhelming majority of its nondemocratic coalition.

How could I live in a society based on such an essential contradiction in terms and content alike? How could I appease my moral maximalism in order to function in this unpredictable society? Was it worth sacrificing my family's well-being for an abstract cause like establishing democratic rule? Was it worth working against the leading principles of my life? Most importantly, such a decision would only be justifiable if I was motivated by a moral duty to assist the people to which *I belonged.* But did I belong to those people anymore? Moreover, was it worth applying moral principles that once again might prove fragile and wind up on the losing side? This time I was left on my own to make a choice.

I began to realize that my life had been broken because of the procommunist mentality of the people I was supposed to work with toward the fulfillment of common social goals. On top of that, I already realized that the democratic alternative was about to fail. There thus was nothing left to bolster my sense of national identity. Blood ties would not make me safer, happier, or a better achiever. By contrast, getting free of this belonging and relying on my individual identity appeared to be the only way to escape communism. It did not matter that it was impossible to unchain oneself from the blood links. There was actually no need to do so.

To be an observer of this political hullabaloo turned out to be a privileged position. I refined my sense of tolerance and respectable neutrality. Most importantly, I detached myself from the communist body. There was no question about my family staying any longer, however, since at the same time my wife and I realized that our democratic dreams were doomed to fail. I was also more accepting of the idea that the form in which totalitarian communism was bequeathed to the coming generation was the right way for my country to move ahead in her yearning for material well-being. I did not, however, see myself participating in that process. That made all the difference.

Today, I am a staunch anticommunist. To be sure, though, my anticommunism refers to the totalitarian communist body, which still lives in my memory and in the memories of my fellow intellectuals and friends, and in mankind. As far as the post-totalitarian communist body is concerned, I fled from it because it is heavily laden with communist remains, but I recognize its legacy and accept its necessity. Now, I look at Bulgaria from a distance with mixed feelings of frustration and love. I am a Bulgarian Westerner rather than a Bulgarian.

It is really startling how most of my dear Western friends continue to be captives of the same illusions that had a firm grip on me during my younger years, when I was still infected with the virus of a "just socialist society." Deep down in my heart, I fully subscribe to their idealism and basic human empathy with the deprived and disfranchised, and also with their hatred for the venal self-seeking wrath of unbridled capitalism.

However, I cannot make a political philosophy out of this elevated ethics. I am quite sure that the Western world prevailed because it was built upon better social values, such as freedom, individualism, and so forth. These values happened to be nurtured in the West. Indeed, even though the initial disintegration of the former socialist world was in part triggered by Western economic might, the communist regimes lost the Cold War competition *because* the West is a morally better world and *because* it is progressive—not because it is socially or culturally superior. Although it appeared that the immediate cause of communism's failure was economic—mismanagement and corruption of the people in power—the profound reason for the failure was moral. Much to the dismay of all of us progressively thinking individuals, the cause of communism's disintegration was not political. While I was living there, I did not know what democracy meant or was all about. But I knew, and still know quite well, what people thought about those things and that they did not give a damn about democracy.

Moreover, from the perspective of social values, there is little doubt that the West is a better world! It is obviously not the best we can imagine or the world we would like it to be, but at this moment in history, there is no better place to live, work, enjoy life, and philosophize about life and the future of humankind than the West. The larger question is whether the idea of exporting Western values—among which are civil democracy, humanitarian concerns and human rights, the supremacy of the law, the sense of social equality, social justice, and the possibility to nurture liberal values through education—is a sustainable idea.

The big issue facing us all in the so-called postcommunist era is whether the West has a moral and political right (as well as credibility, perhaps) to export these values. Do not various peoples deserve their own destiny? Should not people develop their political systems on the basis of their own historical development and cultural values? Can Western values work *everywhere* in the world? During the decade of ethnic cleansing in Yugoslavia, and in particular during the Kosovo war, I thought that NATO's cause was better and worthier than Milošević's, no matter what. But is this reason enough for intervention?

The flip side of the same problem is whether someone who has moved to the West can claim equal social and cultural status with his Western fellow citizens. Or, do people deserve only the status they acquire by birth? There are so many people who would like to come to the West and benefit from Western standards of living without having contributed to them. I think the vast majority of these people have a good case for their move to be granted. However, is this reason enough to grant them full social and cultural equality? Who is to decide? How can one decide?

I left my sea, my mountain ivory tower, some of my children, and my grandma's tomb in exchange for a social shelter. I hesitate to say that my nostalgia impairs the joy of being sheltered. To the contrary, it adds a touch of irrationality to this mostly rational experience. I cannot now exclude the possibility that in seeking an escape from communism (in facing it with reason and resolve, and rebutting its claims for a justified extension, but not just physically going away from it) my moral stance may collapse. I will certainly never know for certain whether I have become a full and integral part of this sheltering culture.

Now, sitting in my waterfront yard along the Saint Lawrence River, I contemplate a mad desire: Why was it not possible to transfer the fig tree from my native home's tiny yard, the herring gulls squawking above, and the silver sunrise over the Black Sea to North America? At the same time, I repeat to myself a maxim uttered once by photographer Robert Mapplethorpe: "I will take responsibility for my actions, but I want the freedom to act." That is my dilemma.

To be sure, everyone who immigrates to North America deposits here his or her soul's obstacles to freedom. No matter how many personal resources we immigrants mobilize to overcome this stumbling block, we will never be reborn free. It renders us close to each other. Here again, however, my obstacle is ex-Soviet communism, and this makes a great deal of difference.

I am not simply an immigrant. I am an immigrant who survived communism, distinguished, if at all, by a particularly robust instinct of compliance and serfdom. My instinct may be hidden under civilized manners, attitudes, and philosophies. Intelligence is an admirable quality, but it fails to reign over instincts and cultural roots.

The British ambassador to Sofia saw my wife and me off on our journey away from Bulgaria. Our British friends, who in their capacity as freelance correspondents to the British media took part in the Bulgarian first-year post-totalitarian euphoria, had introduced us to the ambassador and his wife late in 1990. Those friends had challenged my lost self-confidence, and it was by virtue of their sound judgments that I came to achieve my status as a high-profile journalist of the new trend. Before returning to London, they wanted to extend my links among the scarce British emissaries of Western support to the anticipated post-totalitarian democracy in the country. The ambassador himself was conspicuously one of them.

During the ensuing eighteen months, we had many happy occasions to see the ambassador, his wife, and several civil servants among the embassy staff. It was no secret that my wife and I were among the suitable "targets" for implementing the British government's humanitarian strategy vis-à-vis the countries of the ex-socialist camp of Eastern Europe. This strategy consisted of helping local intellectuals and promising politicians to promote a truly democratic alternative within the ongoing political changes throughout the region. As far as I am concerned, the role the British ambassador assigned to himself in those years was largely that of an enlightened mentor rather than rugged politician. Yet, enlightenment itself seemed a far-seeing politics. In return, people like us served the embassy with natural feedback on what was happening in the country.

Regardless of the formal reason that brought us together, we had established warm human relations. I realized with astonishment that British hospitality was in no way inferior to the famous Bulgarian style. I also realized, without being explicitly told, that England would abstain from interfering with the Balkan communist aftermath unless a force of circumstances dragged her in. (The events in Kosovo proved to be just such a force.) To be sure, this was not high-mindedness, but cold calculation. Perhaps other Bulgarians got different signals from other Western European ambassadors to Sofia, but in the British case the message was clear, although never discussed in private. I also realized that friendship is a universal relation among people who share common intellectual capacities and morals, cultural differences notwithstanding.

The ambassador's final gesture surpassed my expectations, however. It goes without saying that he received the news that our family was preparing to immigrate to Canada with the required neutrality of tone and posture. He asked me a few questions and readily accepted the validity of the personal reasons I divulged to him. A slightly higher pitch of enthusiasm, even within the protocol, would have indicated that he really enjoyed the prospect of our move. I perceived nothing of the sort. Several days later he called me to say that he intended to organize a farewell party in our honor and asked me to provide him with a list of guests we would like to invite. We scheduled the party three days before our departure.

On a wonderful, hot, and unusually still evening in August, the ambassador praised our involvement in the democratization process and in upgrading Bulgaria's human rights record. Everyone was more sentimental than usual. I could not help feeling an undercurrent of puzzlement at something unusual in the fact that "hopeful," "trustworthy" Bulgarian intellectuals were being seen off on their travel away from their native land by the British ambassador.

This fact is remarkable for several reasons. It reveals the disunited character of the movement toward democracy allegedly unleashed by the cream of Bulgaria's intelligentsia. My own involvement in the process was not peripheral, yet none of my peers ever objected to my decision to leave, nor have they ever sought to get me to reverse it. That *is* evidence that the battle for the communist legacy was led only inside the partisan old and new elites.

I was an openly nonpartisan commentator, driven by humanitarian goals, motivated by a cosmopolitan democratic ideology, and thus ignored by the fighters for political power. Elites from all sides of the political arena actually agreed upon the need to change the totalitarian character of communism but cared only rhetorically about the democratic alternative. They felt self-confident enough to ignore impartial voices, since they instinctively knew that such voices would have no serious impact on the electorate. Other impartial voices operated in isolation, with no common cause in sight to bother them should one of their own quit the fold. Our enemies included ourselves.

Thus, I see no justification for calling the post-totalitarian transition of power a revolutionary one. A revolution requires the disagreement of the elites, a certain degree of mass uprising, and (without question) a nonpartisan intellectual elite consisting of visionary ideologues, philosophers, and strategists to design the broad context of the radical change. A spiritual union around a new social strategy must fill the air, preparing all social strata for the abrupt and, by historical experience, violent transition. Communist societies were basically a deviation from history. The return to history is painful and dramatic, but by no means revolutionary. It is nothing more than recognition of a failure.

The ambassador's British gentility exemplifies the role Westerners have long attributed to intellectuals. The respect of free choice competed in the ambassador's mind with his duty to support real anticommunism. He, or Bulgaria, to be more precise, was losing a soldier, although the soldier himself would presumably be rewarded for his retreat. The ambassador was a person in the field, so, unlike frivolous Western commentators and historiographers, he knew the real value of every single soldier.

The communist system was not the deed of its dictators and its nomenclature. It was a national enterprise in which everyone's participation was equally important. Likewise, change in the communist system was not to be a performance of several personalities led by a spirit of alleged good will. It would come true only if the combined efforts of all layers in those societies unleashed an irreversible transition. Change is not just a political endeavor. Change requires a fundamental shift in mentality, which can be anything but fast.

In my mind, communism's worst legacy is the deep, long-term damage to the fabric of Bulgarian society. I could not agree to vegetate as a useless thread in such a moth-eaten garment. I was not threatened, I was excised.

TO WHOM IT MAY CONCERN

MR ZLATKO ANGUELOV

Zlatko Anguelov was well known to the British Embassy from 1989-1992.
During these years Bulgaria went through a revolution generally known
as "the changes". It entered them as a hardline communist state,
the subject of wide condemnation for its human rights abuses, and
emerged as the parliamentary democracy which it now is.

Zlatko Anguelov was a key figure during those years in the
field of human rights. He worked tirelessly, in his personal
capacity, and as a journalist, to bring to attention and ameliorate
the plight of the ethnic Turkish community. This was a brave
position to adopt, since he himself is ethnically Bulgarian and was
thus constantly subject to misunderstanding, criticism and hostility
at the hands of his ethnic peers. He never allowed this hostility to
deflect him from his single-minded work for the cause of greater
understanding and reconciliation between the two ethnic communities.

Zlatko Anguelov was also a good friend of the British Embassy in
all manner of ways, personal and official, as was his wife, Roumi
Slabakova. Without their advice and the contacts which they were
able to provide, especially during the difficult months of late 1989
and early 1990, the Embassy would have been far less effective in its
work on human rights and related political issues. They took great
risks in adopting what was, during that period, essentially a dissident
attitude. They did this for the good of their country and of its
persecuted and disadvantaged minorities, without thought to the
consequences for their own personal circumstances.

Zlatko Anguelov's knowledge and experience of human rights issues
and political change in general, in Bulgaria and throughout the former
communist states of Central and Eastern Europe, is extensive, possibly
unsurpassed. He is also articulate and sociable. He communicates
with ease in both English and French.

I commend him unreservedly.

Richard Thomas

R Thomas
British Ambassador
17 September 1992

EPILOGUE

———————

To Whom We Belong

Creativity is no longer trusted to speak for itself; as in tabloid journalism, existence (the life) enjoys priority over essence (the performance, the works).

—*John Updike,* The Man Within

Bulgaria is as beautiful as Switzerland. At the start of the twenty-first century, the life expectancy of Bulgarian men and women is still the highest among the former communist countries. However, the Bulgarian population is shrinking: a very low birth rate and the continuous flow of young people out of the country account for this thus far irreversible trend. The only value Bulgarians have not yet questioned is patriotism. That is why cheerful crowds frenetically applauded the tsar, who made a comeback on the Bulgarian political stage after fifty-five years of exile in Spain.

"How can we reach the Americans?" is the key question a famous Bulgarian comedian asks in a song. "How can we even pass them over?" And then there is the story of a Bulgarian who wants to know why someone stole his windshield wipers. How is it possible, he wonders, to steal the wipers from my modest car? I had just been seized by the ambition to drive forward and reach far, reach the Americans, and Look! Rain came over. How can I drive farther in such rain and fog when they steal my windshield wipers? Even in Albania and Zimbabwe, there is no such bad luck: someone steals your windshield wipers and rain starts just as you decide to act.

This song captures an ultimate truth about Bulgaria's postcommunist character: there is always someone or something responsible for my failure but it is never me! Patriotism and unaccountability: that is a burdensome legacy. One wonders what others would do in a similar situation, but Bulgarians seem not to care.

Last summer, I received an unexpected phone call from a classmate of mine. I had not seen this guy for thirty-five years: since we graduated from the French school. He said he was calling from Florida. I gather I am now among the few who know that his story had a happy end. In 1987, I heard that he had defected from his post as a high-ranking Bulgarian counterintelligence agent serving abroad, and was in hiding. No one knew where he, along with his wife and two children, had gone. Everyone understood, however, that his life was in mortal danger. Using a computer-based telephone line, he told me that he had fled to Switzerland and shortly thereafter gone to the United States. He is now an American citizen.

However, he still does not have a publicly disclosed telephone number or mailing address. I cannot call him or send him a letter. I cannot even be sure he called from Florida, since I am unable to check. He told me that he fears retaliation. He knows for sure that the majority of his former colleagues from the Bulgarian SS have kept their jobs in the postcommunist state security services. The same is true in Russia, he claims. Thanks to the old connections, Russian KGB officers still mess with Bulgarian political life using secure and unbreakable professional channels.

Should one believe his story? It quite likely may be true. It is equally likely he became a double agent and is now on hold, or recruiting, or even actively working. In any event, his story is another face of the postcommunist unaccountability: impunity.

Should you believe *my* life story? If your idea of communism comes from George Orwell, it is likely you will not. If your idea of communism comes from John Le Carré, it is again more likely you will not, but for different reasons. The ambiguity of any generalized account of communism is astounding. It still appears as a world enveloped in suspicion and mystery. If we take these with a healthy dose of irony, as we should, we also ought to acknowledge the fact that Slobodan Milošević, surrendered to the postcommunist authorities in Serbia on April Fool's Day.

Zlatko in Iowa City, Iowa, in the fall of 2000. (Author's collection.)

Yet, we all (without irony) lived under communism, and we survived to tell our stories, albeit with broken destinies, but unfazed regarding the possibilities of our resuscitation. My own life cannot be fictional. Such a life cannot be created by even the wildest imagination.

At first, I belonged *in* communism. There, in that unforgotten past, we *all* belonged in communism. Therefore, we know what communism was all about. Our stories ought to be heard as a lesson learned that must be passed on to our children.

Entirely on my own account, I did my best not to belong *to* communism. It is the result of that effort that is ambiguous, not my truth about communism. If freedom is a synonym of not belonging, I could not set myself entirely free within communism, hence, I also partly belonged to communism. So did Westerners who from outside embraced the illusion that communist regimes were bringing a just socialist society into the world.

Freedom is what I acquired in the second part of my life. How can I be so sure? First off, I do not belong in communism anymore. Secondly, I acknowledged and confessed my sins of being dragged into belonging to communism as well. Finally, I do not belong to Bulgaria anymore.

However, there is yet another perspective to this. In my experience, freedom means to be free from the authority of another or something. I am free from the authority of the Bulgarian communists. I am free from the authority of communism as a social project. In this sense, I am freer than many philosophers, sociologists, and liberal intellectuals in America and Western Europe. I am free from the authority of patriotism as well.

Nonetheless, I do belong. No, I do not belong to my past, since I have overcome it, although not with impunity. Rather, my past belongs to me. My family saga ends with me. Or, if I am able to extend it outside communism, it begins anew with me. I am no longer alone in my reflexivity, as I have always been. I now know there is no superior sage to tell me what is right and what is wrong. Unchained from communism, I live in harmony with my closest community and myself. I hope I do not delude myself that I also live in harmony with the larger world. My grandma's moral code (never lie, never break your word, be good and gentle, be a man of honor) is still a guiding light above my path. Yet, I believe that my own experience is a much brighter guide in moral matters. Of one thing I am sure: right and wrong, my light tells me, is not at all the same as good and evil.

Although excised from my motherland, I am thankful and full of love. I know that my children come after me. They will carry on my experience, my cosmopolitanism, my love, and the memory of me. I do belong to my children.

Index

ZLATKO ANGUELOV was born in Bulgaria in 1946. After earning his M.D., he taught anatomy in Varna and worked as a general practitioner in Sofia. He later contributed to western newspapers, worked with Bulgaria's Turkish minority, and wrote extensively on AIDS. In 1992, Anguelov moved to Canada, where he earned a degree in medical sociology. He currently edits a medical journal in Iowa.

ISBN 1-58544-195-3